MW01595257

VENETIAN STUDIES

BY

HORATIO F. BROWN

LONDON

KEGAN PAUL, TRENCH & CO., 1, PATERNOSTER SQUARE

1887

OF the following Studies, No 5 appeared, in a slightly different form, in the *Quarterly Review*, and No. 11 in the *English Illustrated Magazine*. To the proprietors and editors of these thanks are due for permission to reprint.

TO

MY MOTHER.

CONTENTS.

VENETIAN STUDIES.

THE CITY OF RIALTO.

"Quid est mare? refugium in periculis."—ALCUIN.

THE origin of Venice is one of the most obscure points in Italian history. Tradition marks the incursion of Attila as the birth-moment of that republic, which was destined to grow in silence, fed from the East, during the Middle Ages; to embark upon the troubled waters of Renaissance politics; to put forth the blossom of a glorious art; to stand as a bulwark for Europe against the Ottoman power; to flame in sinister splendour down the road of corruption, and to be extinguished at last, the oldest state in Europe, by the convulsions of the French Revolution. But long before Attila came with his Huns, before the Goths or the Lombards or the Franks seized on the plains of Northern Italy, those mud islands of the lagoon must have had their population—a race of fishermen, poor, hardy, independent, sea-bred and sea-nurtured. Cassiodorius, secretary of Theodoric the Great, writes to the Venetians of the Lagoons as to a people who had already achieved a certain

B

amount of unity and self-government. From his famous epistle of A.D. 523,* we gather the impression of a community simple, industrious, republican, and we obtain our earliest view of the Venetian villages; the houses rising on the shoals, saved from destruction in the ever-shifting waters by the frail palisade twisted from withes of osier. There is a breath of the salt, free air in the secretary's phrase. "Hic vobis, aquatilium avium more, domus est." But no eye noted the first low huts, built of mud bricks, nor measured those light and shallow boats which stood, stabled like horses, at the door of every house ; no historian traced the internal growth of these fishing stations; and we have been left to suppose what has often been stated, that the refugees from the mainland, flying before the frequent foreign occupations, found the islands, where they sought shelter, deserted mud-banks out at sea. This could not have been the case. Venice was not peopled solely by exiles from Aquileia, Oderzo, Concordia, or Padua. Through the obscurity of the records which have reached us, we can trace a long-continued struggle raging inside Venice,† before a thorough fusion of the original and the immigrant populations could be brought about. There were years of quarrelling between Malamocco, where the older race predominated, and Heraclea,

---

* See Hazlitt, " Hist. of Venetian Republic" (London : 1860), vol. iv. doc. i. ; "Viminibus enim flexilibus illigatis, terrena illis soliditas aggregatur . . . proinde naves quas, more animalium, vestris parietis illigastis, diligenti cura reficite."

† Throughout this essay I shall use the name "Venice" for the whole lagoon district, reserving "Rialto" for the city we now call Venice.

peopled chiefly by refugees from Feltre and Oderzo. The union was not effected until the city of Rialto, the city we now call Venice, rose to pre-eminence on the ruins of Heraclea and of Malamocco, as the monument of Pipin's attack and defeat. The choice of Rialto as the seat of the government is the starting-point of sequent Venetian history. Around Rialto we gather all those memories which are chiefly associated with the name of Venice—the wealth, the splendour, the pride of the Adriatic's Queen; Rialto floating on the water, a city that is "always just putting out to sea." A discussion, therefore, of the causes which led to the final selection of Rialto as the capital of Venice will form a fit prelude to any studies in the history of the Venetian republic.

Rialto was the city of compromise and of survival, —of compromise between those internal and discordant elements which constituted the population of the fishing villages ; of survival between two great external and antagonistic powers, the East and the West. On one side of Venice lay the mythic splendour, the dim grandeur, the august name of "the Golden Emperor;" on the other the barbaric power, the juvenile force, the mighty hand and out-stretched arm of the Frankish king. Constantinople displayed the civilization of the world, the long-in-herited lordship of the Cæsars; while the court of Charles the Great seemed instinct with the might of some unmeasured natural force, eruptive and volcanic. The Eastern Empire was old * and mythical through

---

* " τὴν γραῦν τὴν Βασιλείαν, ὡς κόρην χρυσοστάταλον, ὡς μαργαροφο-ροῦσαν." Manasses in Constant., vii.

age; but it still retained some of its pristine vigour, though the hand of sovereignty began to fall, here and there, from the government. The Frankish power, on the contrary, bounded forward with the impetuosity of youth; yet destiny reserved for it too. although so young, only a brief life in Italy. It fell to pieces on the death of its creator; and "Charlemagne. with all his peerage," faded away into the shadowy region of poetical myth—the only region where their mark remained as conquerors. Between these two forces Italy, and with her Venice, pursued their task of developing themselves as states. The action and reaction of East and West determined the evolution of Venice; and Rialto emerged as the result of their operation on that portion of the Roman world.

The Eastern Empire, though surely settling towards dissolution, still presented the greatest power in existence. Its longevity, its centuries of vigorous old age, were continually proving how massively the structure of the Roman constitution had been framed. The repeated recovery of vital force, the re-organization of the whole system, the new leases of life effected by Constantine, by Heraclius, by Leo the Isaurian, by Nicephorus, and by Basil, demonstrated the solid ribwork of the Roman body politic. Under the protection of the law we may believe that the subjects of the Eastern Empire were well governed. Its chroniclers have chosen to dwell upon the exceptions, recording, chiefly, instances of imperial caprice; but the enormous wealth of the merchants would rather prove that property was secure, commerce active, and justice strictly administered. Nicephorus I. could never have incurred such a torrent of obloquy for his alleged extortions, nor could Theodora have bequeathed so vast a treasury to her son Michael the Drunkard, had the people been impoverished, or the country ruined, by years of fiscal oppression. The gigantic scale of the imperial operations for the encouragement of agriculture shows at once the power of the emperors and their earnestness in good government. We have only to call to mind the colony of two hundred thousand Sclavs transferred by Constantine V. to Bithynia, and the corresponding establishment of Asiatic agriculturists on the borders of Sclavonia, to perceive that the Roman emperor was both the successor of the Great King and the ruler bred in the political principles of the early Cæsars. And the same profundity of resource appeared in the military, no less than in the financial administration. Constantine Copronymus found no difficulty, after the loss of an army and fleet numbering two thousand transports, in taking the field against the Bulgarians the following year with a new army of eighty thousand men and two thousand vessels.*

During the eighth and ninth centuries the Eastern Empire was, on the whole, prosperous. Nor could the continual dynastic changes upset, or even seriously shake, the solid strength of the constitution. The emergence of successful soldiers like Leo, of feeble princes like the Amorian family, of pure adventurers like Basil I., left the general lines of government

---

* See Finlay's "History of Greece" (Oxford: 1877), vol. ii. p. 230.

unchanged. That policy of careful finance and vigorous military administration, initiated by Augustus,
and laid down by him as the basis of imperial authority, was maintained, for the most part, by those who
subsequently bore the title of emperor. The maxims
of Cæsarship were held by them as something hardly
dependent upon their personal character. The prince
was not to be confounded with the administration ; that
was hereditary and traditional, the expression of the
Roman idea. No doubt the vigour and efficiency of
the government varied with the qualities of the
Augustus, but the substantial principles never altered.
And so, distinct from the national life, severed from
the interests of the people and almost unobserved by
them, there existed the life of the Great Palace, the
private economy of Cæsar as sovereign of a court, not
as minister of finance or emperor of the Roman
armies. We know more of this palace life than we
know of the imperial executive, for the chroniclers
have busied themselves over the details of it. We
see it sumptuous and fantastic under Theophilus, the
emperor who played the Paris to the virgins assembled
in his stepmother's house, and chose his wife by the
gift of a golden apple.* He is the Augustus whose
chief glory lay in building the Palace of Bryas,† an
imitation of the caliph's home in Bagdad. The

* Symeon Mag., Ann. Corpus Script. Hist. Byz. (Bonn:
1838), tom. 46, p. 415.

† Sym. Mag, *op. cit.*, p. 421 ; Theophanes, "Contin." Corp.
Hist. Byz. (Bonn), tom. 46, pp. 86–91 ; Leo, Gram. Script.
Hist. Byz. (Venetiis : 1729), tom. vi. p. 362 ; Gibbon, "Dec.
and Fall," capp. 52, 53.

porphyry chamber for the lying-in of empresses; the long colonnades with tessellated floors and marble pillars made for cool promenades; the sleeping-rooms arranged to suit each season of the year; the dining-halls named Erôs and Margarite; the golden tree with artificial birds that piped and fluttered in the branches; the organs hidden in the ceilings that played soft music while the emperor passed below; the system of sun telegraphs that flashed their messages from the borders of the empire and wrote them on a disc inside the council hall; the telephone and whispering gallery that joined one corner of the gardens to another—these and a hundred other such toys and curious inventions occupied the leisure and amused the fancy of Theophilus the Unfortunate. Or we may see the court bigoted and fanatical, ruled by monks, clamorous with arguments in favour or in condemnation of image-worship; settling the nature of the Trinity by blows and blood; engrossed by no more actual care. Constantine VI. lost his throne for a breach of the canon law in divorcing his wife to marry Theodota; and earlier still, in the year 669, the troops of the Orient Theme, catching the religious infection from their chief Constantine IV., claimed that the emperor's two brothers should also be crowned, and thus a Trinity would reign on earth, the counterpart of that in heaven. Leo V., the Armenian, owed his death partly to a scruple about Christmas Day which forbade him to slay his enemy, Michael, before receiving the sacrament, and partly to the military precision with which he attended matins and joined in the psalms. The assassins recognized the emperor by his deep, sonorous voice, and stabbed him before the altar in the chill grey Christmas morning. Or once again, and in opposition to this passionate earnestness in matters of dogmatic dispute, we may see the court scurrilous and ribald under Michael the Drunkard, the emperor who made Gryllus, his buffoon, ride in procession through the streets of Constantinople, robed in the patriarch's vestments, seated on a white mule, and attended by eleven mimic metropolitans chosen from among Augustus's boon companions.* Michael himself followed in the train, and the rout sang profane songs and obscene psalms to popular hymn tunes ; while, in mockery of the sacred cup, they administered a loathsome draught of vinegar and mustard to any among the crowd whom they could catch and compel to drink it.

But whatever the personal character of the prince may have been, frivolous or passionate or profane, affected the well-being of the people very remotely. The stories which crept out from the palace helped to fill their minds with curious astonishment and wonder as for something heard in a dream ; they helped to create that atmosphere of mystery and fascination which made the private life of their emperors take place side by side with that of Haroun al Raschid and the caliphs of Bagdad.

And the almost superhuman greatness of the imperial title, coupled with the number of adventurers who attained to it, gave the popular imagination ample food for the construction of myths. The popular version of the facts alone was often romantic enough.

* Theophanes, "Continuat.," p. 124 ; Sym. Mag., p. 437.

Leo the Isaurian, while yet a poor lad, known by the name of Conon, determined to leave his native hills to try his fortune in the richer lands below. One day, as he was journeying across the plain, he rested from the noontide heat in a grove of ilex, near a spring of water, and turned his pack mule loose to graze. As he lay upon the turf he found that he was not alone, but that two other travellers were also resting in the shade. From their talk he learned that they were Jews and astrologers, and the two strangers, taken by the beauty and grace and strength of Conon, readily satisfied his desire to know what the future might have in store for him. To his astonishment he heard that he was destined to rule the Eastern Empire; and in return for their brilliant forecast, the Jews exacted a promise that when Conon should come to the throne, he would root out the idolatrous worship of images that now disgraced God's Church. The prophecy was fulfilled; and Conon became the second refounder of the Roman Empire.

The legend of Basil I., though more closely related to the truth, is hardly less picturesque. Born a poor groom, but gifted with beauty, great strength, and a singular magnetic power which made the most intractable horses quiet at his merest touch, Basil determined to leave his father's farm to push his way in the large world. His wanderings brought him to Patras, where he fell under the notice of a rich widow named Danielis. Through her kindness he accumulated money enough to purchase estates in Macedonia, and he became a member of the family by the religious ceremony of "adelphosis" with the widow's son. But

Patras offered too narrow a field for Basil's growing ambition. He quitted the Peloponnese for Constantinople. Another tradition of his life, but one which hardly accords with the story of his Macedonian properties, represents the young groom entering the capital alone one evening, with a wallet on his back and nothing in his pockets. He went to sleep on the steps of a church near the gate. That night the priest of the church was troubled with a dream which told him to go out and bring the emperor in, for he lay sleeping at the door. Twice he obeyed, but found no emperor, only a young man lying on the church steps asleep. The third time, to exorcise the dream, he roused up Basil, brought him into the house, and gave him supper and a bed. The young groom rose rapidly into favour through his skill in horse training, till he at length attracted the notice of the court. His fortunes were secured when one day, in the presence of the Emperor Michael, he wrestled with a Bulgarian champion and overthrew him. Michael made him his prime favourite, and never took his riotious pleasures but with Basil at his side. At last two successful murders, first of Bardas Cæsar and then of Michael himself, placed Basil on the throne. He founded the great Basilian dynasty and reigned himself for nineteen years.

There are many other stories from the lives of emperors, patriarchs, and generals to be met with in the Byzantine chroniclers. They are half real, picturesque, and all deeply tinged with Eastern fancy; but they have little connection with the movement of the government. They appealed to the imagination in the distant provinces of the empire—in Venice or in Naples, for example—making Constantinople a place where men desired to go, a city of dreamland wonders. They created a strong bias of curiosity, of attraction, of sympathy in favour of Byzantium, as opposed to the repulsion exercised by the nearer and more positive power of the Lombards or the Franks. The doge's sons sought Constantinople when they could; the doges themselves coveted honorary titles * conferred by the emperor; the people answered Pipin's summons to surrender with the cry, "We choose to be the subjects of the Roman king, and not of you."

But, in spite of the emotional bonds which bound the distant members of the empire to Constantinople as their head, the hand of government began to fall away from many provinces. Italy was lost. Venice and Naples, though they acknowledged the suzerainty of Constantinople, enjoyed an independence virtually complete. Venice was in a position to ignore Byzantium when it suited her to do so; to continue uninterruptedly her own line of development, and yet to make use of her nominal dependence as a bulwark against invasion from the west. Only in the extreme east the great empire still stood firm, keeping the Saracens always at bay. Under the shelter of its unconscious protection the nations of modern Europe found leisure to ferment, to seethe and settle down; taking slowly that form under which we recognize them now.† This is the eternal benefit conferred by the Byzantine Empire. Venice, when her day of

---

* Armingaud, "Venise et le Bas Empire" (Paris : 1868).
† See Rambaud, "L'Empire Grec" (Paris : 1870).

power arrived, performed, though on a smaller scale, a similar service for civilization by her almost single-handed opposition to the Turk.

The forces at work upon the other side of Venice, towards the west, operating upon her in such a way as to determine the evolution of her independence and the creation of Rialto, were the powers of the Lombard and the Frank. But Italy herself modified the action of these powers that came in contact with her. And perhaps the most powerful, the most Italian factor in all Italy, was the Church of Rome. It is, therefore, by observing the policy of the Church and of the popes, that we obtain the most accurate view of the part played by the foreigners in the development of the peninsula.* When the suppressive weight of the empire was lifted from Italy, partly through the decay of the imperial power, partly by the removal of the emperor to Constantinople and the consequent accentuation of the Roman See, a rebound towards individuality and self-government manifested itself. In isolated portions of Italy, in Venice, in Rome, in Naples, Amalfi, and Bari, the people became conscious of a passionate desire for self-realization, for separation, for the assertion of their own peculiar qualities, which the empire had so long suppressed. But these fragments were scattered and weak. Byzantium was not dead ; an exarch still ruled in Ravenna; Lombardy, Beneventum, and Spoleto were in the power of a foreigner who would not be sorry to extend his borders. Politically, and quite apart from any religious

---

* I must acknowledge my debt to Ferrari's brilliant essay, " Storia delle Rivoluzioni d'Italia " (Milan : 1870).

considerations, salvation could come from the Church alone. The Goths had respected the Eternal City; the Lombards never effected a thorough conquest. Round the See of Rome the democratic impulse, an impulse by no means foreign to the essence of the Church, might crystallize and grow solid. A front of resistance might be offered to their foes if the pope would consent to become the core of a federation of states that aimed, first and foremost, at individuality, but who were forced to seek some central support upon which to lean until their own position should be secured. The Church itself, however, no less than the other fragments of Italy, obeyed the state-making appetite and sought a temporal dominion. The opportunity seemed favourable to its designs. But one imperative condition lay behind, tacitly implied by all who demanded assistance from the Church: the condition that the Church itself should not endeavour to become sovereign at the expense of its confederates; that the pope should never attempt to make himself doge or prince or emperor; in fact, that the Holy See should allow its spiritual authority to be used, as long as it might be required, for a bulwark against Byzantium, Pavia, or any other absorbing power, so that behind it Venice, Naples, Amalfi might pursue their own self-chosen course of development. The Church accepted the position. Italy stood with the Church or against it as it showed readiness to satisfy the imperious desire of the people, or gave signs that it, too, was seeking a temporal power for itself. So long as the pope consented to act as a shelter to the embryonic communities and shared the struggle for individual preservation, now against the Lombards, and now against the Eastern Empire, he commanded the sympathy of Italy. But the moment he manifested the least disposition to yield for his own advantage to either of the regnant powers, or on the slightest suspicion that he was aiming at sovereignty, the people threw their passions and their action violently into the opposite scale.

The popes accepted the position; but the condition imposed upon them was just one they could not fulfill. For, while undertaking the duties of confederate chiefs, while consenting to be no more than "primus inter pares," they could not escape the spirit of the age acting upon them in their narrower political capacities as heads of the Church and individual men. They embraced the policy of creating a temporal dominion, and Italy swayed in obedience to the fluctuations of their course. The danger that beset the popes from the Lombards and from the East determined their action as continual see-saw. They stood now with Pavia, achieving a little more liberty as they saw Byzantium weak; now with Constantinople, bolstering up the imperial authority if the Lombards showed a tendency to encroach. All the time their conduct was eagerly scanned by confederate Italy. The iconoclasm of Leo the Isaurian, condemned as a heresy by the Western Church, and dividing the East into two furious and hostile camps, presented a favourable opportunity to deal a blow at the emperor's ascendency in Italy. Accordingly, Gregory II. bound himself in close alliance with Luitprand, king of the Lombards. The pope preached the enormity of iconoclasm, and the king lent him the secular arm wherewith to give weight to his words. The Lombard troops entered the exarchate and drove the exarch Paul out of Ravenna to seek refuge in Venice. But the pope immediately found himself compelled to undo his own work. For Luitprand claimed the Pentapolis as his own, by right of conquest. This extension of Lombard power disclosed a danger to the independent growth of papal authority. A rapid backward sweep took place. The restoration of Paul to his exarchate, at the instance of the pope and by the help of Venice, marked the extent of the reaction against the Lombards.

The head of the Church was now placed in difficulties. His struggles to keep the balance adjusted between the two forces which dominated Italy, a struggle from which he hoped to emerge sovereign, had raised up for the Church an enemy, both in Pavia and in Constantinople. Luitprand's vigour infused new life into the Lombards, and his conquest of Ravenna reawakened the desire for enlargement ; his successors were sure to follow the lines laid down by him. On the other hand, Byzantium, though by no means strong, had gained considerable weight in Italy, thanks to the reaction in her favour which sent the exarch Paul back to Ravenna. Venice experienced a shock of alarm at the results of the pope's Lombard policy. The capture of the Pentapolis threw her into the arms of Constantinople, and there she was held by the commercial privileges granted to her on the restoration of the exarch. For the moment she stood isolated from the Church and suspicious. The pope had shown his hand a little too openly. Under these circumstances the Church was forced to look for support elsewhere. To restore the equation between itself, Pavia, and Byzantium, the introduction of a fourth factor became necessary. The victory of Charles Martel, saving Western Christendom as it did, drew all eyes to the race of the Franks. The popes selected them as their champions for the next move in the game. Zachary sanctioned —as far as such sanction had any meaning—the substitution of the Carolingian for the Merovingian dynasty. The house of Charles Martel became the defender of the Church ; and Pipin I.'s coronation by Stephen, at Paris, sealed the alliance.

The results of this union were at once felt in the peninsula. The Lombards now learned the quarter whence danger threatened. The Church pointed clearly to the Franks as the new race that was girding itself behind the Alps, to try its fortune too in battle for that phantom Helen of the Middle Ages, the crown of Italy. The Lombard kingdom grew restless under the presentiment of death. Astolfo, Luitprand's successor, by his decided enmity alarmed the pope, and warned him to precipitate the ruin of his foes. In 755 Pipin came to Italy. He is said to have made a gift of the Pentapolis and the exarchate, which he took from Astolfo, to his ally of the Holy See. But though Astolfo was humbled, the Lombards were not annihilated. No sooner had Pipin left Italy, than Desiderius, the last king of Pavia, prepared himself to recover the lost cities and to chastise the pope. The Lombards made their final effort to retain their kingdom. Desiderius occupied Comacchio, the Pentapolis, the city of Ferrara. He pressed on to Gubbio and Urbino ; he even threatened Rome itself. But at Viterbo he hesitated before the excommunication hurled against him by the Holy See.* The Lombards had made the fatal mistake of becoming orthodox ; they could not worship the pope and fight him too. Desiderius recoiled and was lost. In the year 774 Adrian sent for his ally, Charles the Great, who had succeeded his father, Pipin. Charles crossed the Cenis, blockaded Desiderius in Pavia, and, after a protracted siege, captured both the city and the king.

The pope had advanced rapidly towards the object which the Church desired. By the help of the Franks it now seemed probable that a temporal dominion would be added to the spiritual empire of the Holy See. Though the donation of Pipin never took effect, yet its suggestion marked in unmistakable characters the ambition of the pope. He was violating the tacit understanding upon which alone he enjoyed the political sympathy and support of Italy. Everywhere appeared signs of reaction against the Church. In Venice, in Ravenna, in its own city of Rome, the people protested against the political direction which the Church threatened to impose on the country. The popes passed through stormy years of hostility from their own subjects, until at length Leo III. was assailed by the mob, beaten, imprisoned, and only escaped the loss of his tongue by a secret flight to Charles the Great at Paderborn.

* Muratori, "Annali d'Italia," ad. ann. 772.

C

And now the consummation was almost reached. Charles brought back the pope to Rome, and there he himself was crowned Emperor of the West, King of the Franks and Lombards. On the other hand, Leo received the temporal sovereignty over Parma, Reggio, Mantua, the exarchate, Istria, Venice, Beneventum, and Spoleto.* The Church and the Franks concocted the pact and donation between them. Leo believed that he had restored the Augustan Cæsars in the person of Charles; Charles believed that he could confer a veritable kingdom upon his ally the pope. But both beliefs were groundless, and proved to be so almost on the day of their birth. Charles never was a Roman emperor; he did not so much as reside in Italy. The pope never could be a reigning prince; he could not so much as levy a tax. This country which they were partitioning so lightly had never been consulted, and its voice was of paramount importance. The pope and the emperor had no sooner conceived the idea of an Italy based upon their double power than their mutual gifts began to prove themselves unsubstantial. The emperor made a present of that which was not his to give; the pope committed treason against the passions and the instincts of the people. He sought to become a king where no kings were to be. The country swung around in violent contradiction to the Church and to the Franks. In every direction rose the cry of " Save the country," and the pope was left standing alone, deserted by those upon whom he endeavoured to impose himself. But the pact and donation, though

* Anastasius, quoted by Ferrari, *op. cit.*, vol. i. p. 122.

wanting in solid reality, stood over Italy with all the force and potency of an idea; always in evidence; passing from lip to lip; fixed in the imagination; a permanent threat against the desire for self-effectuation, the state-forming appetite which was swaying the peninsula. Their effect remained as a determining factor in the course adopted by such communities as Venice; their power to affect the political imagination endured just because they were an idea and not a reality, therefore more difficult to refute, to negative, to destroy.

The early history of Venice illustrates accurately the movements of an Italian state labouring towards independence, between the triple forces of the East, the West, and the Church. For Venice lay, in a certain sense, at the heart of the struggle; she formed a part of the Byzantine Empire, and she had been included in Charles's donation to the Church; she felt the full stress of the conflict. It has been well said that "Venice on her *lidi* stood exposed to every wind." The interest of her earliest development depends on the courage and determination with which she resisted all conquest, Gothic, Lombard, Byzantine, or Frank. Venice enjoyed a position both peculiar and ill defined. She acknowledged a titular allegiance to the court of Byzantium, and yet by her acts she recognized the supremacy of the barbarian kingdoms on the mainland of Italy. Her tribunes received orders from Cassiodorius, and, later on, her first doge paid tribute to Luitprand in return for certain privileges of commerce. On the other hand, her public deeds were superscribed with the name of the Eastern Emperor.

Yet neither Byzantium nor Ravenna nor Pavia could claim the lagoons as an undisputed portion of their empires. The twelve confederate islands * were in fact attempting to steer a difficult course towards independence of any power. These twelve islands, lying close together along the shore of the Adriatic, formed the nucleus of what was to be the state of Venice. It is probable that, originally, they were little more than fishing stations and salt-pans belonging to the wealthier towns of the mainland. And the famous document, recounting the despatch of the three Paduan consuls † sent to govern the village of Rialto, though in all likelihood a forgery, yet represents the facts of the case—that the islands were under the charge of the rectors or consuls appointed by the neighbouring cities, Monselice, Padua, Oderzo, and Aquileia.

But in the stillness of the lagoons, in the freshness

* Sagornino, "Cronacon Venetum," edit. Zanetti (Venetiis: 1765). Sagornino probably lived at the beginning of the eleventh century. He is therefore one of the earliest authorities we possess. He gives the names of the twelve islands—Grado, Bibbione, Caprule, Eraclea, Equilio or Jesolo, Torcello, Poveglia, Murano, Rivvalto, Malamocco, Chioggia, Cavarzere. This last is not an island, but is on the mainland, not far from Chioggia. We miss the names of Mazzorbo and Burano.

† Romanin, "Storia documentata di Venezia" (Venezia: 1858), ignores the story. Romanin's history is a work full of scholarship and learning, accumulated by long and patient research. It is the most complete and accurate history of Venice. I shall have to refer to it constantly. For the Paduan document see Daru, "Histoire de la Rep. de Venise," and Hodgkin, "Italy and her Invaders" (Oxford, 1880), vol. ii. ; Andreæ Danduli, "Chronicon," ap. Muratori, "Rer. It. Scrip.," tom. xii. lib. v. cap. i. p. x.

and freedom of the sea air, those germs of individuality and liberty which began to quicken as the pressure of imperial Rome was lightened, found a congenial soil and fitting nutriment. The islands, unorganized and disconnected as yet, gained two solid advantages from the sufferings of the mainland under foreign invasion: their population increased through the in-flux of refugees, and the ruin of the mainland cities prompted them to claim their freedom. In 466 the twelve islands drew together in federation; each governed by its own tribune, elected by itself, but all meeting in parliament for the consideration of points affecting the common weal.* This was the first organic movement of the lagoon villages; the bursting of the seed destined to ripen into such a fruit. About a century later the results of their consolida-tion became apparent when Narses arrived in Italy. The Paduans in vain appealed to the imperial general, begging him to restore to them their rights over the mouths of the Brenta and the Bacchiglione which fall into the lagoon. The islanders argued that the outlets of these streams belonged to the lagoon-dwellers in virtue of the labour, which kept them open. Narses refused to decide either way, and the mainlanders were too weak to enforce their will without his aid. The general, by this conduct, distinctly acknowledged the twelve islands as an element in the empire, and they gained a solid standing ground. The people, by the realization of a portion of their desire, became con-

* Dandolo, *op. cit.*, lib. vii. cap. i. p. 1; Janotii, "Dialogus de Rep. Venet.," cum notis Crassi (Lugd. Bat. 1722), ap. Groev. "Thesaur. Antiquit. It.," p. 40.

scious of the whole of it. The sequence of Venetian history from this point, down to the establishment of Rialto as the capital, is governed by a series of actions and reactions rapidly initiated and as rapidly exhausted, by a process of attraction and repulsion, now towards Byzantium, now away from it. It is the people who move; throwing their weight now into this scale, now into that, as they saw that the dreaded danger of absorption threatened from Italy or from the East. Always with the passion for independence alight in them, they were not Roman or Frankish with their bishops, nor Byzantine with their doges, but Venetian, with a strong resolution to make themselves recognized as such. They stretched ever forward to the object of their desire, and rejected all that might prove inimical to their hopes of attaining it.

But this very desire for self-realization, while it wrought in the core of the state as a whole, quickened a similar appetite in each individual member. If Venice craved to stand sole and independent in Italy, each tribune also craved to rule sole and alone in Venice. Jealousy between Malamocco and Heraclea, rivalry for the leadership inside Venice, summed itself up in feuds and quarrels between the tribunes of the principal towns, until the federation seemed in danger of falling to pieces through the intensity of its own passion. Only one solution offered itself—to waive individual claims and to create a personal head of the state, to concentrate the functions of government in his hands. The Venetians elected their first doge, Luccio Paolo Anafesto, in the year 697.* Internal

---

* Dandolo, *loc. cit.*

discord necessitated this change in the constitution ; the antagonism of minute particles inside Venice had brought about the revolution. It followed, therefore, that the colour first given to the dukedom would depend upon the character of the city which chanced to be in the ascendant at the moment, of the sympathies of that tribunate which succeeded in imposing itself upon its federate brothers. Anafesto was a Heraclean, and his election proclaimed the leadership of Heraclea. That city had always been aristocratic in sympathy, with a strong leaning towards Byzantium. This quality in Heraclea was determined in part by opposition to its rival Malamocco, the very kernel of the democratic factor. And so the doges first emerged tinctured with aristocratic proclivities, leaning towards autocracy and ready to court Byzantium and the emperor.

Though the creation of a doge had been a voluntary act and clearly necessary for the salvation of the state, yet it concentrated and intensified the internal oppositions it was designed to allay. For the doges and Heraclea stood there now as the embodiment of the danger from Byzantium, and drew upon themselves all that popular jealousy which was only appeased by the ruin of the reigning city. The solution that Venice had chosen placed her in the same difficulty as that which the action of the popes imposed upon the whole independent movement in Italy. Like the popes, the doges might either lean too much upon one or other of the external forces which were threatening to absorb their state, or, by a skilful manipulation of internal discords, they might succeed in making themselves sovereign. The people desired their doge to be a bulwark against any encroachment by the Church upon civil liberty; prince of themselves, but not agent for Byzantium. The least swerving from the prescribed line, the slightest suspicion of an ambitious policy, the first note of a servile submission to any dominant power, sufficed to rouse the people, who deposed, blinded, tonsured, or even slew their dukes. In the same light the people regarded their bishops. They desired them to be the safeguards of their faith against heretical Byzantium; but they would not tolerate that their spiritual pastors should act as political agents for the Church or for the Church's allies. In fact, the people submitted to their doges and their bishops solely with a view to their one engrossing object, the evolution of their own independence. The attempt of either bishop or doge to impose his will upon the state was sufficient to insure his ruin.

Resuming the course of Venetian history, we find it obeying the impulses just noticed. In the year 728 the pope, for his own purpose of aggrandizement, had united with Luitprand against Leo the Isaurian. But the results of this policy, the capture of Ravenna by the Lombards, proved so alarming to Venice, that when the pope discovered his mistake and desired to undo his work, he had little difficulty in persuading Orso, the doge, to restore the exarch Paul to his capital.* For the moment Venice, obeying the impulse given by her doge, held with Byzantium. In reward the Venetian merchants obtained from Constantinople

* Dandolo, *op. cit.*, lib. vii. cap. iii. pp. 2, 3, 4.

large commercial privileges in the Pentapolis ; while Orso himself received the honorary title of " hypatos " or consul. The sympathies of Venice set towards the East, in alarm at the danger from the Lombards. But, while the state was in process of formation, any movement implied a counter movement. The stronger the action showed itself the more rapid and positive the reaction was sure to be. To the people it seemed that they had gone far enough with their doge. He had achieved one object of his desire ; he might reckon himself a noble of the empire, within a measurable distance of the Augustan majesty. The people whom he governed, however, were intensely sensitive. These dignities bore too much the character of a pledge committing the duke and Venice to dependence on Byzantium. A doge of Venice should not wear that title as a lesser one, nor think it honourable to hold a subordinate office of the Eastern cour:. The knowledge of their own weakness forced the Venetians into violence. They murdered Orso, and abolished the dukedom in favour of a yearly magistracy, called the " mastership of the soldiery." * They revolted fiercely from Byzantium, whither their doge seemed to be leading them.

The reaction had, of necessity, been excessive ; part of its effect required to be undone. Experience proved that the dukedom was essential to the coherence of the state. The mastership of the soldiery recalled the evils of the tribunate. Another current of feeling, opposed to the violence which had abolished the dukedom, set in, and Heraclea profited

---

* Dandolo, *op. cit.*, p. 13 ; cap. iv. p. 1.

by it. She desired to resume the prestige she had lost through the suspension of the dukedom. In the year 742 a Heraclean victory over its democratic neighbour Jesolo brought back the doges, in the person of Deodato, a noble of the victorious city.* But the permanent result of the whole revolution made itself felt in the removal of the government from Heraclea to Malamocco, the democratic centre. This was a step towards the thorough compromise of Rialto. A Heraclean, an aristocrat, a Byzantine in sympathy, still reigns, but reigns at Malamocco, democratic and anti-Byzantine. Both the factors of the future Rialto were modified towards the point where union became possible. The restoration of the dukedom, however, in spite of this modification, was the work of Heraclea —a proof of its ascendency regained, and therefore a sign that the state had taken a swing towards Byzantium again.

And the course of Italian politics generally determined Venice, for a while, in her present direction. For the reciprocal attraction between the Church and the Franks had just begun. The two powers hostile to Constantinople, and standing together for the attainment of their respective objects, the mastery of Italy and a temporal sovereignty, were becoming solid. The results of this union were felt at once by Venice. The Venetians had saved the exarchate from the Lombards ; Charles now desired to see these protectors of Byzantium expelled from the Pentapolis, in order to pave the way for his own occupation of that district. Accordingly,

* Dandolo, *op. cit.*, cap. ix. p. 1.

under the direction of Pope Hadrian, an organized attack upon the Venetian merchants took place, and the pope was able to write to his ally informing him that his will had been done, and that Venice no longer held a single garrison or factory in the Ravennate.*

This action of the pope awakened the greatest alarm in Venice; an alarm which resulted in the accentuation of Byzantine sympathies, and in strengthening the hands of the doges, to whom the state looked for protection from the imminent danger. How close the peril had come the Venetians learned when they discovered that the pope, not content with his attack upon them in the Pentapolis, had actually negotiated with Giovanni, patriarch of Grado, for the creation of a Papal and Frankish party inside Venice itself.† The materials ready to the patriarch's hand were, naturally, the democratic faction, who still eyed Heraclea and the Heraclean doges with bitter jealousy. A crisis could not be long delayed. The questions which now agitated the whole of Italy were faithfully reflected in the lagoons. Like a sensitive flame, Venice responded to the least movement on the mainland. She was not yet strong enough to declare her independence between two such powers as the Franks and the Eastern Empire; therefore, for the moment, her perception of her own aims, her intuition of the political problem, became confused. The question appeared to be submission to East or West; the parties of Frank and anti-Frank seemed to express

---

* "Codex Carolinus" (Romæ: 1761), Epist. 84, ad. ann. 785.
† Ibid., Epist. 52.

her central difficulty. But in reality the desire for individual freedom remained in the background, as the vital and motive force inside the state. How long a crisis could be delayed depended largely upon the character of the doge. Maurice Galbaio had succeeded in guiding Venice clear of embroglios on the mainland, though he could not fence her round from infection by the general turbulence of the political atmosphere.* His son Giovanni succeeded him ; a man of very different temperament, violent and headstrong, and moreover placed in a position of greater difficulty, for the crisis was ripening to the acuter phase of its progress. The pact, the donation, the crowning of Charles, were all notorious now; hung out like a danger signal for those communities who felt the impulse towards self-government, leaving no doubt as to the intentions of the emperor and the pope. Venice had to look to herself. By a violent deed of blood she wrote her refusal to be included in the donation. She repelled the assumption that she belonged to Charles and was his chattel to gift away. She denied her allegiance to a pope who could presume to claim the imperial title, and then to sell it ; to that head of the Church who dared to prove a traitor to the passions of his country.

In this fervour of opposition to the Church events centred round two ecclesiastics. The bishopric of Olivolo, in Venice, fell vacant, and, at the request of the Emperor Nicephorus, the doge appointed to that

---

* Dandolo, *op. cit.*, cap. xii. p. 1 ; cap. xiii. p. 1 ; Filiasi, "Veneti Primi e Secondi" (Padova : 1822), tom. v. cap. xxi. p. 265.

See a young Greek, named Christopher, a mere boy, sixteen years old at most.* Giovanni, patriarch of Grado, seized the opportunity to test the strength of himself and his party against the doge and the Byzantine element. He believed that he was powerful enough to show a mastery which would determine the waverers, and hasten the subjection of Venice to Charles and to the pope. Giovanni refused to consecrate Christopher. The doge remained firm in the support of his appointment. Giovanni replied by excommunicating not only the young Greek, but all his adherents, including the doge. The heat of party fury and his own violent nature determined Galbaio's action. He sent his son Maurice with a fleet to Grado. The patriarch was besieged in his palace, pressed closer and closer, and finally thrown from the highest tower. Giovanni had shown himself a traitor to the instincts of Venice, as his master, the pope, had proved a traitor to the desires of Italy. Yet the vengeance which overtook the patriarch savoured too strongly of tyranny. It came as a culminating point to a long series of masterful deeds on the part of the Galbaij.

But Venice was no sooner relieved from a danger threatened by her bishop and the Church than she found herself face to face with the opposite danger from her doge relying on Byzantium, whose triumph seemed secured by the murder of Giovanni. True, Venice would not allow her patriarchs to act as agents and procurers for the Church and for the Franks, but neither did she desire her doges to become tyrants

---

* Sagornino, *op. cit.*, p. 18 ; Dandolo, *op. cit.*, cap. xiii. p. 23 ; Filiasi, *op. cit.*, cap. xxii.

of the state. The murder of Giovanni was an act of excessive violence, and warned her of that ever-present menace. The sympathy of the people swerved from the Galbaij and claimed the elevation of Fortunatus, nephew of the murdered patriarch and a man of the same political complexion, to the See of Grado, as a check to the tyrannical tendency of the doge, and as an expiation for the sacrilege he had committed.*

A crisis such as that which was agitating Venice could not fail to produce men of strong personality. Of all who appear upon the scene at this moment, none is more remarkable than Fortunatus, the new patriarch of Grado. In page after page of that populous chronicle bequeathed to us by Andrew Dandolo, we meet him again and again—here borne high upon some wave of reaction, there sunk deep in that troublous sea of politics, but always present, active, restless, intriguing ; now at Venice, leading his party, the party of Charles and of the Church ; now in exile, flying from his country, hurriedly crossing "the white Alps alone." In Germany, in France, in Istria, at Constantinople, we find him ; anywhere but at Grado and his episcopal seat. He is courtier, merchant, virtuoso, engineer, and architect ; anything but pastor of that quiet church among the still lagoons. Restlessness, movement, diplomacy, were passions with the man. It is almost impossible to follow him closely through his journeys or his intrigues ; yet around him are grouped the chief actors and the principal events that contributed to the emergence of Rialto. The intimate friend of Charles the Great,

* Dandolo, *op. cit.*, cap. xv. p. 24; Sagornino, *loc. cit.*

known only too well to the popes, dreaded by Nicephorus, and counsellor of Pipin, Fortunatus moves about among these great personages, the outward and visible sign of the spirit which was troubling them.

The appointment of Fortunatus to the See of Grado was made in obedience to a reaction against ducal tyranny. His politics were known to be decidedly in favour of the Church and the Franks. Pope Leo at once sent him the pallium and his blessing on the work he should do for the Holy See. That work was to carry on his uncle's course of action; to establish and strengthen the party that sympathized with Charles; to pave the way for the reduction of Venice as a province of the West. But Leo knew the shifty nature of the man, and thought it necessary to urge upon him the duty of strenuous action. "Remember," he writes to Fortunatus, "that the place you have now undertaken is not a place of rest, but of labour." * So it proved to the patriarch— a place of labour, indeed, from the beginning to the end. The pope, however, need have felt no such fears. Fortunatus had not occupied his See more than three months when a conspiracy against the doges was discovered and stamped out.† The author of the conspiracy proved to be the patriarch, who, relying on the enthusiasm which had raised him to his dignity, concerted the measures of the plot with Obelerio, tribune of Malamocco and chief of the democratic party. But the treason took wind. Obelerio and

---

* See Ughello, "Italia Sacra" (Venetiis : 1720), tom. v. pp. 1075 *et seq.*, for the history of the See of Grado.

† Dandolo, *op. cit.*, cap. xv. p. 26 ; Sagornino, *op. cit.*, p. 19.

his brother conspirators retired to Treviso, while Fortunatus experienced his first exodus. He fled across the Alps to Charles the Great, whose court he found at Salz.*

His reason for taking so long a journey and seeking such a distant asylum was his hope to move Charles to active measures which should render the donation of solid effect—to urge him to undertake the reduction of the lagoons. Fortunatus never showed himself less than whole hearted in his service of the Church and of the Franks as its ally. He brought to bear upon the emperor many cogent arguments.† Setting aside his own faithful adherence to the cause of Charles, the proof of which lay patent in his exile, Fortunatus dwelt upon the strong Byzantine sympathies of Venice. Here was a small province which the emperor claimed as his own and had given away to his friend the pope; yet that province, so far from acknowledging the Emperor's authority or bowing to his will had expelled his partisans and professed allegiance to a court which scorned his imperial title and laughed at his pretensions to the lordship of Italy.‡ But more than that; Fortunatus insisted on the wisdom of subduing Venice, and so establishing a naval power upon the Adriatic; for it was through those waters that Constantinople must be attacked,

* Dandolo, *loc. cit.;* Sagornino, *loc. cit.;* "Monumenta German. Hist," edit. Pertz (Hanov.: 1826), tom. i. ; Einhard, "Annales," p. 191, ad ann. 803.

† "Cod. Carol.," tom. ii. p. 47 ; Dandolo, *op. cit.*, cap. xvi. p. 3.

‡ See Baronius, "Annales Eccles. cum crit. Pagii" (Luca: 1743), tom. xiii. p. 379.

should Charles ever find the leisure to prosecute a dream of his ambition, the union of East and West in his own person. The emperor listened to the patriarch, and the advice then given bore fruit seven years later in Pipin's attack upon Venice.

Fortunatus's success at the Frankish court was very great. Charles not only felt the political value of the man who had made himself the leading spirit of the anti-Byzantine party in Venice, but he was also conciliated by the presents Fortunatus had brought with him to Salz. The emperor's cathedral at Aachen was occupying much of his attention, and the patriarch's presents came most timely. They consisted of hangings of tapestry and silk, church ornaments in gold and silver, and, above all, two ivory doors of exquisite workmanship.* We are curious to know how the patriarch carried all this heavy luggage with him, in his hurried flight over almost pathless mountains; but here the chronicle fails us, as on many another point. In return for his gifts Fortunatus received an imperial diploma,† granting him the full use of all his ecclesiastical emoluments in Istria and Romagna, together with freedom to trade untaxed in any port of the new empire. His exile, however, prevented him from actually realizing the revenues of his Church, and to meet his present wants Charles made him abbot of Moyen Moutier,‡ near Bordeaux. The

---

* Monum. Germ. Hist. ; Einhard, *loc. cit.*

† Baronius, *op. cit.*, tom. xiii. p. 389 ; Ughello, *op. et loc. cit.* : Dandolo, *op. cit.*, cap. xvi. p. 4.

‡ Mabillon, "Annales Benedictini" (Luca : 1749), tom. ii. p. 316.

D

patriarch's treatment of his abbey was characteristic of the man. He could not endure to live away from the court and active politics near the person of Charles. Nevertheless, he demanded that the whole income of Moyen Moutier should be paid to him for his private use; intending to let the brothers fare as best they might, while he remained an absentee. The corporation protested. After litigation, appeals, and arbitration, in all of which the restless spirit of Fortunatus took a keen delight, the matter was arranged by compromise. The new abbot received half the revenues of the monastery, and remained at Charles's court, where we must leave him for the present.

When Fortunatus concerted his measures for the overthrow of the Galbaij, he counted on that reaction against the doges which he perceived had set in after the murder of the patriarch Giovanni. His own impetuosity of spirit, however, misled him; he acted too precipitately and failed. But his failure did not stay the course of popular feeling in Venice, nor prove that it was weak and transitory. Obelerio, the partner in the plot, who had sought refuge at Treviso, reaped the benefit of waiting. From his hiding-place he continued his antagonism to the doge. When he saw that hatred of the Galbaij had reached its highest point, he made a sudden entry into Malamocco,* his native town; the people welcomed him with enthusiasm and proclaimed him doge. The Galbaij were forced to fly from Venice, whither they never returned. As a result of Doge Giovanni's high-handed action in murdering Fortunatus's uncle,

---

* Dandolo, *op. cit.*, cap. xv. p. 26; Sagornino, *loc. cit.*

and in consequence of the apparent tyranny of his conduct, the state, forgetful for the moment of the ever-present danger from the Church and from the Franks, swept violently away from Heraclea and Byzantium into the arms of Malamocco and of Charles. Malamocco, in the person of her tribune, Obelerio, assumed the leadership, and a further step towards the union and fusion at Rialto was effected. For Obelerio reigned as the first Malamoccan, or democratic, doge. Heraclea no longer absorbed the governing functions; they were becoming common to all inhabitants of Venice. But stability was not yet secured; nor could it be until both Heraclea and Malamocco, with all the internal jealousy and discord which they represented, had been still further subdued and toned away.

The political sympathies of the new doge were well known. There could be no doubt as to the direction in which he would endeavour to lead Venice, if allowed to work his will freely and unrestrained. His devotion to the cause of Charles and of the Church admitted no question. But, by the law which was governing the development of Venice, this very outburst of popular feeling, that had raised Obelerio to the dukedom and given the leadership to Malamocco, implied a reaction. An undercurrent of opposition to the doge set in, slowly and barely perceptible at first, but gaining power as it went on. The impulse, however, that had carried Obelerio to the head of the state was not exhausted by its first effort. It still possessed force enough to enable the doge to accomplish a deed personally grateful to himself, and infinitely important in paving the way for the appearance of Rialto as the capital—the destruction of Heraclea. The Heracleans themselves supplied the pretext for their own annihilation. When Fortunatus fled to Charles, the nobles of that city seized on some of the patriarchal lands which lay along the coast. The people of Jesolo, envious of this extension on the part of their neighbours, and under cover of a pious wish to restore to the Church its due, attacked Heraclea and were themselves nearly destroyed. In these straits Jesolo appealed to the democratic centre, to Obelerio and Malamocco. The doge convened an assembly which solemnly decreed the destruction of Heraclea. The people of Jesolo and Malamocco razed the aristocratic city to the ground, and forcibly distributed its inhabitants among the other townships of the lagoon.*

The overthrow of Heraclea marks the furthest point attained by the wave of popular feeling which had placed Obelerio and the Frankish party in power. Hitherto Obelerio had carried the people with him. But this deed seemed to derange the balance in the state. The tide of sympathy began to recede from the doge, and he was left to continue his course towards Charles and the Franks, alone. Each step that he took showed the distance between himself and his people to be growing steadily greater; proved more and more clearly that ruin lay in his path. For

* Cronaca Veneta detta "Altinate," ap. Archivio Storico Italiano (Firenz : 1845), tom. viii. lib. iii., with a commentary by Prof. Rossi. The author lived about A.D. 1210. Dandolo, *op. cit.*, cap. xvi. p. 10.

him there was no alternative and no hope. He may have heard the waters sinking away behind him, and foreseen that he must be stranded and deserted before his policy could bear its fruit ; yet to fall back with the tide was impossible. He could not stay its inevitable sweep towards Byzantium again. He might not put off the pre-eminence he had won, and, by sinking into obscurity, escape the vengeance of the opposite faction. Nothing remained for him but to press on towards an unattainable goal, to face the impossible task of carrying his country with him into the arms of Charles.

When Fortunatus heard of Obelerio's success, and of his elevation to the dukedom, he left the court of the emperor and hurried down to Venice. But the hopes he entertained of sharing in the victory of his friends and returning to his See at Grado were not realized. After the discovery of Fortunatus's plot, the Galbaij had created a new patriarch, and Obelerio deemed it prudent to leave that appointment undisturbed. Fortunatus was so restless an intriguer, that the doge rightly declined to place him in his See again. Obelerio felt that the patriarch would only be a source of danger to his newly established authority, and that his presence would needlessly exasperate the defeated party of Byzantium. So Fortunatus received no encouragement and no invitation to Malamocco. He wandered like an unquiet spirit round the borders of the lagoon ; now at Campalto near Mestre, now at Torcello ; always revolving some scheme for his return. Fortune favoured him so far, that one day John the Deacon, bishop of Olivolo, fell into his hands, and he carried him prisoner to Mestre.* But, while he was considering the best method of turning this advantage to account, John slipped through his fingers and escaped to Malamocco. Fortunatus saw that his game was ruined for the present. He abandoned all hope of recovering Grado, and betook himself to Istria, to make what profit he could out of the privilege that had been granted him by Charles. There he established himself as a merchant, owning four large vessels and accumulating a vast fortune from the cargoes which they carried. Some of this wealth he invested politically in buying interest at the Frankish court, and in securing connections among the chiefs of the Dalmatian seaports which still belonged to the Eastern Empire.† Some, again, he stored up in works of art, in silks, in hangings, in silver and gold ornaments. He filled the high office of imperial judge,‡ and kept a little court of dependents about him. He formed a company of military engineers, for whom he acted as *impresario;* ready to hire them out to the best bidder. In his capacity of political agent for the Frankish emperor he endeavoured to sap the allegiance of the Dalmatian towns, and seduced them to acknowledge a dependence on the Emperor of the West. Ceaselessly active, plotting, governing, amassing money; all the while intent

* Ughello, *loc. cit.;* Sagornino, *loc. cit.;* Dandolo, *op. cit.,* cap. xvi. p. 14.

† By the treaty of 802, between Charles and Nicephorus. See Filiasi, *op. cit.,* cap. xxii.

‡ Dandolo, *op. cit.,* cap. xvi. p. 8.

upon his return to Venice and to Grado, where his heart really lay. The bishopric of Pola fell vacant, and, at the request of Charles, Leo most reluctantly conferred it upon Fortunatus, stipulating that should he ever recover his patriarchal See, he should be bound to relinquish that of Pola, with all its emoluments. The pope dreaded Fortunatus's rapacity. In a letter to Charles he begged the emperor to be moderate in his favours to the patriarch. "I pray you," he says, "while you are labouring for the temporal well-being of this man, think of his immortal soul; that through the fear of you he may the better fulfil his ministry. For we have heard no good report of him, such as becomes an archbishop, neither from these parts, nor yet from France, where you have lent him such powerful support. But, thank God, all is not unknown to you. Ask men whom you can trust; for those who praise him to you do so for a purpose and bought thereto." * But Charles still remained the patriarch's firm friend, and Fortunatus still retained sufficient weight to influence Venice and the Adriatic. Fortunatus may possibly have been the cause of that explosion which ruined Heraclea. In any case, he heard of it in Istria and rejoiced over the triumph of his friends. Its importance to him proved great. For Obelerio now believed himself strong enough to invite the patriarch to return to Grado. He hoped that the reappearance of Fortunatus in his See would add life and vigour to that party, whose victory he deemed secure upon the wreck of Heraclea.

* "Cod. Carol.," tom. ii. p. 47.

But reaction was active in the air of Venice, and the presence of Fortunatus served to stimulate it. Obelerio had steadily pursued his Frankish policy, and as steadily the temper of the people set against Charles and towards Byzantium once more. The conduct of their doge offered a continual subject for alarm ; and the growing power of the Franks, the consolidation of Pipin's kingdom in Italy, all tended to heighten that sentiment. Obelerio married a Frankish wife ; and, still further to parade his union with the conquerors, in the year 806 he left his capital to attend the court of Charles. While there he received, with all the submission of a subject, instructions as to the government and policy of Venice.* The Venetians could not accept in quiet the position of dependence which Obelerio designed for them. It seemed to them that their doge proposed to make Venice a fief of the Western Empire. The people felt that their ruler had proved once more unfaithful to the permanent instinct of his race. The pressure upon them was becoming severe. Their doge and their patriarch acted no longer as checks and counterpoises to each other ; on the contrary, they were at one, and both were working towards a consummation to which the whole instincts of the people were opposed. The ferment of popular feeling

---

* Mon. Germ. Hist., tom. i. p. 193 ; Einhard, ad ann. 806 ; Cod. DLI. alla Marciana ap. Romanin., *op. cit.*, cap. iv. Chronicon Reginonis, ap. Mon. Germ. Hist., *loc. cit.*, p. 558. The Marcian manuscript says, " De Obelerio alii scripserunt quo tum Gallicam quidem nobilem haberet uxorem, promissionibus allectis ad regem perexit offerens dominium sibi contradere."

manifested itself in a revolution against Obelerio and his party.* The Doge, however, was still strong enough to retain his hold upon the reins of government. The presentiment of the final crisis, which was clearly now approaching, accentuated all political passions, and while it raised a violent opposition to the doge, it forbade any one to stand aside, and confirmed all those who had originally held with Obelerio. The revolution failed in its object.

Hitherto the Empire of the East had hardly been an active agent in the development of Venice. Byzantium had not interfered directly with the politics of the lagoons. But the idea of the Great Roman Empire was ever present to the imagination of the people—a rock to which they could cling for support in any reaction against aggression from the West. Now, however, East and West were about to clash over Venice. Byzantium began to be an active factor in the movement of Venetian politics. The causes which immediately led to the awakening of the East were due to Fortunatus's conduct while an exile in Istria. His intrigues among the Dalmatian towns had resulted in the creation of a party favourably inclined towards Charles. The loyalty of the Dalmatian seaports was seriously shaken. Their attitude alarmed Nicephorus, the Emperor of the East; for at this moment the whole Italian policy of the Franks pointed to their desire to establish a fleet in the Adriatic. Nicephorus was a man of vigorous character, an able financier, and a brave, though unsuccessful, soldier. He had deposed Irene, and ascended the throne as the

* Chronicon Reginonis, *loc. cit.*

professed defender of the imperial majesty against the new-fangled Empire of the West. It was therefore impossible for Nicephorus to neglect the ominous signs along the Dalmatian coast. He despatched the patrician Niceta to the Adriatic with the imperial fleet, and Venice, as a vassal of the East, received a summons to furnish a contingent.* Obelerio would gladly have refused ; but the Franks, his allies, were not prepared to support him at the moment, and the temper of the people he governed had been steadily setting towards Byzantium ever since the fall of Heraclea. The Venetian squadron joined the fleet under the command of Niceta, and, after awing the Dalmatian towns, the patrician sailed to Venice. The policy of Obelerio and of Fortunatus, their intentions and actions as regards Venice and Dalmatia, were well known to the Eastern court. Niceta had been instructed to destroy their authority and to exact guarantees for the loyalty of the lagoons. The patriarch did not wait his coming, but fled again to Charles. An assembly convened by Niceta declared his See vacant and himself an outlaw. The patrician sailed to Constantinople, taking with him Beato, Obelerio's brother, as hostage for the doge's future conduct.†

The pressure upon Venice was growing more severe. Both East and West were beginning to put the question whose she meant to be ; nor would they

---

* Mon. Germ. Hist. ; Einhard, *loc. cit.;* Finlay, *op. cit.;* Filiasi, *op. cit.,* cap. xxiii. ; Romanin, *op. cit.,* cap. ix. ; Dandolo *op. cit.,* cap. xvi. p. 16.

† Einhard, *op. cit.,* p. 194 ; Sagornino, *loc. cit.;* Dandolo, *loc. cit.,* p. 18.

wait long for an answer. It would soon become impossible for Venice any further to conceal her hand, to continue that outward play between the policy of loyalty to the East and obedience to the West, while inwardly pursuing the problem of her own individual preservation. Inside Venice the respective power of the Frank and Byzantine factions had not yet been fairly tested. In the scene which had just been enacted under the guidance of Niceta, the presence of the imperial fleet and the absence of the Franks had terrified the followers of Obelerio into silence. But the doge declined to accept the action of Venice as a proof that his policy had lost the support of the people. He believed that the balance yet hung undetermined.

The question of their allegiance was again put to the Venetians the following year, and this time in more categorical form, requiring a more decisive answer. The result proved Obelerio's supposition to be correct; the balance had not yet finally dipped towards Byzantium and against Charles. The doge, living in the heat of the struggle, could not see that the conduct of Venice was in reality predetermined by the weakness of the East and the greater proximity of the Franks. He was not aware that the people, always bent on independence, would certainly declare their allegiance to that power which was least able to enforce it. Nicephorus again sent the imperial fleet into the Adriatic; * this time for the purpose of recovering Commacchio and the exarchate, in retaliation for Fortunatus's attempt to

* Einhard, *op. cit.*, p. 196 ; Romanin, *loc. cit.*

seduce the Dalmatian towns. Venice again received orders to furnish a contingent to the admiral Paul. To obey meant war on Pipin; to refuse meant defiance to Nicephorus. The critical moment for the future of Venice was at hand; while for the present either course was dangerous, perhaps fatal. A decided step either way would at least have secured to the Venetians an ally, Frank or Byzantine. But the balance of parties prevented the state from taking any positive line of action. Out of three possible issues, Venice pursued the most perilous, and by her conduct she severed herself both from East and West. The result, however, proved only fortunate, for it threw the state upon its own resources, and compelled Venice eventually to save herself by her own unaided energy. The party opposed to Obelerio forced the doge to supply the contingent to Paul's fleet. The expedition sailed to Commacchio and was defeated. This check roused the spirits of the Frankish faction; and when Paul returned with the remnants of his squadron to Venice, he encountered every kind of opposition. Obstacles were thrown in the way of his signing a treaty with Pipin, and his life was in such danger that he found himself obliged to fly.* This, then, was the result of the momentary balance between parties in Venice, apparently disastrous, but really propitious for the aspirations of the people. Pipin was now their enemy, for they had fought against him at Commacchio; Nicephorus had been alienated by the insults offered to his admiral Paul. Venice was face to face with the crisis.

* Einhard, *op. cit.*, p. 196; Filiasi, *loc. cit.*

Pipin did not long delay his action.* The advice given by Fortunatus seven years before, when he was at the court of Charles, had fallen on no unfruitful soil. The son of Charles was young, vigorous, courageous, eager to increase and consolidate his kingdom of Italy. The reduction of the lagoons offered an enterprise at once productive and glorious. The affair of Commacchio determined him to subdue those islanders who so stubbornly refused to acknowledge his sovereignty. But first his policy required the reduction of Dalmatia. He sent to ask Venice to join him in the undertaking.† For Venice there could be now no rest, no quiet, no standing aside. The forces which were determining her formation required this repeated and intensified pressure; she had reached the moment of fusion and fiery heat which precedes crystallization. Obelerio exerted every power at his disposal to induce his compatriots to accept the offered alliance with the king. He urged that the state could look for nothing from Nicephorus; that here was presented an opportunity to repair the error of the previous year, an occasion to obliterate animosity and secure her safety by union with the Franks. But the instincts of the people told them that salvation lay only in their own exertion, not in reliance on the power of any prince. The wave of reaction set in motion by the overthrow of Heraclea had gathered volume enough to claim its way. The Venetians declined to follow Obelerio; he found himself stranded and alone, the ruler of a people who refused to obey.

* Dandolo, *op. cit.*, cap. xvi. p. 23.   † Romanin, *loc. cit.*

Venice rejected Pipin's invitation, and prepared to defend herself, trusting to no other aid than the courage of her men and the intricacy of her lagoon channels. The king made ready for an immediate attack. His fleet lay at Ravenna, and in Friuli an army was at his disposal. From north and south he could concentrate his forces upon Venice. Victory seemed easy to him. But he left out of his calculation the natural defences of those sea-born cities ; he did not know the shoals and deeps of their sea home. By the advice of Angelo Participazio, a Heraclean noble, who assumed the lead as Obelerio's influence waned, the people removed their wives, their children, and their goods from Malamocco to a little island in the mid lagoon, Rialto, inaccessible by land or sea. The fighting men took up their post at Albiola, now Porto Secco, a village between Pelestrina and the port of Malamocco. There they awaited the attack of the Franks. Pipin seized on Brondolo, Chioggia, and Pelestrina. He endeavoured to press his squadrons on towards the capital, but the shoals opposed him. His vessels ran aground ; his pilots missed the channels; the Venetians from the further shore plied him with darts and stones. He could not force a passage to Malamocco, and even then Rialto was not reached ; it lay in view, but far away across seven miles of winding canals and undiscovered banks. For six months, through the winter of 809–810, Pipin and his Frankish chivalry wasted their energy in the struggle to advance. At length the summer heats drew on, and rumours of the approach of an Eastern fleet warned Pipin of his failure. He ventured on one last appeal. "Own yourselves my subjects," he cried to the Venetians, "for are you not within the borders of my kingdom?" "No! we are resolved to be the subjects of the Roman emperor, and not of you." * The king was forced to retire. He signed a treaty with the cities of the lagoons, whereby they consented to pay the nominal tribute formerly due to the Lombard kings, whose heir Pipin claimed to be. The debt was never discharged. Pipin left Venice filled with the bitterest mortification, and died the same year at Milan.†

Venice emerged from her trial an independent state. She had attained the object of her long desire. Byzantium owed her a deep debt for having checked the progress of the Frankish arms eastward. The empire of the West would trouble her no more. The agony and the victory completed her spiritual self-consciousness and the union of her various parts. Venice was homogeneous now, a whole, undivided, liberated from internal discord, and at peace. And not only was there fusion between her rival elements, but her people also became one with the place of

---

* Our most trustworthy authorities for this episode of Pipin's attack are Sagornino, *loc. cit.*, and Constantine Porphyrog., "De Adminis. Imp.," cap. xxviii. They are both of the following century. Einhard, a contemporary, is suspect through his Frankish sympathies and the manner in which he hurries over the event. The later Venetian historians, including Dandolo, are anxious to magnify the victory, and fill their accounts with legends and myths.

"ὑπὸ τὴν ἐμὴν χεῖρα καὶ πρόνοιαν γίνεσθε ἐπειδὴ ἀπὸ τῆς ἐμῆς χώρας καὶ ἐξουσίας ἐστέ." "ἡμεῖς δοῦλοι θέλομεν εἶναι τοῦ βασιλέως τῶν Ῥωμαίων καὶ οὐχὶ σοῦ" (Constantine, *loc. cit.*).

† Einhard, *op. cit.*, p. 197.

their habitation. Venetian men and Venetian lagoons had made and saved the state. The spirit of the waters, free, vigorous, and pungent, had passed in that stern moment of struggle into the being of the men who dwelt upon them; now the men were about to impose something of their spirit too, and build that incomparatively lovely city of the sea. Venice, in this union of the people and the place, declared the nature of her personality; a personality so infinitely various, so rich, so pliant, and so free, that to this day she wakens, and in a measure satisfies, a passion such as we feel for some life deeply beloved.

The island of Rialto had proved the advantage of its situation, and established a claim for gratitude as the asylum of Venice in her hour of need. The raids of Attila demonstrated the insecurity of the mainland; the attack of Pipin showed that the sea-coast was not more safe. Experience led to the final choice of this middle point. In the year 813 the seat of the government was removed to Rialto, under Angelo Participazio as doge.* Rialto became the capital of Venice—a city of compromise between the perils of terra firma and the banishment of the extreme *lidi*, Malamocco had destroyed Heraclea; she now renounced her supremacy in favour of Rialto, founded by a noble of the city she had ruined. Rialto became as it were a sacrament of reconciliation between Heraclea and Malamocco. Venice, battling blindly inside herself to win her freedom, found herself and achieved a unity with qualities which belong to her alone. It was the singular glory of Venice

* Dandolo, *op. cit.*, lib. viii. cap. i. p. 1; Sagornino, *loc. cit.*

that, of all Italy, she alone remained unscathed alike by the foreign ravages of the fifth century and the conquest of the eighth. The seed sown during the incursions of Attila bore fruit, and came to the birth when the Franks overthrew the Lombard kingdom. Venice was the virgin child of Italy's ruin; conceived in the midst of anguish and distress. born to the very manner of invasion, and from invasion she alone escaped, pure and undefiled. The achievement of Venice, the repulse of the Franks and the creation of herself, requires the embellishment of no fables to render it more glorious; yet we cannot wonder that the Venetians have loved to gather round this central victory a whole mythology of persons and events. The cannon-balls of bread, fired into the Frankish camp in mockery of Pipin's hopes to starve Rialto to surrender; the old woman, king of council (*rex consilii*), who lured the invader to that fatal effort where half his forces were lost, the bridge across the lagoon; the Canal Orfano, that ran with foreign blood and won its name from countless Frankish homes that day made desolate; above all, the sword of Charles, flung far into the sea when the great emperor acknowledged his repulse and cried, "As this, my brand, sinks out of sight, nor ever shall rise again, so let all thought to conquer Venice sink from out men's hearts, or they will feel, as I have felt, the heavy displeasure of God;" *—all these are myths, born of

* See Sanudo, "Vite dei Duchi," ap. Murat. Rer. It. Script., tom. xxii.; Cronaca Veneta da Canale, ap. Archiv. St. It., tom. viii. par. 7; Cron. Altinate, bk. viii. p. 219; Dandolo, *op. cit.*, cap. xvi. p. 23.

E

a pardonable pride; but Venice still remains her own most splendid monument.

The limit of this essay has been reached. Its course has shown the impulse of federal Venetia effecting itself in the creation of Rialto. Yet it is hardly possible to come to a full stop without a word about two principal actors in the drama, Fortunatus and Obelerio. Venice had attained to rest; for these two restless souls there was no longer any place in her. Their mission was fulfilled, their epoch passed them by, and they had not been blessed in dying with it. They were not born, but they had the equal misery to live, out of due season. The doge faded out of Venetian politics from the moment when he failed to carry the people with him to an alliance with Pipin. The victory of the Venetians and the creation of the new capital were achieved under the auspices of a Byzantine reaction and the guidance of a Heraclean noble. A nuncio from the court of Constantinople formally deposed Obelerio, and banished him.* From his place of exile he yearned ever towards his native waters, and nursed delusive hopes of restoration. But his influence died when he was deposed. He made one fruitless descent on Malamocco, hoping to waken the city by the outworn cry of democracy and hatred of Heraclea, still vital in the person of the Doge Participazio. He failed miserably. Party feuds and watchwords were old and meaningless for the Venetians now, merged in the new fact of Rialto. Participazio dispersed the

* Dandolo, *op. cit.*, lib. vii. cap. xvi. p. 24; Sagornino, *loc. cit.*

handful of revolutionists, and Obelerio forfeited his head. With him the last sparks of Malamoccan supremacy were quenched for ever.

Fortunatus, who had fled before the presence of Niceta and the imperial fleet, returned to Grado for a brief space under the wing of Pipin and the Franks. But the king's repulse warned the patriarch not to try the temper of the victorious Byzantine party. For the third time he quitted his little island for the Frankish court. When Angelo Participazio had established the government securely in Rialto, Fortunatus applied for a safe conduct and permission to return. The doge believed that now, at least, there could be no more danger from the patriarch's Frankizing policy, and permission was granted. Fortunatus came back to Grado, and, at first, devoted himself with his wonted vigour to the adornment of his church and to the cultivation of the episcopal lands. We hear of him at Grado, a small island, like Torcello as we know it now, with a large brick church, and solid, square, self-sustaining campanile shining rather redly across the waters. A few straggling, low brick houses, a winding canal, and banks trailing with creepers in spring, over the tops of which rise the dusky red-tipped leaves of the young pomegranate trees, or blazing in autumn with the endlessly varied crimsons of the dying tamarisk and sea-lavender. Behind Grado the hills rise in the distance—sharp dolomite peaks that catch the sunset lights and flame rosily across the grey lagoon. Between the shore and the hills the country is all broken and rough with limestone rocks cropping out everywhere, so rugged and untilled that there is just sufficient herbage to pasture some flocks of thin and meagre sheep. The land is scarred with white ghiarre, the rubbish of stony desolation swept down from the mountains every spring by the Tàgliamento and the Isonzo.

Here, then, Fortunatus busied himself with the masons whom he called from France;* pouring out the treasures he had amassed in Istria, importing precious marbles for his church's façade, for the colonnades and porticoes; filling his cathedral with altars of gold, altars of silver, pictures, purple hangings, tapestries, carpets, *panni d'oro*, jewels, crowns, "the like of which are not to be found in all Italy," chandeliers of rare workmanship with branching lights. And the bishop in the midst of all this growing magnificence, superintending the builders, laying the beams, designing the patterns for the inlaid stones. The care of his church was not enough to occupy him. Agriculture, too, claimed a share of his inordinate activity, and at San Pelegrino he established a stud farm for the breeding of horses.† It would have been well for him if he had rested there. But he could not keep his mind from political intrigue; a demon of restlessness pursued him to the end. He thought that the Frankish party might still be revived in Venice; he, at least, never despaired of final success. The Venetians more than suspected his influence in the

* "Feci venire magistros di Francia" (Fortunatus's will, ap. Hazlitt, *op. cit.*, Doc. II., and Marin, "Storia Civile e Politica del Commercio d. Venez" (Venezia : 1798), tom. i. cap. vii.).

† See Filiasi, *op. cit.*, tom. vi. cap. 1.

family feuds which tore the household of the doge in two, and drove his younger son, Giovanni, into exile.* The presence of Fortunatus was a never-failing source of disquiet to the whole of Venice. At length a plot against the life of Angelo Participazio himself roused the extreme wrath of the people. The plot clearly had its origin among the broken fragments of the Frankish party, and as surely Fortunatus was its prime instigator. The Venetians deposed, and for the last time expelled the patriarch from his See.† His own passion for intrigue, his own inability to perceive that Venice had taken a new direction when Rialto rose to be the capital, that the old formulæ of Frank or Byzantine had little import now, were the causes of Fortunatus's ruin. He passed from the sphere of Venetian politics, where he had played so active and so perilous a part, into a region of obscurity whither we can hardly follow him. Henceforth he ceased to exercise any considerable influence on Venetian affairs. His name appears less and less frequently in the chronicles ; yet we may be sure he was not quiet nor at rest. Whenever he does appear, it is always in connection with some plot or some intrigue, each scheme wilder and more hopeless than its predecessor, as the patriarch's authority dwindled, as his strength failed, as he sank surely down the decline of a life that had been so full and yet so fruitless. On his expulsion from the lagoons, Fortunatus crossed to Dalmatia, where he had already secured connections, and applied himself to estab-

---

* Dandolo, *op. cit.*, lib. viii. cap. i. p. 17 ; Sagornino, *loc. cit.*
† Dandolo, *loc. cit.*, p. 35.

lishing these upon a firmer basis. His friend Charles
had died in the year 813, and the patriarch could look
for little help from the Frankish court, torn to pieces
by the feuds of the great emperor's successors. He
turned to seek for aid from Constantinople, from
that court whose persistent enemy he had always
shown himself. His personal policy wavered ominously; the power had gone out of the man. He
sought to gain the favour of Byzantium, under whose
influence he hoped to be restored to Grado. With
that object in view, he applied himself to harass the
Emperor Lewis, as far as in him lay. He sent into
the service of the rebel duke of Pannonia that band
of military engineers which he had raised in Istria,*
and thus materially assisted the duke in fortifying his
country. For this conduct Lewis cited the patriarch
to the Frankish court. Fortunatus feigned obedience
and set out; but on the way he turned aside and fled
to Zara, whence he took ship for Constantinople.†
There he remained three years, labouring, we may
believe, to secure support : but in vain, as the sequel
proved. In the year 824 he left the capital in the
train of an embassy sent to treat with the Emperor of
the West. He trusted that his case would be mentioned among other points, and that so, at peace with
East and West, he might return to Grado, for which
he never ceased to long. But Lewis refused to pardon
or to listen to him. The ambassadors declined to
jeopardize the success of their mission by any un-

---

* Einhard, *op. cit.*, p. 208, ap. ann. 821, " artifices et muria-
rios mittendo."

† Mabillon, *op. cit.*, tom. ii. p. 458 ; Einhard, *loc. cit.*

welcome proviso in favour of Fortunatus; they repudiated and ignored him. Lewis ordered him to Rome, under a kind of arrest, there to answer before the pope for his share in the Pannonian revolt.* Fortunatus commenced his journey, but never accomplished it. He died upon the way, a broken and a failing man; a restless end to a restless life. His last thoughts were turned, with that indomitable hope of his, to the quiet church among the lagoons, whose bishop he had been for so many unquiet years. The closing words of his will, bequeathing his vast fortune to his See, have an almost pathetic ring when we remember all the failure of his career, the hope against hope deferred: "I will pay my debts before God," he writes; "and so it shall be when I am come back to my own Holy Church, in peace and tranquillity I will rejoice with you all the days of my life."

* Einhard, *op. cit.*, p. 212, ad. ann. 824; Dandolo, *loc. cit.*, p. 36.

BAJAMONTE TIEPOLO AND THE CLOSING OF THE GREAT COUNCIL.

AMONG the many memorial stones of Venice, there is one likely enough to escape notice. It is a little square of white marble, let into the pavement of the Campo Sant' Agostino; and on it are these letters: "LOC. COL. BAI. TIE. MCCCX." Right in the heart of Venice, between the Frari and Campo San Polo, the feet of strangers rarely bring them by it. Yet the events, the closing act of which this stone commemorates, are among the most important in the constitutional growth of the city. This slab marks the place of the *colonna infame* raised on the site of Bajamonte Tiepolo's house to perpetuate the recollection of his conspiracy and failure by this inscription—

> "De Bajamonte fo questo tereno
> E mò per suo iniquo tradimento
> Posto in comun e per l'altrui spavento
> E per mostrar a tutti sempre seno."

Time has come to cover this among other sore places; the column is gone; it rests now, far away, cracked and riven, in a quiet garden by the Lake of Como; the little marble slab is found only by eyes that look for it. But over Tiepolo's name has been piled a cairn of obloquy more hard to move. Chronicler after chronicler has flung his stone on the heap, and Tiepolo still remains "Bajamonte traditore."

Is this just? The chronicles are too frequently partial; they are too readily and too often the mouth-piece of success, which has won its privilege of open and uncontradicted speech. They trumpet the fame of victory; the character and motives of the defeated they leave—

> "black
> To all the growing calumnies of time,
> Which never spare the fame of him who fails,
> But try the Cæsar or the Cataline
> By the true touchstone of desert—success."

We cannot accept the portraits which they draw without reserve. Tiepolo, as they present him to us, is a restless, ambitious, and turbulent noble, aiming at the overthrow of an excellent paternal government for the sole purpose of satisfying his individual appetite for sovereignty. We are asked to believe that his conspiracy was based on nothing but per-sonal jealousy and ambition. It is hardly as such that we can accept him. He was, very likely, no single-minded hero; his motives may not have been unmixed; but the question he raised was a question worth raising—it touched the very core of Venetian home politics. Her past history justified Tiepolo's attempt; his failure determined the course she was to pursue. Tiepolo represented one of the essential elements in the original composition of the Venetian state. His conspiracy was the death-throe of an older order of government. We cannot look upon him as a merely factious rebel and traitor.

In the earliest years of its life the vital spark had been evoked in Venice by the friction between the nobility of Heraclea and the primitive fishing population of Malamocco. Under external pressure these two elements had come together at Rialto and founded the modern city of Venice. A rapid increase of wealth was the result of the internal quiet obtained by the fusion of discordant elements in Rialto. Venice profited by her period of rest to apply her energies to commerce and trade with the East. But this very augmentation of prosperity prepared the way for new internal difficulties. The old aristocratic factor, the Heraclean party, still retained many of its characteristics, claiming a superiority in virtue of its descent; while, on the other hand, from the people arose a class of men who by commercial activity had acquired a wealth far exceeding that of the old nobility. These men were drawn together by the common desire to assert themselves, to obtain the full value of their wealth, and the recognition of themselves as a distinct element in the polity. It was inevitable that they should seek to develop themselves as an aristocracy. No other course was open to them. But, as inevitably, such a development brought them into collision with the old hereditary nobility, already firmly rooted, and also with the people from whom they wished to differentiate themselves, but from whom they had really sprung. The achievement of their object could only tend to the creation of a plutocracy, absorbing in itself the rights of the people and the powers of the doge, round whom the elder aristocracy gathered. The apparition of this third party in the state gave presage of internal rupture which was destined to end in revolution ; and the epoch was marked by the quarrels between the families of Dandolo and Tiepolo.*

Neither the people nor the old nobility were as powerful as this new party, and, accordingly, in the face of their common and aggressive foe they displayed a tendency to draw to one another. It was doubtful, however, whether the bond which united them was of sufficient strength to bear the strain of inherently opposite impulses ; indeed, in the end it proved not to be strong enough. But for the present, however, they were at one ; and we shall see the people in their last constitutional effort calling for a Tiepolo rather than a Gradenigo as their doge.

The constitutional history of Venice, from 1084 to the date of Tiepolo's conspiracy in 1310, turns upon the progressive movement of the new commercial aristocracy and the various steps by which it made itself paramount. This aristocracy had three primary objects in view, and its development was regulated accordingly. Its first desire was to crush the power of the doge, for he was the crown and centre of the old nobility, and frequently chosen from among them. The new party intended to use the ducal title and the ducal publicity as a cloak for their own tyranny ; as a mask behind which they could shelter, and through which they might, as through a mouthpiece, issue their crushing and repressive edicts. They suc-

* Romanin, *op. cit.*, vol. ii. lib. vii. cap. i. p. 288, note 1.

ceeded. Before the close of the thirteenth century, the dukedom was no longer an office of real honour or of power. The ducal palace was too often merely a prison into which this cold and determined aristocracy could thrust any one of their own number who had the misfortune to incur their suspicion. The head of the state was deprived of almost all real weight, and left with empty dignities alone. The tragedy of Francesco Foscari and his family in the fifteenth century illustrates terribly the fate in store for any prince who should try to resuscitate the ducal authority.

The second object which directed the policy of the commercial aristocracy was the constitutional extinction of the people on the one hand, and, on the other, the reduction of the old nobility. So long as the people still retained their ancient right to share in the election of the doge, so long as the members of the more ancient families were still the successful candidates for the dukedom, the new party felt that it was not yet supreme, and nothing short of supremacy would satisfy it. The third determining object was its own consolidation. While it repressed everything external to itself, it was continually remodelling, rebuilding, reforming, internally strengthening itself, so that when the final struggle came, it was able to offer an impregnable front to the attack of its foes. The new aristocracy forced itself like a solid, irresistible wedge, like the ploughshare of an alpine glacier, into the living body of the Venetian constitution, and, in the end, froze the whole organism to that rigidity which, for a time, proved strength, but, in the end, was death. It tore its way between the doge and the people, severing, annihilating, and thrusting out the older aristocracy, the living matter which bound the two together. It retained the dukedom simply as a veneer upon its own solid surface, structurally unconnected with it; while the people were ground down to a smooth bed upon which it might rest.

The steps by which this third party, the new aristocracy, worked towards its goal, destroyed all other powers in the state, and emerged as sole lord of Venice, must be noted, for they form the long prelude to the closing of the Great Council and Tiepolo's conspiracy, which resulted from that revolution. For some time previous to the year 1172, the aristocracy had been curtailing the functions and privileges of the dukedom. Its judicial attributes had long disappeared; they had been transferred to the three Guidici del Palazzo, and even the appeal from this court, which formerly lay to the duke, had been vested in the supreme court of Venice, the Quarantia. But it was not till the election of the Doge Sebastian Ziani, in the year 1172, that the aristocracy obtained a solid and independent standing ground in the constitution. A gap of six months intervened between the assassination of Doge Michele II. and the election of Ziani. In those six months the nobles drew together into a legislative council, called henceforth by the name of the Maggior Consiglio;* the base of the pyramidal

* It is improbable that this was the first appearance of such

Venetian constitution, the largest cylinder, out of which all the lesser cylinders of the various executive and legislative colleges were drawn. The immediate object of this cohesion on the part of the aristocracy, old and new alike, was to secure to themselves the sole voice in the election of the doge; to rob the people of their share in appointing the head of the state. And this they did; the election of Ziani was unconstitutional, for it lacked the seal of popular acclaim.* But the robbery was veiled under the specious formula with which the new doge was presented to the people, "Questo è il vostro doge si vi piacerà," and, *subauditur*, whether it please you or not.†

And now, from this solid basis of the Maggior Consiglio, the aristocracy could thrust itself forward and upward, until every office in the state was an emanation from itself alone. But this operation required time. Owing to the mode of election, the Great Council was not a close body; a seat in it was still open to all citizens of Venice. The new aristocracy were resolved to purge themselves of this popular element, not because they had any

a council in Venice, but it is certain that its existence was reckoned as an undisputed fact from this date. The manner of electing was originally this : Twelve electors were appointed, two from each sestieri, or division of the city ; each elector named forty citizens, noble or plebeian ; these 480 formed the Maggior Consiglio (Rom., *op. cit.*, vol. ii. p. 89; Giannoti, "Dialogus de Rep. Ven.," p. 40, and the notes of Crassus to the same ; Ap. Grœv. Thesaur. Anti. Ital.).

　* Bernardo Guistiniano, "Dell' Origine di Venetia," lib. xi.

　† Marin, "Storia Civile e Politica del Com. dei Venez.," vol. iii. lib. iii. cap. vii.

true aristocratic bias, but because, for the purposes of such a government as they contemplated, they felt that a body like theirs must be made a caste— must become oligarchical. But as yet their party was young, with many difficulties to overcome; notably the power of the doge, and the power of the old aristocracy; the one supporting the other as integral portions of the same political system.

Nevertheless, the immense stride which the commercial aristocracy had taken towards a real sovereignty in the state was soon shown by the establishment of the college of six Consiglieri Ducali,* in some respects a sort of privy council board. The creation of this office was a decided blow to the ducal independence. It robbed the doge of his power of initiative in the legislature; it curtailed his personal freedom of action; for now constitutional measures were proposed not by the doge alone, but by the doge in council, and in council with the aristocracy. Questions of foreign policy—especially as regarded commerce—the audiences granted to ambassadors, were entrusted no longer to the doge alone, but to the doge in council. The invention and development of this college placed two of the most important ducal functions in commission, and that commission was the appointment and the servant of the aristocracy. But while restricting the real power of their doge, the aristocracy continued to augment the outward pomp attendant on him.

* Originally this board had consisted of two councillors. This was now held to be too weak a check on the doge, and four more were added. See Roman., *op. cit.*, vol. ii. p. 92.

This could be of no danger to themselves; it only added a splendour to the state and helped to flatter their vanity. On the day of his election the doge was carried round the piazza,* like the Eastern Emperors, scattering gold. He received an oath of allegiance from all the citizens every four years. He never now left his palace without an escort of nobles and citizens. His person was declared sacrosanct. The ducal position was becoming defined—"Dux in foro, servus in consilio;" later on he was to be "captivus in palatio" as well.

This first attack was soon followed by a further restriction of the constitutional powers and privileges pertaining to the dukedom. During the first thirty years of the thirteenth century the College of the Pregadi † (the invited), usually known as the Senate, was established as a permanent branch of the legislature. Formerly the doge, like the kings of England, had been free to ask any citizen to assist him with advice on matters of state. But now the Great Council issued two decrees: the first,‡ that for the future the members of the Pregadi should be elected by the Great Council itself, and out of that body, as the other members of the government were; the second, that the number of the Pregadi be fixed at

---

* Dandolo, "Chronicon," lib. x. cap. 1; Marin., *op. cit.*, vol. iii. lib. ii. cap. vii.; Sansovino, "Venezia, città Nobili"* e Singolare," lib. xiii.; Vita di Seb. Ziani. Muazzo; "St. d. governo d. Rep. d. Venez;" Roman., *op. cit.*, vol. ii. p. 255, note 5.

† Sandi., "I Principi di Storia Civ. d. Rep. d. Ven." (Venezia: 1755), lib. iv. p. 507, cap. ii.

‡ Sandi., *loc. cit.*

sixty. Here, then, was the Senate constituted beyond the power or the pleasure of the doge; constituted as a limb of the aristocracy. Undoubtedly this was a curtailment of the ducal freedom, a further tying of the doge's hands. For he was no longer able, by choosing his council himself, to determine what kind of advice he should receive, and to flavour it according to his own liking; but he was compelled to accept such advice as the Great Council chose to give him, and it was now seasoned to the palate of the aristocracy. Advice, when not self-chosen, is frequently a constitutional synonym for command. By the election of his councillors from the Maggior Consiglio, the doge was rendered more than ever a servant of the new aristocratic party.

But while the new party have been pinioning their doge, they have also been advancing on their other wing, pressing forward the other side of their attack against the ancient nobility. On the abdication of Pietro Ziani in the year 1229, two competitors for the ducal chair presented themselves—Jacopo Tiepolo, of the old conservative party,* and Marino Dandolo, a member of a family which had declared for the party of revolution. It was doubtless of great moment to the new aristocracy, now that it had succeeded in limiting the ducal power, to seat one of its own number on the ducal throne. With a man after their own heart established in the palace, there was no reason why they should not succeed in baffling the old aristocracy. The contest was

* Tiepolo had been *podestà* at Constantinople and duke of Candia (Rom., *op. cit.*, vol. ii. p. 212).

F

therefore a keen one. At this period the number of ducal electors was forty, and so close was the voting that the forty were equally divided. The election was decided by lot, and fell in favour of Tiepolo. But this check to the new aristocracy only served to call forth a vigorous display of their real power. The Maggior Consiglio appointed the five Correttori della Promissione Ducale,* or committee for supervising the oath of allegiance tendered by the doge on assuming office. The Correttori received authority to alter and amend the oath in any direction they might think fit, subject always to the sanction of the Great Council. At the same time, and with the same object, the new aristocracy appointed the three inquisitors,† whose duty it was to review the life and actions of a deceased doge, and to note where he had violated his oath. The inquisitors were armed with power over the heirs and property of the late doge, in order that the fear of them might weigh with him when alive. The glory of the ducal office could not be much further reduced. It only remained to add some vexatious personal restrictions in order to render the possession of the dukedom an honour not to be desired by any man of high pride or sensitiveness.

There was, however, a second important result

---

* Rom., *op. cit.*, vol. ii. p. 244. The earliest *promissione* extant is that of the Doge Henry Dandolo, 1193. The *promissione* of Tiepolo is given as Doc. No. VI. in Mr. Hazlitt's "History of the Venetian Republic," where it may be compared with that of Dandolo, which precedes it (Sandi., *op. cit.*, lib. iv. cap. iii.).

† Sandi., *loc. cit.*

arising from the election of Tiepolo. It became obvious that if the electoral body could be divided always, as it had been on this occasion, some reform of the whole elective machinery was required. The new party, with their special objects steadily in view, determined to use the opportunity for their own purposes. Accordingly they elaborated that extraordinarily complex system of combined lot and ballot which resulted in the appointment of the forty-one electors to the dukedom.* They hoped that this system would prevent any powerful group in the Maggior Consiglio from ever being able to nominate a doge at their own pleasure. This reform was really a blow to the old aristocracy, who, up to this time, had undoubtedly the larger experience in affairs

---

* The first election by the forty-one was that of Marin Morosini in 1249. See Rom., *op. cit.*, vol. ii. p. 249.

This was the process :—

1. All who sat in the Maggior Consiglio, and were above thirty years of age, elected by ballot thirty members.
2. Thirty reduced themselves by lot to nine.
3. Nine elected by ballot, with at least six votes each, forty.
4. Forty reduced themselves by lot to twelve.
5. Twelve elected by ballot twenty-five.
6. Twenty-five reduced themselves by lot to nine.
7. Nine elected by ballot forty-five.
8. Forty-five reduced themselves by lot to eleven.
9. Eleven elected by ballot forty-one.
10. Forty-one elected doge with at least twenty-five votes.

See Rom., *op. cit.*, vol. ii. pp. 289, 290, note 3 ; also the long account of the election of Lorenzo Tiepolo in the "Cronaca Veneta" of Martin de Canal, capp. 257–259; "Arch. St. It.," tom. viii. ; Sandi., *loc. cit.* Daru, " Histoire de la Rep. de Venise " (Paris : 1819), vol. i. p. 378, gives some popular doggerels on the mode of election.

of state, and therefore the larger control in the selection of the doge. Besides this result, the new aristocracy possibly foresaw that when they had succeeded in obliterating or swamping the old nobility in the Great Council, such a purely fortuitous method of election as the one now created would greatly help to prevent their own party from falling to pieces through internal jealousies, when the day came that they, and they alone, should possess the field.

After the year 1250 the annihilation of the ducal authority was completed by a series of restrictions on the personal private action of the doge. He was no longer the real head of the state, above all offices, and from whom all other branches of the government fell away in descending and spreading lines. The position was just reversed; he was for the future to be simply the ornamental apex of the aristocracy, drawing all his existence from below him, from the base of the constitutional pyramid. A clause was added to the *promissione* by which the doge pledged himself to execute the orders of the Great Council, or of any other council, be they what they might.* Nor dared the doge exhibit his portrait, his bust, or his coat-of-arms † anywhere outside the walls of the ducal palace, that all might

---

* Sandi., *op. cit.*, lib. iv. cap. iv. p. 2.

† On the death of Renier Zeno in 1268, the quarrels between the two parties in the state, represented by the Dandolo and the Tiepolo respectively, grew so dangerous and began to spread so far, that a law was passed forbidding a citizen to display the arms of any great house as a note of his politics—the first warning of the constitutional struggle about to take place (Rom., *op. cit.*, vol. ii. p. 288, note 1).

know that the essence of the dukedom was not resident in the doge, but in the whole aristocratic body. The doge was, in fact, to be the phenomenon of the aristocracy, with no individual existence, but living only as the outward and visible sign of the inward aristocratic spirit.* In this view he was held to be incompetent to announce his accession to the throne in any foreign court, except that of Rome. No one was to kneel to him, kiss hands, make presents, or render him any act of homage which could possibly be construed as homage to the individual rather than homage to the spirit of the aristocracy in which alone the doge lived and moved. The elevation of a member of any family to the supreme office barred all other members of that family from holding posts under government either in Venice or in Venetian territory. The sons of the doge were ineligible as members of any councils except the Maggior Consiglio and the Pregadi,† and in this latter they had no vote. Finally, to complete the isolation of the ducal throne, to close the doors of the princely prison, it was decreed that no one who might be elected to the office of doge should have the right to refuse that appointment; that no doge could of his own choice resign his office, nor ever quit Venice. ‡

* He was not allowed to trade either in person or by proxy (Rom., *op. cit.*, vol. ii. p. 292, note 1).

† Rom., *op. cit.*, vol. ii. p. 250; Sandi., *loc. cit.* Neither the doge, nor his sons, nor his nephews might contract a foreign marriage without the consent of the Maggior Consiglio. See the *promissione* of Jacopo Contarini, 1275 (Rom., *loc. cit.*, p. 305, note 2).

‡ Sandi., *loc. cit.*

So far, then, we have followed the advancing steps of the new aristocracy. It had absorbed the ducal authority, and had delivered two well-planted blows— one at the old nobility, by introducing a mode of election to the dogado which destroyed the ancient influence of that body; the other at the people, by robbing them of their constitutional privilege of a voice in the election of the doge. But complete victory over these powers had not yet been won. The new party had yet to establish and consolidate itself internally, and in the process the final collision was brought about—a collision which terminated in the Tiepolo-Querini conspiracy. As long as a seat in the Great Council was open to the people there still remained a large and indefinite popular element in the constitution; from this element the aristocracy determined to free themselves.

The tumultuous nature of democratic assemblies will usually lend a handle to those who desire to establish a tyranny. It was upon the necessity for curbing the jealousy, the ambition, the feud engendered by a yearly struggle for a seat in the Great Council, that the new party based their proposals of October 5, 1286. By these proposals it was intended to define the right to a seat in the council for all future time. Accordingly the three heads of the Quarantia moved,* first, that none should be eligible for a seat who could not prove that a paternal ancestor had already sat; second, that the doge, the majority of

* See Teutori, "Il vero Caratere Polit. d. Baj. Tiep.," p. 74; Romanin, *op. cit.*, vol. ii. p. 342, note 3; Sandi., *op. cit.*, lib. v. cap. i. p. 1.

the Consiglieri Ducali, and the majority of the Great Council should have the power to elect to a seat in the council any who should be excluded by the preceding clause. The doge opposed the motion, and carried his opposition by eighty-two against forty. Although the motion was thus lost, yet it was a distinct declaration of programme, and to this programme the new aristocracy devoted itself for the next ten years. In this policy there were two intentions visible : one was to make the aristocracy a close body for the future, sharply defined, rigid, capable of very little further expansion ; the other, to make membership in this close body an indispensable qualification to all officers of state. These objects were the logical conclusion following from the creation of the Great Council in the year 1172; though the realization of them would undoubtedly be a violation of the constitution.

They were, however, to be realized ; the constitution was to be violated, but by another doge. In the year 1289 Giovanni Dandolo died. He was buried in the Church of San Giovanni e Paolo. As the crowd of senators, councillors, procurators, and magistrates issued from the great door of the church, after the funeral service was over, they found the piazza thronged by the people. They were there once more, and for the last time, to assert their right to be heard in the election of the doge.* Their cry was not for a Dandolo or a Gradenigo, but for Jacopo Tiepolo, a representative of the old nobility, and closely connected with those families who were violently

* Rom., *op. cit.*, vol. ii. p. 323.

opposed to the revolution which was silently going on in the state. No choice could have been less fortunate. Tiepolo was a man of good abilities; he had held many important posts under the government. But he was certainly timid; perhaps at heart averse to bloodshed and filled with horror at the prospect of civil war. He knew that his elevation to the dukedom would exasperate the new party to such a pitch as to render a violent explosion inevitable. He was not the man to lead the people and the old nobility at a crisis like the present; he suffered himself to be over-persuaded, and withdrew to his villa on the mainland. A great occasion for the anti-reform party was lost, and civil war became more probable than ever.

The popular cries from the piazza of Zanipolo rang in the ears of the new aristocracy, and warned them that they were as yet far from success. Much depended on the selection of a doge. It was necessary to find a man who should be at once devoted to their cause and yet of commanding powers. Their choice was happily directed; it fell upon a young man, comparatively young for so high an honour, Piero Gradenigo. He was thirty-eight years old at that time, and *podestà* of Capo d'Istria. In every way he was suited to the occasion. From his birth devoted to the new party, fully grasping their political intentions, rapid and intrepid in action, he at the same time possessed a coolness of judgment which made him pre-eminently fitted to guide his party through a crisis like the present. His unpopularity with the people, which won for him the name of " Pierazzo," was only a further recommendation in the eyes of the new aristocracy. He summed up in his person the essence of the party he was now called upon to lead.

Gradenigo arrived from Capo d'Istria, and was received in ominous silence by the populace. The new doge at once applied himself to the work that was expected of him. The propositions of 1286 clearly indicated the wishes of his party. Nothing remained for him but to reformulate them and propose them afresh in the council. In the year 1296 he moved the famous measure which has since been known as the *Serrata del Maggior Consiglio*, the closing of the Great Council.* The terms of this act were :—

" 1. That all who have sat in the Maggior Consiglio during the last four years shall present themselves for ballot before the Forty, and, on obtaining twelve votes, shall be members of the Maggior Consiglio for one year.

" 2. That those who fail to present themselves now, owing to absence from Venice, shall do so on their return.

" 3. That three electors be appointed, who, on the indication of the doge and his council, may nominate certain citizens from among those who are excluded by the first clause. That those nominated shall go through the ballot before the Forty, and, on obtaining twelve votes, shall sit in the Maggior Consiglio.

---

* The measure was not carried till February, 1297 (Rom., *op. cit.*, vol. ii. pp. 343, 344, note 2 ; Tentori, *op. cit.*, pp. 74, 75, 76, where the act is given in full ; Sandi., *loc. cit.* ; Gianotii, *op. cit.*, p. 53.

"4. That the three electors shall be members of the Maggior Consiglio.

"5. That this statute may not be repealed except on the vote of five out of the six Consiglieri Ducali, twenty-five of the Forty, and two-thirds of the Great Council.

"6. That, within the first fifteen days of each year, the Consiglieri Ducali shall move the question whether the whole act is to stand or to be modified or repealed.

"7. That the heads of the Forty shall post the names of those who are about to be balloted for three days before the election takes place. That thirty shall constitute a quorum of the Forty."

This measure was carried. But its terms were not stringent enough to satisfy the new aristocracy. Their body was not yet sufficiently close; a seat in the Great Council could be too easily obtained. In 1298 the act was amended; a majority of the Forty, in place of only twelve votes, became indispensable to secure a seat. In the same year the list of selected candidates was confined to those who could prove that a paternal ancestor had at some time sat in the Great Council. In the year 1315 the government opened the " Libro d'Oro"—an official record of all those who possessed the requisite qualifications, and whose names could be submitted to the ballot. A rush of citizens to establish their nobility, to secure a place in the governing class before it should be too late, took place. Abuses soon appeared in the golden book : parents entered the names of illegitimate children, and the severe decrees of 1316 and 1319 became necessary to purge the list. The avvogadori del commun were entrusted with inquisitorial powers to examine family history; the duties of a herald's office were added to their functions. If they admitted a name to the " Libro d'Oro " that was taken as sufficient proof of its qualification. The office of the three electors was abolished. All whose names appeared on the lists of the golden book were, on attaining the age of twenty-five, considered eligible to a seat in the Maggior Consiglio.

It would be a mistake to suppose that the closing of the Great Council was in any sense a *coup d'état.* The constitutional history of Venice had been tending in that direction for more than a century; and the actual measure was not passed at one stroke, or by unconstitutional violence, but occupied several years before it could be finally established. Nor was it an absolute and rigid closing of the council; a little stream of fresh blood might still creep in through the grace of the doge and the three electors, although it is true that the free circulation from the people, the heart of the state, was effectually choked. The decree virtually cancelled family history previous to 1172, the date when the Great Council was formally established. It did not matter how old a family might be, nor what services it might have rendered to the state; if, by some accident, none of its members, during these hundred and twenty-four years, had sat in the Maggior Consiglio, that family now became disfranchised, unrepresented, robbed of all share in ruling the state it may have helped to make. The result of the statute was to divide the population into two classes. The one, by an accident of parentage, had a right to claim a seat in the Great Council of Venice; the other had no such right, nor any hope of obtaining it, but by the exceptional grace of men who, before the passing of the act, were, constitutionally, their equals. And these graces were rendered more and more difficult to secure, till, in the year 1328, they seem to have ceased altogether; nor were they renewed till after the war of Chioggia, in the year 1380, when an addition of thirty families was made to the roll of the Venetian patriciate. To be deprived of a seat in the Great Council was to be doomed for life to silence in Venice. The way to all honours, to all activity, lay through that assembly; those who were condemned to live outside it were, in fact, disfranchised. The aristocracy had effected their object; they had robbed a free people of their rights and converted them to their own sole use. When we think of the injustice of the act we cannot wonder that the closing of the Great Council caused a conspiracy which shook Venice to her foundations; nay, we are almost tempted to regret that it did not succeed.

The new aristocracy triumphed; but doubtless they did not expect to be left in undisturbed enjoyment of their victory. Nor were they, although their opponents, the old aristocracy and the people, failed to unite their forces, the only course which offered any prospect of success against the victorious party. The popular indignation was the first to make itself felt. In the year 1300 Marco Bocconio, a man of respectable but not of noble family, organized a rising of the populace.* He was not equal to his task. The doge was warned in time; the conspiracy

* See Rom., *op. cit.*, vol. iii. cap. i.

never had the deadliness of secrecy. We may dismiss this futile attempt almost as curtly as the chronicler Sanudo does.* "It is written," he says, "that the doge took good means to have the conspirators in his hands, and had them." Good means truly. Bocconio and his friends had determined on a physical assertion of their right to enter the Great Council. Followed by a mass of the people, they presented themselves at the door of the chamber and knocked. Those inside were ready; the door was opened, and, in the doge's name, the leaders were invited to enter, one by one, that they might submit to the ballot and win their seat. Bocconio and ten of his followers passed in; they were instantly seized and executed in the prisons; the voice of this revolt was stifled beneath the waters of the lagoon that hid so many of Venice's secrets. After the leaders were despatched, between five and six hundred of their supporters are said to have suffered death. "And so," to quote the chronicler again, "ended this sedition, in such wise that no one dared any more to open his mouth after a like fashion." †

Not after a like fashion, it is true; for the people had entered their protest, had struck their blow, and had failed. It remained for the old conservative party to make their attempt against the revolution which had been effected. But they were not ready yet, and were by no means unwilling to wait. Time was all in their favour, for the foreign policy of Gradenigo and his followers was daily deepening

---

* Sanudo, "Vite dei Duchi," ap. Muratori, Rer. It. Scrip., tom. xxii. p. 581.

† Ibid., *loc. cit.*

the hatred against them. The doge's insistance on the Venetian claim to Ferrara had involved the republic in a disastrous war; but worse than that, it had brought Venice into collision with the pope. The Holy See had revived an obsolete title to the Ferrarese; after repeated orders to the Venetians to retire from before Ferrara, there came a sentence of excommunication against the whole state of Venice. The clergy left the city; the sacraments were refused; burial, even, with religious rites was denied. The sentence weighed heavily on the people. But worse was to follow. The excommunication was supported by the publication of a crusade; liberty and indulgence were given to any attack upon Venetian subjects or property. In England, in France, in Italy, in the East, the merchants were robbed. From Southampton to Pera the Venetian counting-houses, banks, and factories were forced, sacked, and destroyed. The commerce of Venice trembled on the verge of extinction; and all these evils were laid at the door of the doge and the new aristocracy. But the party in power never wavered; their determination was the result and the proof of their youth, their confidence, their real capacity for governing. Though they were surrounded by a people suffering intensely from physical and spiritual want, as well as by a nobility who openly declared their hatred of the new policy and of its authors, yet they never deviated for a single moment from the predetermined line. Everything was done to win the regard and the support of the people. The doge instituted a yearly banquet to the poor and the picturesque ceremony of washing and kissing twelve fishermen from the lagoons. Everything also was done to humble, insult, and ridicule the old nobility. Marco Querini was refused a seat among the ducal councillors, and the place was bestowed on Doimo, count of Veglia,* in spite of a statute which forbade a Dalmatian to hold that office. The law against carrying arms in the streets was enforced with rigour. Marco Morosini, a "signor of the night,"† met Pietro Querini one evening in the piazza; in spite of Querini's protest Morosini insisted upon searching him; Querini knocked him down, and was, of course, fined heavily. It was clear that matters were coming to a crisis.

But the real difficulty of the old nobility lay in the want of a leader. After holding several meetings at the house of Marco Querini, they determined to invite Bajamonte Tiepolo,‡ the son-in-law of Marco, to come

* Rom., *op. cit.*, vol. iii. p. 27.

† This was the picturesque name for the three heads of the police patrol in Venice. "Il diavolo che attendava alla rovina di questo governo porse in animo a Marco Morosini, Signore di Notte, di voler sapere se Pietro Querini della casa Grande, fratello di Messier Marco, aveva armi; et accostandosi a lui li disse; lasciati cercare; perciò lui irato gettò per terra esso Morosini" (Marco Barbaro, Chronicle, quoted by Rom., *loc. cit., sup.*).

‡ Bartolo Tiepolo, 1062.
Marco, 1137.
Giacomo, doge, m. Gualdrada, dr. of Tancred of Sicily.
Lorenzo, doge, m. Marchesina of Brienne.
Giacomo.
Bajamonte.
See Litta, "Famig. celebri Italiane," *in voce* "Tiepolo;"

to Venice and lead the party. He was the grandson of the Doge Lorenzo Tiepolo and Marchesina, daughter of Boemond of Brienne, king of Servia. He was. therefore, great-grandnephew of John of Brienne, the emperor of Constantinople and king of Jerusalem. In the year 1300 he had been condemned for peculation in one of the governments he had held. But execution of the sentence was postponed, and two years later he was elected one of the Quarantia.* But in the same year he withdrew to his villa of Marocco,† near Mestre, where he remained until 1310, when the invitation of his brother nobles reached him. He readily answered their appeal, and his arrival in Venice was of the greatest service to his party. For Bajamonte was a man of strong, impetuous, and decided character, the owner of large wealth and of an almost unbounded popularity with the people, who called him the *gran cavaliere;*‡ while, on the other hand, he was connected with most of the noble families who were strenuously opposing the new aristocracy.

On the arrival of Bajamonte the ferment of discontent was precipitated. Meetings were held at the house of Marco Querini, in which the hopes and

Laurentius de Monacis, " Chronicon," lib. xiv. p. 274 ; Roman., *op. cit.*, vol. ii. p. 294; "Cronaca Veneta, da Canal," cap. cclxiii. note 351.

* Caresini, "Contin. Chron. And. Dand.," p. 492, ap. Murator., Rer. It. Scrip., xii. ; Vianoli, " Hist. Venet." (Venetia : 1680), lib. xii.

† Rom., *op. cit.*, vol. iii. p. 28.

‡ Navagero, "St. Venez.," ad ann. 1310, ap. Murat., Rer. It. Scrip., xxiii.

designs of the party were discussed, and steps taken to achieve them. Marco himself led the way, dwelling bitterly on the ruin which the new aristocracy had brought upon the state, urging the dangers of the Ferrarese war and the horrors of the excommunication. But above all he insisted on the injustice of the act that closed the Great Council, whereby many noble and virtuous citizens were excluded from all share in the government of the state. Bajamonte followed his father-in-law, enforcing his argument and urging immediate action. He concluded thus: " Let us leave, let us leave words on one side now, and come to deeds. Let us place a good prince at the head of this state; one who shall be acceptable to all classes, beloved by the people, ready so to act that our city may be restored to her ancient ordinances, that public freedom may be preserved and increased." Tiepolo expressed the general feeling. The party were eager for action; but Jacopo Querini, the oldest and most cautious of their number, now rose to counsel moderation. He implored them to move by constitutional, not by revolutionary steps; he warned them not to trust the people for support;* while, fully recognizing the unendurable position in which they were placed by the closing of the Great Council, he insisted that this should be corrected by legal, not by illegal and violent measures. But the nobles felt that the advice of Jacopo Querini came too late.

* " Sperate aver il popolo favorevole? ma il popolo, come a tutti è noto, è cosa vana ed instabile." A true warning as it proved. See "Cronaca del Barbaro," quoted by Rom., vol. iii. p. 31 ; also Vianoli, " Hist. Venet." (Venetia : 1680), lib. xii.

G

Pacific measures were out of the question. The speech of Tiepolo indicated the lines on which they must act. Nothing remained but to develop the plot. The conspirators agreed that the doge should be attacked in his palace, and that he and as many as possible of the new aristocracy should be slain. One of their own party, Badoer Badoer, was sent to Padua, with instructions to bring with him as many men as he could induce to help in the attack. They fixed on the 15th of June as the day for the execution of their design. The associates were to meet in the house of Querini on the evening of the 14th, a Sunday.

The evening came and the nobles assembled. So far these meetings had been conducted with the utmost secrecy. But now information was brought to the doge * that there was an unusual and suspicious stir about the houses of the Querini and in all the quarter beyond the Rialto. Gradenigo at first refused to believe that this movement had any significance, but he thought it prudent to send three members of the government to inquire into the meaning of the report. The officials were met with drawn swords whenever they crossed the Rialto, and were forced to fly for their lives. The doge grasped the situation at once, and lost no time. He sent messengers to the *podestà* of Chioggia, and to the governors of Murano, Burano, and Torcello, demanding their help. The officers of state, the Consiglieri, the Avvogadori, the Signori di Notte, were summoned to the palace armed. The town on St. Mark's side of the canal

---

* The traitor was Marco Donato, who had at first joined the conspiracy.

was roused from its sleep—for the night had already far advanced towards morning—and all good citizens were called upon to march to the piazza, there to defend the doge and the state.* These measures, rapidly as they were carried out, occupied some time, and the day was already dawning. In the dim twilight, and under a threatening sky, the doge and his company left the ducal palace and descended into the piazza. There guards were stationed at the mouths of the different streets that opened on the square, while the main body was drawn up in the piazza itself, eagerly expecting help from Chioggia and waiting the event.

Meantime, on the other side of the canal, affairs had nearly reached the climax. The piazza, then as now the heart of the city, was the point at which Tiepolo intended to aim his blow. The conspirators had determined to divide their forces. One body, under Bajamonte, was to march through the Merceria, emerging on the piazza by the street where the clock tower now stands; the other, under Marco Querini, was to find its way to the same point by the Ponte di Malpasso.† All was ready for the start, when a violent storm broke over Venice; wind, thunder, lightning, and rain descending in torrents. The storm seemed ominous and terrified Tiepolo's followers. He delayed his departure, hoping that it might pass by, and, in order to amuse and occupy his company, he gave them permission to sack the offices of the police magistrates and the Corn Exchange.

* Laurentius de Mon., *op. cit.*, lib. xiv. p. 275.
† Now the Ponte de Dai.

But the rain did not cease, and precious time could not be wasted to an unlimited extent. Too much had been lost already; every instant lessened the chances of success. The conspirators crossed the Rialto. But they soon found, as they advanced, that they had miscalculated in reckoning on the support of the people. Each step towards the piazza showed the temper of the populace to be more and more hostile. The vigour and calmness of the doge had overawed those who were immediately within his reach, and had counselled them to be on that side which their instinct told them was the winning one. But more than that, the present rebellion was the protest of the nobles against the *serratta*, as that of Bocconio had been the popular protest. This latter had failed, and the people were not prepared to try their fortune again. Perhaps they were more than doubtful whether the success of Tiepolo would really restore to them their lost rights. However that might be, the conspirators found no support, no signs of a rising in their favour. In accordance with the plan agreed upon, they divided into two companies. By some miscalculation Quirini arrived at the piazza first; as he debouched upon the square, the doge's troops charged with the cry of "Ah! traditore; ammazza! ammazza!" Marco and his two sons were instantly killed, and his followers routed before Tiepolo could come to his assistance. A like defeat awaited him. As he passed along the Merceria, a woman hurled a stone from a balcony, which slew Bajamonte's standard-bearer, who was marching foremost with a banner on which was embroidered the word "Liberty." A few moments later, Tiepolo himself and his followers were flying from the piazza in confusion, to seek safety on the other side of the Rialto. They broke down the bridge and destroyed the boats, and thus gained for themselves a breathing space. They were still in considerable force; and if Badoer had arrived from Padua, it might yet have been possible for them to make some head against the doge. The news, however, that Badoer with his boats had run aground in the lagoon, where the *podestà* of Chioggia had captured him and all his men, dashed that hope. The game had been played and lost. Nothing remained but to make such terms as they could with Gradenigo and his victorious party.

The leniency of the conditions offered by the doge prove how unwilling the new aristocracy were to push their victory too hard. All the citizens who had followed Tiepolo were allowed to make their peace by swearing allegiance to the doge and the constitution. The heads of the conspiracy were banished for four years to certain defined localities; but all of them, including their chief, broke their confines.* This violation of their bounds resulted in a decree of perpetual exile against Tiepolo, and the confiscation of all his goods. The houses of the Tiepolo and the Querini were razed, and their site marked by a *colonna infame*, and the family arms of both were cancelled.†

* Sanudo, "Vite dei Duchi," p. 586, ap. Murat., Rer. It. Script., tom. xxii.

† The Querini bore parte per fesse azure and gules; the

Tiepolo was banished in perpetuity, and, for the years that remained to him, he flitted like an unlaid ghost round the borders of his native land. From Dalmatia, from Padua, from Treviso, he looked towards Venice, and sighed for the *campi*, the *contrade*, the water-ways of that home no longer his. But each sigh was a menace to the new party now consolidating itself on the ruins of the older nobility. The government was never at rest for a moment while the spectral form of Tiepolo remained unburied We find proposals for an amnesty to be extended to him, invitations to him to return. These may have been ruses to get him into their power—we cannot tell; in any case, they were not accepted. Bajamonte is the centre of innumerable plots, all doomed to failure; but he could not abandon them while he lived. He was the spirit of the old aristocracy that would not cease to hope as long as there was breath. In the year 1311 we find him conspiring at Padua;[*] later

Tiepolo, azure, a castle of three towers, argent. See Coronelli, "Blazone Veneto," and Freschot, "La Nobilità Veneta;" "Commem.," lib. i. No. 435, 448; Laurentius, *op. cit.*, lib. xiv. p. 277, where a list of the conspirators is given, together with their places of exile; And. Dand., "Chronicon," p. 410, ap. Murat., Rer. It. Scrip., xii.; Caresini, "Contin. Chron. Dand.," pp. 490, 491, 492, where the sentences are recorded; also see p. 483 for the letters of Gradenigo recounting the conspiracy.

[*] Laurentius, *loc. cit.*, pp. 277, 278; "Commem.," lib. i. No. 476; 1876. Tiepolo tried to interest some of the family of Carrara in his designs. Scrovegno, on their behalf, went so far as to promise him eight hundred men. Venice was seriously alarmed, and increased the guards on the lagoon shores at San Giuliano. But the scheme fell through (Rom., *op. cit.*, vol. iii. pp. 43, 44 Verci, "St. della Marca Trivigiana," vol. viii. Doc. 862, ann. 1318, Feb. 21).

he is hunted from Treviso. In 1322 the Ten offer a sum for his capture in Dalmatia. In 1328 the doge is imperatively ordered to take steps to secure his person, if possible; but he escaped his enemies to the very last, and, on the point of falling into their hands, he died.

Tiepolo died, and with him died the old nobility as a dominant party in the state. He and it were killed by the new aristocracy. Tiepolo's object had been to preserve the old constitution of Venice; for in it he and his order, by long prescriptive right of birth and rule, were powerful. But this party failed to make common cause with the people, they neglected to win their confidence, and they went down before the younger and stronger order. Had Tiepolo succeeded it is not impossible that Venice might have developed a constitutional government based on the three estates of prince, nobles, and people; but it was not given to her to escape the tendency which was bringing all Italy under the power of individual families of despots.

The new aristocracy triumphed and proceeded to follow unimpeded the law of its growth. Externally the government of the city was crystallized after the fall of Tiepolo. A full police system was developed— the patrols for the streets, the guards for the canals, the piazza, and the Palazzo Ducale. A native militia was raised by a levy of five hundred men from each of the six quarters of the city.* But freedom was

---

* Rom., *op. cit.*, vol. iii. p. 40; "Commem.," lib. i. July, 1310, No. 438, 439; Marin., *op. cit.*, vol. v. p. 320, Doc. II., "Provisions for the Defence of Venice."

not in the nature of the new aristocracy; its essence was opposed to liberty, and so it was doomed in turn to submit to itself as its own most tyrannous master. The danger it had just escaped was so great that, for its own immediate safety, it had recourse to a dictator. But following the inherent bent in the Venetian political constitution, that dictator was not an individual, but a committee, a college. The Council of Ten was appointed to examine the causes and to trace the ramifications of the Tiepoline conspiracy. Its tenure of office was first limited to a few days, then extended to two months, then to five years; finally it was declared permanent, July 20, 1335, and became the lord, the Signore, the tyrant of Venice *— more terrible than any personal despot, because impalpable, impervious to the dagger of the assassin. It was no concrete despotism, but the very essence of tyranny. To seek its overthrow was vain. Those who strove to wrestle with it clasped empty air; they struck at it, but the blow was wasted on space. Evasive and pervasive, this dark, inscrutable body

* Rom., *op. cit.*, vol. iii. cap. iii.; Giannotti, "Della Rep. d. Venez." (Firenze: 1850), pp. 122–124; Sanudo, *op. cit.*, p. 586; Baschet, "Les Archives de Venise" (Paris: 1870), p. 514. It is shown by the researches of Sig. Cecchetti that in all probability a Council of Ten did exist before the year 1310. But it is certain that that year saw the creation of the Ten as the power which was destined to rule Venice. See "Dell' Istituz. d. Magist. d. Rep.," Cecchetti (Venezia: 1865). And popular tradition was right when it fixed the date in the well-known rhyme—

> "Del mille tresento e diese
> A mezzo el mese delle ceriese
> Bagiamonte passò el ponte (the Rialto).
> E per esso fo fatto el consegio di diese."

ruled Venice with a rod of iron. For good or for bad the Council of Ten was the very child of the new aristocracy, which had won its battle against both the people and the old nobility. The victorious party breathed and their breath became the Ten, and it is the Ten which determined the internal aspect of Venice for the remainder of her existence.

Such is the reading of events which facts seem to warrant. But, in the dense obscurity which hangs over all that might indicate beyond a doubt the true relations of the old aristocracy, the new party and the people, it has to be admitted that a somewhat different view is possible. It might be urged that the struggle was nothing more than one between a *primo* and a *secondo popolo*, in which the people, properly so called, had little or no interest; that the issue lay between an old semi-feudal nobility and a wealthy middle class, eager to seize the reins of government; that each party was running a selfish race for the mastery in the state, and that a species of tyranny was inevitable, whichever won. It would be possible to urge that the apparition, the struggle, and the victory of the new nobility was only one step in a necessary evolution; that the victory brought with it not the element of death, but just that quality of rigid stability which preserved Venice longer than her sister Italian states. What remains, however, as important to Venetian history in this period is that the Tiepoline conspiracy marks the point at which the central element in the government was fixed. From that moment Venice appears with the peculiar constitution which, for better or for worse, was to distinguish her from the rest of Italy.

THE CARRARESI.

"Si trova sulla terra delle catastrofi."—FERRARI.

ITALY, it has often been said, is not the country of chivalrous romance. In nothing is the truth of the observation more clearly shown than in the history of her great families. There is no lack of adventure, and often an excess of startling incidents; but the aroma of romance is not there, the peculiar charm of chivalry is wanting; there is no mystery. Italian character is true to Italian landscape, "the little blue-hilled, pastoral, sceptical landscape," perfect in form, delicious and delicate in colour, but grand or mysterious seldom. Italy never had a feudal system; and people of Northern temperament miss that sympathetic thrill that even now runs through us as we read of actions gentle, loyal, knightly, or true.* No doubt much of the charm in our family history is due to its vague outline. We look at the deeds of our forefathers that begat us through the obscurity of ages. The lines grow mellowed and softened, toned to fit subjects for a ballad; the traditions of family history

* This whole category of words is wanting in Italian. They are flowers of a foreign soil, and have to be transplanted from the North. They pine and droop, as "*leale*," or change their nature altogether, as "*virtu*" and "*onore.*"

live as sacred legends, of deep interest to the family, but still legends, myths robbed of the cold clearness of an historical outline. In Italy family story emerges only to become at once an integral portion of the country's history, to pass directly into the cold light, to be immediately tested by the critical standards of historical accuracy; it has from the moment of its birth that clearness and crudeness which belongs to fact. The early deeds of the Visconti, the Scala family, or the Carraresi live not in ballads but in chronicles, our main fountain-heads for picturesque Italian history generally. Yet it would be a mistake to suppose that these chronicles are devoid of interest or of fascination. They have, after all, many of the qualities of the ballad; they make their pictures, they touch the human passion with that simplicity which is consummate art, and, almost in spite of the deeds they relate, there is a tenderness about them. No one can read the Perugian chronicle of Matarazzo,* or the Paduan history of the Gattari, without feeling that they have a charm and romance of their own—not the clannish romance of feudalism, steeped in mystery and weirdness, but the charm of highly developed individualities in play with other characters their like. The men of these chronicles are beautiful as highly finished products of civilization; but we can never think of them as

" Beauty making beautiful old rhyme."

The family of Carrara, with whose intricate growth

---

* See the essay " Perugia " in Mr. Symonds' " Sketches in Greece and Italy."

and tragical death we have now to deal, lived in the very heart of that curious period of Italian history when the Signori rose to the height of their illegal power. The Carraresi grew up side by side with the Visconti, the Gonzaghi, the Estensi, the Polentani, the Rossi, the Scaligeri, and with the last of these they fell. Venice alone among all these princelings pursued a steady policy. In common with her neighbours she had passed through the crisis of the Signori, those pangs which issued in the birth of a despot for nearly every Italian town. But with her the revolution took a complexion peculiar to herself. When the ferment of the Tiepoline conspiracy subsided, Venice found herself not under the rule of a single tyrant, an individual who might be assassinated and who was doomed, sooner or later, to extinction with his whole race, but with the permanent, unassailable Ten as her lord. She was a republic only in name ; the Ten was her despot, without the dangers of a despot's throne. Venice was secure ; freed from the fatal need for incessant and feverish action, that curse on all the other Signori, she could bide her time and choose her moment to strike her foes. That moment was never chosen wantonly, but always with a distinct and reasoned view to her own requirements. The Venetian Republic was the one stable element in all North Italy.

It was an age of exciting change, of deep and riveting interest, and the Carraresi were typical of their period, not only in their politics and in the vicissitudes of their fortune, but in their private life as well.

The men of those days were "born to strange sights;" they sought them, courted them, delighted in them: nothing could be too strange or bizarre for that insatiable thirst for novelty with which they burned. They rung the joy out of violent changes and contrasts. All they touched was embraced with ardour, from a headlong debauch to a religious revival. At one moment these men were tearing along in a mad orgy, at the next they were covered with sackcloth and ashes, marching in the rear of the Bianchi procession,* joining fervidly in the cry, " Repent! repent!" swelling the chorus of " Stabat Mater." Few were greater proficients in the invention of new arts, for public as for private life, than the Visconti. But nothing could save these men from the doom they dreaded; they were condemned to plagiarism, to repetition and sameness. Each draught of pleasure or of power only intensified the thirst that mocked their impotence to satisfy it. The forty days' tortures of Galeazzo Visconti were repeated by Francesco Carrara at Bassano;† but the master had at the same moment created and exhausted the idea. All that human bodies are capable of enduring he had forced them to endure. It was in vain that Carrara cried for a fiftieth day; the limit was

* " Chronicon Patavinum," ap. Muratori, " Antiquit. Ital. Med. Œv.," tom. iv. ad. ann. 1399 (Milano: 1741).

† Azzari, " Storia di Milano," ap. Muratori, Rer. It. Script., tom. xvi.; Galeazzo Gattaro, " Istoria Padovana," ap. Murat., Rer. It. Script., tom. xvii.; Verci, " Storia della Marca Trivigiana" (Venezia: 1789), bk. xvi. ad ann. 1373. The enormous learning of this work is too well known to require any praise from me, but I must here acknowledge my deep debt to it throughout this essay.

reached ; he was face to face with the impossible. At another time the operation of diverting all its rivers from an enemy's territory, or its converse of drowning the foe by piercing the banks of a river in flood, was devised. The labour was enormous. but delightful, for there was a new power to contend with, a new opposing element even more incalculable than man, and that was Nature. But the ruse became hackneyed at once, and we grow tired of reading the story of works on the Brenta, the Bachiglione,* the Mincio, unrelieved by any variation except that now and then Nature refuses to bow to the whims of a Lombard lord, and. bursting out. sweeps a Scala's or a Visconti's dams and embankments to perdition. Again. Can Signorio della Scala resolved to murder his brother—that was common enough ; but coming from his mistress. there was the new touch. The plan succeeded, and was soon after adopted by Antonio Scala, who killed his brother Bartholomew on his way home from a rendezvous ; and certain of the Carrara family proposed a like fate, under like circumstances, for the head of their house. The idea was run to death in a moment, but the honours remained with the inventor ; Can Signorio alone put the finishing touch to his work by accusing his brother's mistress of the murder and torturing her till she died. The number of family murders was enormous. In seven generations of the Scala house we can count nine such treacherous deaths, an allowance of one and two-sevenths of a murder to

* See Gattari, *op. cit.*, ad ann. 1387, and *passim;* Verci, *op. cit.*, bk. xv. ad ann. 1368.

each generation, and that inside their own walls.*
The heads of houses had this fate constantly before
their eyes, and yet they never seemed to have expected it to overtake themselves ; so Bernabò Vistonti,
when his nephew arrested him, cried, "O Gian
Galeazzo non esser traditor del tuo sangue ; " but he
might have known from his own experience the value
of such an appeal.

These men were "born to strange sights ; " perhaps to no stranger one than the mixture of chivalry
and treachery in the story of so many noble houses.
Francesco Carrara the elder was dubbed by Charles
IV. on the field ; and no doubt he deserved it,
for he was a brave soldier : but he immediately
conferred a like honour on a number of Paduan
gentlemen ; among them, on one Zanibone Dotto,
who at that very moment had the poisons in his
pocket to give to Francesco, and money for doing
so from Jacopino Francesco's uncle.† We cannot help
feeling that these men looked upon life as a game to
be made as intricate as possible for the pleasure of
playing it. Anything which added a new colour to
life or imposed a new condition on the game was
at once adopted ; and so we find knighthood and
treachery side by side, accepted as facts and elements
to be manipulated. Anything, on the other hand,
which, like moral considerations, interfered with the

* See Litta, " Famiglie Celebri d'Italia," *in voce* "Scaligeri."
† Cortusiorum, " Historia," ap. Mur., Rer. It. Script., tom.
xii. ad ann. 1354 ; Gattari, *op. cit.* ; Verci, *op. cit.*, ad ann. ;
Cittadella, " Storia della Dominazione Carrarese in Padova "
(Padova : 1842), vol. i. cap. xxiv.—an excellent history of the
Carrara family.

development of the game, or crossed the path to the end in view, must be left aside—" Si violandum est jus regnandi gratia, violandum est ; " if virtue "like not the play, why then she likes it not, perdy." All things were pardoned to the man who played the game successfully. Here it was not a soft but a witty answer which turned away wrath. Ubertino Carrara invented a grim amusement for himself, to while away the time till he should succeed to the Signory. He and his companions used to roam about Padua at night ; if they met a citizen or a merchant going home, a bag was slipped over the unfortunate man's head, and he was dragged about, up and down the streets, until he lost all sense of where he might be ; he was then taken to some house, where the band mystified, bullied, and frightened him, sometimes to death and always until he had paid a large sum to his tormentors. One day Ubertino caught a Florentine. The man was treated in the usual way. When the bag was taken from his head, Lappo—that was his name—asked where he was. "In Trebizond," was the answer. "A good wind and a fair passage, gentlemen!" The company relished the wit of this reply, and they allowed Lappo to go scot-free.*

It is not a pleasant picture ; but as these men treated life like a problem in chess, so their lives have the interest of a problem for us. If we referred to the pages indexed as *ejus mores* in Muratori's vast storehouse, we should find much that is terrible and revolting, while making a large allowance for the

* Vergerius, "Vitæ Carrariensium," in vit. "Marsilii," ap. Murat. Rer. It. Script. tom. xii.

exaggeration which not improbably exists; but we should also find an infinite variety of strongly developed characters, each one defining itself clearly before us; and this individuality seems to be the real point of interest in that curious age. They were people full of passion, which they obeyed unhesitatingly—"Quando vienne il desiderio non c'è mai troppo," said a modern Italian; and so these elder Italians felt and acted. But they paid dearly for this loyal obedience to desire. They did not perceive that this was not true liberty, that it landed them in a *cul-de-sac*. The attainable was exhausted and grew insipid, the unattainable alone had any attraction for them, and so they were condemned to an endless heaven of hope and hell of realization.

As in private so it was in public life. Politics was a game which no one wished to see ended. Wars were dragged on to an interminable length without one decisive blow, because, of the men who conducted them, no two were pursuing exactly the same object. Treaties public and secret crossed and recrossed each other, covering the face of Italy with an intricate web. Each new ruse of politics became irresistibly infectious: only those at whose destruction it was aimed felt any alarm; the rest stood by to see and learn how the move was played. We might almost draw up a code of political maxims from the complicated history of the time. A treaty or a peace was not used to terminate disputes or to bind allies together; they had definite and special uses other than these. Treaty faith was unknown, and leagues were formed for this purpose—that they enabled a prince, in times

H

of pressure, to buy better terms for himself by selling his allies. He either weakened the league by withdrawing, or he turned his arms absolutely against his former allies; for the latter service the pay would be higher. A peace might be concluded for ten years or a hundred, though it was intended to observe it just four months. Its real value was to gain breathing time and to allow the universal bad faith to explode a powerful and hostile combination. Another maxim, and one which Bernabò Visconti was never tired of applying, was—" Attack others before they attack you. Choose a weak moment in your neighbour, and strike ; if not, he will infallibly turn on you in your hour of distress." The fatal necessity to extend in order to prevent others from extending proved the ruin of the Signori. Having once entered on the path of lordship, only one course lay open to them : headlong they must go or be lost ; and if they went on they were equally doomed to destruction, but in pressing forward lay their only hope of postponing the day of their ruin as long as possible. Under such imperative compulsion to restlessness and aggression, quiet in the neighbourhood of an Italian prince was absolutely unknown and unenjoyed. The Signori were to the manner born, it was one of the conditions of their life ; but for the people this feverish atmosphere proved an endless source of agony and torment. Again, experience soon taught these politicians that to bend was not to break. Suppleness was a quality they highly prized. Scala and Visconti bowed before the whirlwind of John of

Venice and saved himself for a time; his son Novello refused to do so and was lost. Venice herself yielded to Hungary, and surrendered Dalmatia to avoid worse loss; but she never intended to forego that province for ever. The constant kaleidoscopic changes in Italian politics always gave a hope that what was lost to-day might be regained to-morrow. There was, however, a refinement on this maxim of momentary cession under pressure. It became by no means unusual for a prince to yield, not to the enemy who was harassing him, but to some third party. By this means he mortified his foe, he shifted the burden of the war to other shoulders, and might fairly look to recovering what he had lost some later day. Venice, when in the agony of the Chioggian war, handed Treviso to the duke of Austria; she thereby stole it from Carrara, who must inevitably have captured it, and at the same time she entailed on him a war with Austria which materially crippled his power.

Under the Signori the townsfolk suffered terribly. The government of the despots was the very incarnation of a sole and selfish monarchy. All the resources, all the machinery of the state, were in their hands, to be used for their own individual ends. Milanese interests, Veronese interests, Paduan interests had no existence; the salvation of a Visconti, a Scala, or Carrara were the only purposes to which the lives and wealth of all these unhappy citizens were dedicated. It is true that, in the intervals of self-

monuments; Gian Galeazzo might design and dedicate the Certosa at Pavia, or Francesco Carrara endow the university of Padua and foster the wool trade; but what could that do for people exposed to twenty years' unceasing war and in daily danger of pillage? Venice alone, with singular wisdom, identified herself with her subjects; she did not exist apart from them; all her power was ready at any moment to protect her merchants in England, in Italy, or the East. Venetian interests did exist; and for that reason we cannot wonder at the joy with which the lion of San Marco was hailed as, one by one, Treviso, Verona, Vicenza, and Padua passed under the dominion of the Serene Republic. Partly debauched, partly terrorized, the spirit of the towns was crushed out of them, and they suffered quietly agony on agony. They pass from one master to another, each in turn glutting his avarice or his cruelty with their wretched bodies. Feltre, Belluno, Bassano, change hands, are thrown from the Scala to Hungary, from the Hungarians to Carrara, to Austria, to the Visconti, resting only and at last under the wise rule of Venice. The Signori made a point of holding as many towns as possible—not for the glory nor the strength they gave, but because they passed current as banknotes, or could be sold for 50,000, 70,000, 100,000 ducats, or even, as in the case of Verona, for as much as 440,000 florins, and therefore could be used to buy off a foe or to purchase an ally. It was vain for the people to cry with the citizens of Bologna, "Noi non vogliamo esser venduti." They were sold whether they wished it or not.

Looking at their history as a whole, we feel that these Signori were men of singular force and power; capable of all things, of splendid action, no doubt, as well as of that which they really achieved, ruinous failure. But the spirit which filled them and drove them was a fatal one; it compelled them to the destruction of themselves and the annihilation of their country. Their story is a tragedy.

It was among men like this and in such times that the family of Carrara, nobles of Padua, emerged and made themselves famous. Almost the first we hear of them was a disastrous episode; and a Thyestean destiny dogged their steps unto the end. Padua had always been strongly Guelf in sympathy; the Carraresi were by birth and gifts partisans of the emperor, with imperial diplomas and privileges dating back as far as the tenth century.* They settled at a village about seven miles south of Padua, said to have been famous for its wainwrights, and therefore called Carrara, but now Villa del Bosco. The monstrous excesses of Ezzelino da Romano threw the Carraresi into the arms of the people, and it was owing to this change of politics that they subsequently became lords of Padua; but at first it cost them dear. In A.D. 1240 the head of the house was besieged by Ezzelino in his castle of Agna. The tyrant pressed the siege so vigorously that surrender became inevitable. Jacopo Carrara determined to save as much of his inheritance as he

---

* Cittadella, *op. cit.*, vol. i. cap. vii.; Litta, *in voce* "Carraresi." The family was probably Lombard, to judge by the early names we find, as Gumbert and Litolf. See Vergerius, *op. cit.*

could. The castle stood in the middle of a small
lake. A boat was made ready under the walls, and
one night all the ladies of the house, the jewels, the
gold, and the title-deeds were put on board and the
boat pushed off. But they had been anxious to save
too much, and so lost all ; for before the boat had got
half-way across the lake, it capsized, and everybody
and everything went down. The place afterwards
bore the name of the Lago delle Donne.*

Not only the Carraresi, but Padua also suffered
for her Guelfish sympathies. In the year 1312 Can
Grande della Scala, as imperial vicar, took Vicenza
from the Paduans, and the next six years were spent
in fruitless efforts on the part of Padua to recover the
city. In one of the many assaults on Vicenza, Jacopo
Carrara † and his nephew Marsiglio were taken
prisoners and carried to Verona. There they in-
gratiated themselves with the Scala family, and
eventually effected a peace between Verona and
Padua. The Paduans hailed Jacopo, on his return, as
the saviour of his country ; and in gratitude for the
peace, and to put an end to the agony of the town,
which was being devoured by the rapacity of the

---

* Vergerius, *op. cit.*

† Jacopo seems to have been a man of violent temper. In
this assault he was wounded in the leg before surrendering. He
asked his captor to take off his greaves ; in doing so the man
hurt him, and received a smart box on the ear to teach him
gentleness. At another time he was hearing causes in Padua.
An importunate suitor annoyed him by his persistence ; Jacopo
leaned down and whispered in the man's ear, "I'll cut your tongue
out." The brutality of the threat and its probable execution had
the desired effect. See Vergerius, *op. cit.*

usurers, the Ronchi and Alticlini *—of whom the chronicler remarks, " In iis voluptas peccandi erat summa "—they chose him captain of the people (1318). The relations between Padua and Verona seemed amicably arranged, and at one of the last diplomatic interviews which Jacopo held with Can Grande an amusing incident occurred. Carrara and Scala were walking in a garden under the walls of Padua ; they came to a door too narrow to allow them to pass through arm in arm ; neither would take the precedence, and the grave matters under discussion seemed likely to be indefinitely postponed, when a court jester solved the difficulty by crying, " Let the biggest fool go first ; " instantly both leaped forward to claim that honour, and the obstructing door was cleared.

Jacopo died and left the lordship to his nephew Marsiglio, a man of ready resource and deep cunning— "simulare et dissimulare facile doctus."† But all his powers could not stop the approach of Can Grande, who had resolved to possess Padua as well as Vicenza. Marsiglio was pressed from without and threatened from within by members of his own family ; Nicolo Carrara was jealous of him, and was making a bid for the support of Verona. In the year 1328 Marsiglio

---

* The three young Alticlini and the two Ronchi seem to have tortured Padua to their heart's content. The account of their dungeons and prisons, if true, is horrible, and their misdeeds are thus summed up : " Furta, fraudes, adulteria, stupra quæ apud alios gravia videri solent nihili apud eos æstimabantur. Cædes non nisi per summam crudelitatem placebant, rapinæ non nisi per summam crudelitatem extortæ" (Vergerius, *op. cit.*).

† Ibid., *op. cit.*

found himself compelled to give his cousin Taddea in marriage to Mastino, nephew and heir to Can Grande, and with her the city of Padua for a dowry. Scala became lord of Padua, and Marsiglio received it back from him as his governor. From that moment Marsiglio conceived a violent hatred for the whole house of Scala; but he had to bide the time for his revenge. Next year an opportune death carried off Can Grande at Treviso; he died, and left his vast princedom and his vaster designs to his nephew Mastino. Marsiglio saw his opportunity and set to work; he inflamed the mind of Scala against Venice —the one power able to check the growing power of the Scaligers; he urged Mastino to defy and crush the republic. Differences, chiefly on the subject of the salt-pans,* were fostered and fomented; and Marsiglio, blindly trusted by Scala, accepted an embassy to Venice with full powers to arrange the difficulties. He used his full powers to arrange matters after his own mind. One day he sat at dinner next the doge, and as the story goes, he said, " I wish to speak to you." The doge dropped his napkin; both stooped to pick it up. Marsiglio whispered, " What reward for the man who should give you Padua ?" " We should make him Signore," was the reply. When the two heads rose again above the table the terms had been agreed on. Marsiglio was to seize Padua by the help of Venice and in her name, and to receive in return

* See Romanin, " Storia documentata di Venezia," tom. iii. pp. 118–120 (Venezia) ; " I Commemoriali " (Venezia : 1878), lib. iii. p.384, ad ann. 1336 ; Verci, lib. x., where many documents on the subject may be read.

the lordship of the city at the hands of the republic. Whether the story is true or not, the meaning and result of the episode appeared in that great league, headed by Venice, against the house of Scala, which for ever put a check to Mastino's ambition, and in two years stripped him of Parma, Lucca, Padua, Treviso, Feltre, Belluno, Cividale, and Brescia; leaving him where his uncle had begun, bare lord of Vicenza and Verona. Out of this struggle, which ended in the year 1338, Treviso, her first solid land possession, fell to Venice, and Padua, Castelbaldo, Cittadella, and Bassano to the prime mover in the league, Marsiglio Carrara.

The story of the events in Padua which preceded the recovery of the Signory by the Carraresi is curious and picturesque. Albert Scala, brother to Mastino, undertook the charge of Padua, and Ubertino and Marsiglio Carrara, then unsuspected of hostility, were invited to help him in the government. Albert was a man addicted to pleasure; he had wounded Ubertino in his family honour. Carrara feigned indifference; he laughed,* but he put a couple of horns on his crest to keep his wrath warm, and to remind him to exact vengeance some day. Mastino was not without his suspicions of the Carraresi, and these became confirmed after Marsiglio's visit to Venice. He constantly wrote to his brother Albert, warning him to keep an eye on the two Carraresi. But Albert liked the complacent husband and thought the Carraresi amusing companions; so, by way of joke,

* Muratori, "Antiquit. Ital. Medii Œvi," vol. iii., dissert. 36 (Mediol.: 1741).

he showed his brother's letters to Marsiglio, saying, "You see what he would have me do." Carrara feigned to be hurt, and indignantly replied, "Those who tell your brother these stories of me never gave him as much as a coop of hens, but I have given him Padua." Albert thought the reasoning good, and tried to soothe Marsiglio. Mastino Scala, however, grew daily more alarmed. He sent an imperative order to Albert to arrest and behead the Carraresi. Albert did not relish the commission, but his brother was not to be trifled with. He hired several assassins, and, one evening, stationed them near the great door that leads into the court of the Palazzo de' Signori, on the inner side, under the arcade; he then sent for Marsiglio and Ubertino, and he himself waited outside in the moonlight to see the end. It was late, and the brothers were going to bed when the message arrived. They were surprised, and rather suspicious when they heard that Albert wanted them at such an hour of the night; nevertheless they obeyed. A horse was brought round, and just as they were, in their night-shirts and caps, they set out, Marsiglio in the saddle and Ubertino on the crupper, holding on behind him. Albert, from his place under the outer arcade, saw the brothers come trotting into the piazza; his heart smote him and his purpose wavered. The Carraresi came towards him, and in a cheery voice Marsiglio cried, "What the devil do you want with us now? We have only just left you. We are sleepy, and wish to go to bed. What do you want?" Albert replied, "Oh, I want nothing!" "Well, since we are here we will go in with you," replied Carrara, making for the archway where the assassins lay in ambush. "No, don't go in, don't go in. Go to bed ; I want nothing," cried Albert ; and the two brothers, with their worst suspicions confirmed, turned round and rode off to their own house.

A day or two later, Mastino Scala, seriously enraged, sent a further letter, threatening Albert if his orders were not immediately obeyed. The despatch contained explicit instructions as to the execution of the brothers, and it reached Albert while he was playing chess ; he, without looking at it, passed it to Marsiglio, and went on with his game. When that was finished, he turned to Carrara and said, "Well, how is Messer Mastino, and what does he say?" "I have not read the letter; it is addressed to you," replied Marsiglio. "Take it and read it," said Albert. Carrara opened the letter and read the order for his own and his brother's instant execution. "Messer Mastino is very well," says he to Scala, "and wishes to remind you to procure a peregrine falcon for him, if any be on sale here." "A very important affair indeed," laughed Albert. The danger in which they were placed, however, determined the Carraresi to act at once. Marsiglio stayed with Albert all that day, while Ubertino went to tell Rossi, the Venetian general, to advance next morning, and he would find a gate open. Albert was awakened by the uproar in the town. He went out with Marsiglio to the piazza. When he saw the Venetians he cried, "What troops are these?" "These are the troops of Messer Piero Rossi, who is very anxious to see you," says Marsiglio. "Shall I be killed?" asked Albert. "No. Go back to my room and wait for me." Albert obeyed; but the result of his waiting was that the Carraresi arrested him, and sent him to Venice, where he endured three years' imprisonment, the ennui of which was not relieved even by the dogs, apes, and buffoons so liberally supplied him by the doge.*

Thus the Signory came back to the hands of the Carraresi, after a lapse of ten years; but Marsiglio enjoyed the fruit of his labour one year only; he died in 1338. He was followed by Ubertino, and then by five others of the house of Carrara, as lords of Padua. The family was firmly established. They had their share of political fluctuations, and perhaps more than their share of violence and family murders, three in fifteen years, besides many treacheries and conspiracies which proved abortive. Only one feature is particularly noteworthy; that is the dearth of children, and the erratic course the succession took in consequence. Ubertino was fourth cousin of Marsiglio, and Jacopo third cousin once removed of Marsiglietto, whom he murdered and succeeded.† But we cannot linger over details; we must press on to the catastrophe and tragedy of the house in the reign of the last two princes. Only one more story from the life of Ubertino Carrara, and that because it illustrates the touch of almost Caligulan madness that must have existed in these men.

---

* Gattari, *op. cit.*; Muratori. "Antiq. Ital. Med. Œvi," vol. iii. *loc. cit.*

† See Litta, *op. cit., in voce* "Carraresi."

Ubertino lived, on the whole, in friendly relations with Venice, though not without enemies in the Senate and Great Council. It came to his ears that one Venetian noble in particular was especially bitter against him, and he resolved to revenge himself. Ubertino sent several of his dependents to Venice ; the senator was enticed to drink some wine which had been heavily drugged, and fell into a deep swoon. In this state he was carried to Padua; to the palace, and put to bed in Ubertino's own room. When he woke it was some time before he knew where he was ; but gradually, through the dim light, he saw, on the heavy hangings of the bed, the hateful *carro*, the shield of the house he had lately attacked so violently. It was all round him, on the pillars, the tapestries, the ceiling. He leapt out of bed in terror, and at that moment Ubertino rushed into the room, crying, "What are you doing here? How came you here? I know you for my foe. You are here to seek my life ; but you shall pay for it." The unfortunate Venetian fell on his knees and begged for mercy. Ubertino's mood changed ; he burst out laughing, and said, "Very well ; I only wanted to give you a lesson." The senator was royally treated that evening, and sent home the next day.*

The family went on prospering till we come to Francesco, the seventh prince. Francesco succeeded in joint sovereignty with his uncle Jacopino. But such a division of power never could be acceptable, and almost invariably ended in violence. Jacopino tried to poison his nephew, and Francesco replied by

* Vergerius, *op. cit.,* in vita Ubertini.

deposing and imprisoning his uncle. In the year 1355 he reigned sole lord of Padua. In his hands the policy of the house of Carrara was altered with fatal results. Hitherto the family had leaned much on Venice, and had maintained friendly relations with her. This was only natural; for Venice had saved the Carraresi from the Scaligeri and had replaced them in power. But the dangerous ambition for extended territory and lordship with which the family had been inoculated from the first, now declared itself. Francesco determined to run the race with the Visconti and other Signori. That could only be done by freeing himself from the position of quasi-tutelage to Venice in which he and his family stood. But in adopting this policy he made an irretrievable mistake; he looked for alliance and support in Germany, in Austria, above all, in Hungary—a power far removed from Italy, and with few vital interests in the country. Perhaps no other course was open to him, after once determining his line of action. An alliance with the smaller princes around him, the Estensi, the Gonzaghi, the Polentani, lacked strength, besides being useless on account of the universal bad faith. The Visconti were unscrupulous, greedy, and least of all to be trusted. By union with Venice alone in all Italy could he hope to live, and he had decided against her; for, while she protected, she liked to be obeyed. But it is improbable or even impossible that this could have saved him. He was between two forces—Venice and the Visconti, who were destined to plough their way through or over all the small states of North Italy, to meet at last and struggle for the mastery of Lombardy.

At any rate, Francesco chose his line, and the results of his choice were seen the year after his accession to sole power (1356). Lewis, the king of Hungary, had long cast a greedy eye on the Venetian province of Dalmatia. He attacked Venice there and also in the Marca Trivigiana. Venice called on Carrara to help her, as his family had often done before; but she was met by a refusal; and, more than that, Francesco supplied the Hungarians with food and forage, supporting them where they most needed support, in their commissariat, for they are said to have put in the field an army of forty thousand men.* The conduct of Carrara proved a bitter surprise to Venice, all the more stinging because of the great straits in which the republic then found herself. She had lately been defeated by Genoa at Sapienza; she had just come through the Faliero conspiracy; money was scarce; the king of Hungary was before Treviso; Visconti and Can Grande II. had bought their own immunity by supplying him with troops;† Venice virtually stood alone; and now Carrara, on whom she relied, had failed her. Her pronounced anger showed itself by the withdrawal of her *podestà* from Padua and the suspension of all commercial relations.‡ This only served to throw Carrara more than ever into the arms of Hungary. Venice could not forget or forgive this desertion. But the wound was to be made even more piercing. The Hungarian war

---

* Romanin, *op. cit.*, vol. iii. p. 199; Verci, *op. cit.*, lib. xiv., ad ann.; Gattari, *op. cit.*

† See Verci, lib. xiv.

‡ See Romanin, *op. cit.*, vol. iii. p. 200.

moved disastrously for Venice; Dalmatia was occupied and Treviso closely invested. The pope, however, had been watching with alarm the growing
power of the Turks, and now insisted that a peace
should be effected in Italy to leave room for a
crusade against Islam. No crusade was possible without Venice; and therefore the Hungarian war had
to be extinguished. It was Francesco Carrara who
was called on to bring this about. If anything could
have made this peace more unpalatable to Venice,
it was the mediation of Carrara, the man she hated
more than any other at the moment. By the terms
which he procured, Venice lost Dalmatia and was
compelled to respect the allies of the king of Hungary;
among them, of course, Carrara himself. She could
not help herself, and, with her usual good sense, she
made the best of the present and awaited the future.
So when Carrara came to Venice in 1358, he was well
received, and was presented with a palace at San Polo.*
Thus closed the first rupture between Venice and the
Carraresi, peaceably as it appeared, but in the end it
proved disastrous for Carrara. Francesco had made
an immortal foe.

But Francesco himself was deceived by his apparent success; his ambition grew, and he endeavoured
to secure an alliance by marriage with the Visconti.
Bernabò's wife, Beatrice Scala, called "Regina" for her
pride, discountenanced the match and eventually put
an end to the negotiations. This rebuff stung the

---

* Cittadella, *op. cit.*, vol. i. cap. xxvi.; Verci, *op. cit.*, lib. xiv.
Doc. 1572; Romanin, *op. cit.*, vol. iii. pp. 206, 207; Gattari,
op. cit.

self-esteem of Carrara. and he was not sorry to show his hatred of the Visconti house soon after by assisting the pope to hold Bologna against Bernabò. But it was a fatal policy; all he gained was a distant and doubtful ally, the pope. while he made an enemy of his near and powerful neighbour. He had, in fact, placed himself in a vice, one iron of which was Venice, the other Visconti. Though he could not see the end, it was all the same inevitable—the total destruction of his family. But if his pride was hurt in one direction, it was soothed in another and his ambition encouraged. For Francesco received the cities of Feltre, Belluno, and Cividale from his good friend, the king of Hungary.* This might flatter his vanity, but it proved at best a doubtful gift, for it entailed on him a war with Rudolf of Austria, who claimed these places in virtue of his wife, Margaret Maultasch, the heiress of the Tyrol.

For the next nine years, from 1360 to 1369, Carrara lived in a constant state of covert hostility towards Venice, upon the subject of some debatable frontier territory and the right to work salt on the lagoons. But he dared not come to open war, for his hands were tied by fear of the Visconti on the one side, and by his struggles with Rudolf on the other. Matters at last came to a crisis when Francesco built two forts on the Brenta and Bachiglione respectively, and opened a free market at one of them to the considerable damage of Venetian trade, and when he further confirmed the hatred of the republic by tearing up the terminal stones which

* See Verci, *op. cit.*, lib xv.

I

divided Valsugana from the Trevisan march and planting them some miles nearer Venice. The republic felt that Carrara had recommenced his old policy of annoying her when she was in difficulties. She had just escaped a serious danger, the loss of Trieste. The duke of Austria had appeared before the walls to help the rebel city, intending to make the place his own, but he was repulsed and the town subdued. Then Venice turned her attention to Carrara with concentrated fury. Francesco saw the imminent danger and implored all his friends to pacify the republic. Ambassadors from Hungary, Florence, Pisa, the pope, Siena, and Este flocked to Venice ; their numbers and names show the width and strength of Carrara's connections. But in Venetian councils there existed a steady determination to punish the lord of Padua ; and the various envoys made little way towards a peaceable settlement. Their presence, however, suspended instant action, and a delay of several months was granted to try the effect of arbitration. Carrara made use of the interval, as the Italian politicians usually did, in the preparation and employment of treachery. In the middle of the lull Venice was startled by some alarming discoveries. Three Venetians, women of the people, unearthed a plot to murder several of Francesco's most pronounced foes, and the threads of the scheme were traced to Padua. The rumour gained currency that the same hand had poisoned the wells, and it became necessary to appoint a guard to watch them day and night. Lastly, but most disturbing of all, it appeared that Francesco had secret information concerning the councils and intentions of the government, and that from officials of no less rank than two chiefs of the court of appeal and one of the Avvogadore.* Relations were at once suspended ; war became inevitable, and each party looked to his alliances.

Carrara might count on support from the king of Hungary, who sent the vaivode of Transylvania with a large force into his service. By way of answer Venice tried to obtain the help of the duke of Austria, but Carrara bought him off with Feltre, Belluno, and Cividale ; † only stipulating that he should never sell those towns nor put an Italian in possession. Venice secured Can Signorio Scala in a way even less creditable. Can Grande had deposited with the republic twenty-six thousand ducats for the use of his illegitimate children; this sum was now handed over to Can Signorio, on condition that he should attack the Padovano. Both parties took the field, but the campaign was disastrous for Venice. The *provveditori*, the government commissioners in the camp,‡ quarrelled, as usual, with the captain-general, who retired in a huff.

---

* Gattari, *op. cit.*, Daru, "Storia della Republica di Venezia," lib. viii. (Capolago: 1837); Vettor Sandi, "Storia Civile della Repub. di Venez." par. ii. vol. i. (Venezia : 1755); Romanin, *op. cit.*, vol. iii. pp. 241, 242; Marino Sanuto, "Vite de' Duchi," ad ann. 1369, ap. Murat., Rer. It. Script., tom. xxi.

† Gattari, *op. cit.*

‡ The Venetian government was represented in the camp of their commander-in-chief, by two officers called *provveditori in campo*. Their duties were analogous to those of the Spartan ephors in the field. The general was supposed to consult them, and they kept a watchful eye upon his political relations. They were a necessity created by the mercenary system, and their action was usually disastrous.

Taddeo Guistinian, his successor, was utterly routed and made prisoner. In this battle Novello Carrara, twenty-one years old, the eldest son of Francesco, distinguished himself by his bravery.* He was mounted on a magnificent war horse, himself clad in armour of shining steel, and over it a white surcoat sown with red *carri.* The defeat of Guistinian caused great alarm in Venice. The republic hired five thousand Turkish archers and put a new force in the field. The full power of both armies met at Lova, and, thanks to the Turks, the Venetians won a complete victory. Among their prisoners was the vaivode Stephen, nephew to the king of Hungary.†

Carrara had tried treachery against Venice; Venice now replied in the same manner. The republic made terms with Marsiglio Carrara, offering him every support and a large portion of Paduan territory if he would murder Francesco. At the same time certain Paduans also came to Marsiglio at Venice, assuring him that the city would gladly welcome him as lord in place of Francesco. The leader of these was a cleric, one Giacomo Lione, who seems to have borne no very good character; for the chronicler says of him, " Non avendo Dio nè i santi nel mento, ma il Diavolo solo nel corpo." Giacomo " had tasted the sweets of the Church,"‡ and desired more; he demanded the bishopric of Padua as the price of his share in the murder. All the details were carefully arranged; Francesco was to be stabbed when leaving

---

* Gattari, *op. cit.*; Verci, *op. cit.*, lib. xvi., ad ann. 1373.
† Verci, *loc. cit.*
‡ " Avendo gustato la dolcezza della chiesa."

the door of his mistress's house. But two attempts failed—one because a messenger opened a letter and read it; the other, because the would-be bishop, anxious to kill Novello as well as his father, urged a day's delay.* Affairs were, however, tending towards a peace. The king of Hungary was anxious to recover his nephew, the vaivode; Venice also was ready to treat, because she stood in a position to dictate terms. Francesco, alarmed at the prospect of losing his best ally, the Hungarian, found himself compelled to submit; and peace was concluded in the year 1373.† Venice intended to cripple Carrara, and to secure, by the severity of the terms she imposed, quiet for some time in that quarter. The war indemnity was enormous—as much as two hundred and ninety thousand ducats; the offending forts and villages on the Brenta were razed and their sites desolated, while, as a scourge for Carrara's pride, the republic insisted that either Francesco or his son must come in person to Venice, kneel to the doge, confess their fault, and beg forgiveness. Novello, who had a deep affection for his father, would not allow the old man to go. He went himself, and with him Petrarch, the valued friend of the house, who made a long oration in praise of peace. The part played by the great laureate in the political movements of his generation is not the least singular note of that curious, rich, and diversified fourteenth century. This was the poet's last political act, for he died the following year at Arquà, July 18, 1374.

* Gattari, *op. cit.*
† See Romanin, *op. cit.*, pp. 245, 256; Verci, *op. cit.*, lib. xvi.

The severity of this defeat sobered Carrara, and for the next few years he remained quiet. Not that Lombardy was quiet ; Can Signorio, the last legitimate Scala, died, and Bernabò Visconti claimed Verona in virtue of his wife Regina. After a long and disastrous war the two Scaligeri, Can Signorio's illegitimate children, were forced to buy off Regina's claim at the price of four hundred and forty thousand florins. But this war had another result more intimately connected with our subject—the league between Scala, Genoa, Hungary, and Carrara, which was destined to bring Francesco once more into collision with Venice. Visconti made overtures to Venice, inviting her to join him in an alliance which should be a reply to the Scala league. Bernabò was determined to absorb Genoa as well as Verona, if he saw his opportunity ; he now perceived that a war between the two maritime republics was imminent, and, to further his own views, he determined to hold with Venice.

The never-ending question of Eastern trade, so fruitful of quarrels between Genoa and Venice, was always open ; but at this moment it presented one of its acuter phases in the difficulties which had arisen as to the possession of Tenedos. War was ostensibly brought about by the rivalry for precedence between the consuls of the two republics, when Pierino Lusignan, king of Cyprus, was being crowned at Famagosta. At the coronation banquet the Genoese so far forgot himself as to throw a loaf at the head of his brother consul, and was expelled from the banquetting-hall.*

* Marino Sanuto, *op. cit.*, ad ann. 1378.

The end of this fracas was the war of Chioggia, a war disastrous not only to the states concerned but to all Europe as well; for, by exhausting Venice and Genoa, it freed the Turk from the control of the two naval powers which alone could have held him in check.* This war concerns us now, however, only in so far as it affected the history of the Carrara family. Francesco saw with delight the approaching struggle, for he was eager to shake himself free from the peace of 1373. He joined the Genoese, and at the siege and capture of Chioggia he and his Paduans proved of great help. The town was made over to him, his flag floated from the palazzo, and he added "lord of Chioggia" to his titles. He must have known how bitterly this would sting Venetian pride; but he flattered himself that her days were numbered, that Genoa was about to besiege and sack Venice herself. He indeed, more than any other, urged an attack on the city; and, when the doge petitioned him to receive ambassadors to treat of peace, he replied, "Not before I have bitted the horses on Saint Mark's."† But in Italy no alliance was long lived. The Genoese admiral was greedy, and quarrelled with Francesco over the booty of Chioggia. Carrara withdrew to the Marca, and there joined the Hungarians, who, at his request, were besieging Treviso. But Francesco's hatred of Venice was a more pressing passion than his ill

---

* See Verci, *op. cit.*

† Gattari, *op. cit.*, p. 305; Cittadella, *op. cit.*, cap. xxxviii. Others, among them Chinazzo, put these words into the mout of the Genoese admiral.

humour against Genoa ; so when the fortune of war changed, and the Genoese in their turn were shut up in Chioggia, he continued his supply of provisions and war material, until Brondolo fell and Chioggia was cut off from the friendly support of Padua. The siege of Treviso was pressed so vigorously under Carrara's direction, that Venice, rather than see it fall into his hands, made it and the whole of the Marca Trivigiana over to Leopold, duke of Austria. In fact, Francesco had left no stone unhurled which might wound the Venetians, and it was by no means an adequate retaliation that they thrust him into a war with Austria, over the unhappy city of Treviso.

The peace of Turin put an end to the Chioggian war. The terms, as far as they concerned Carrara, were based on those of the year 1373. But Austria did not appear among the signatories, and Francesco remained free to urge the siege of Treviso, which was only feebly defended by the duke. The town resisted for three years, alone and unsupported, except by her hatred of the Carraresi. But her bravery availed her nothing. In the year 1384 Leopold, rather than continue his feeble resistance, sold her, with Feltre, Belluno, Cividale, and Valsugana, to Francesco. This was a large increase to the lordship of Padua. But the inflation brought its inevitable consequence of jealousy on the part of neighbours, and an access, not a diminution, of the thirst for territory. Antonio Scala had set his heart on Feltre and Belluno; he now saw himself robbed of all hope to win them, and became the covert foe of the Carraresi; while Francesco. holding the important alpine passes commanded by

Feltre, Belluno, and Valsugana, ardently coveted the mastery of all the eastern outlets upon Italy. He saw his opportunity when the pope made an unpopular appointment to the patriarchate of Aquileia. The Udinesi refused to accept Philip d'Alençon, the pope's nominee, and Carrara was called on to compel their obedience. He agreed to do so on condition that he should receive Sacile and Monfalcone.* If Francesco had succeeded in carrying out this project, his territory would have stretched in a semicircle from Padua, round the head of the Adriatic, to within a very short distance of Trieste. That would have been a great danger for Venice; and it was obvious that she could not allow anything of the sort to take place.

The Udinesi were secretly encouraged to resist D'Alençon and Carrara; a league of small towns was formed for the purpose, and Venice supplied the funds at the rate of twenty-five thousand ducats a month. The war did not move rapidly, but it spread, as every war inevitably did in those days, when each prince was armed to the teeth and watching his neighbour hour by hour. Venice abstained from openly taking part in the campaign, but she induced Antonio Scala to attack Francesco. Scala was only too glad to do so, in retaliation for the loss of Feltre and Belluno. No sooner did Scala take the field, than Gian Galeazzo Visconti saw that the moment had come for him to seize Verona, which he claimed through his aunt and mother-in-law, Regina Scala.

The appearance of Gian Galeazzo on the scene was decisive in the fate of the Carrara family. He

* Romanin, vol. iii. p. 318.

was, without exception, the least scrupulous and the most cunning of all the Lombard Signori. He had the largest army and the longest purse. In him all the restless ambition, as well as the deep calculating faculties of his family were summed up. He was perhaps the most powerful prince in Europe at that moment, and as dangerous to the peace and freedom of Italy as Napoleon subsequently was to the liberty of the Continent. But Visconti never lived to win or lose a Waterloo. Gian Galeazzo resolved to possess not only Verona, but Padua as well; the acquisition of the first, however, was sufficient to employ him at present. He proposed to Carrara an alliance by which they should plunder the Scaligeri; Verona to fall to Gian Galeazzo and Vicenza to Francesco. Carrara should have known how fatal it was to touch a Visconti; the bait, however, proved too tempting and was swallowed. The joint forces of Milan and Padua entered the Veronese. In battle after battle Antonio Scala suffered defeat. In vain that he sent to Venice imploring aid and urging that it was she who had thrust him into the war.* The charge might be true, but the interests of the republic did not counsel her to move; and she allowed the Scaligers to fall. The battle of Castagnaro decided their fate. Verona was lost by treachery, and Antonio fled to Venice, from thence to Florence. He was poisoned the following year (1388), between Cesena and Forli. With him ended the house of Scala as lords of

---

* See Gattari, *op. cit.*; Cittadella, *op. cit.*, cap. xlviii.; Romanin, vol. iii. p. 320. "Voi m'avete promesso e ingannato con isperanza d'oviare a questa lega, e hora rimaniamo ingannati."

Verona, after a reign of one hundred and twenty-seven years. Visconti had taken one step forward; only the Gonzaghi and Carraresi now stood between the mistress of the Adriatic and the master of Milan.

Francesco paid dearly for his madness in trusting the faith of the count of Virtù. Visconti was not slow to take a second step eastward. When Verona fell, Gian Galeazzo's captain occupied Vicenza also, before Carrara had time to seize it. Francesco still hoped, however, that it would be handed over to him in accordance with the terms of his treaty. But day after day he was put off, and it began to dawn on him that he had been duped and used as a tool by Visconti, who, at that very moment, meditated his ruin. Beside himself, he turned, but too late, to the only power that could help him. He went to Venice to ask her aid. But it was to no purpose that he pointed out how dangerous Visconti might become to the republic; the Venetians only remembered how dangerous and troublesome Carrara himself had proved. They recalled the poisoned wells, the lordship of Chioggia, the siege of Treviso; they hated him, and he had nothing to offer, while Gian Galeazzo was there promising them Treviso and the Marca back again if they would join him in despoiling Carrara. Venice accepted the league, and the marquis of Este joined it; bought by the bribe of the Castello d'Este, the original home of his race, which had for long been out of the family.*

Francesco Carrara stood on the brink of destruc-

---

* Romanin, vol. iii. p. 321 ; Gattari, *op. cit.* ; Verci. *op. cit.,* lib. xx. ad ann. 1388 ; Cittad., *op. cit.*, cap. li.

tion. He had sown the wind in the war of Chioggia; he now reaped the whirlwind of accumulated Venetian hatred. He found himself alone; his friend the king of Hungary had died six years before, and arrayed against him were the two great powers of North Italy. Nothing could save him; but he made one last effort. He resigned the government into the hands of his son Novello, and himself withdrew to Treviso. He hoped by this act to appease Venice; and Novello wrote to the republic, urging that they had no quarrel with him and his father no longer reigned.* But this time Venice was under no external pressure; her hands were free, and she knew no more satisfactory way of employing them than in chastising the Carraresi. The Milanese and Venetian troops pressed towards Novello's capital. After a brave resistance, and chiefly compelled by dissent and faction inside the walls, he yielded Padua and himself to the count of Virtù. Treviso was occupied by Jacopo dal Verne, the Milanese general, and Francesco, who was captured with the town, reluctantly consented to entrust himself to Visconti, under promise that he should have liberty to go where he chose.† He was invited to Cremona. At Verona he found that the safe-conduct was a blank paper in the eyes of the count of Virtù, and that he was in reality a prisoner under arrest. He never regained his liberty, but, after being moved from one prison to another, each growing more and more rigorous, from Cremona to Como, from

---

* The traditional reply of Venice is pithy and sums up the situation: " He who is born of a cat can't help having fleas."
† Gattari, *op. cit.*

Como to San Colombano, he died in 1393 at Monza. He died in misery and actual want, robbed of his last coin by Gian Galeazzo. Then, as so often happened in Italy, as indeed happened a few years later to Novello himself, all honours were lavished on his lifeless body; it was embalmed and sent with great parade to a splendid funeral in Padua. Treviso was handed to Venice; Verona, Vicenza, and Padua remained under the count of Virtù, and the Carrarese dominion seemed at an end for ever.

Francesco had brought the ruin on himself by his persistent hostility to Venice, and by his greed for territory, which awakened the alarm of the republic. Out of all the long embroglio which followed the war of Chioggia, the result was this: that two noble houses were destroyed, while Venice and Visconti remained the gainers. But Francesco had spoken a true word to Venice, though her hatred prevented her from attending to it: Gian Galeazzo was a great danger, and Novello Carrara was destined to reap the benefit of the jealousy which inevitably arose between him and the republic.

The next two years in Novello's life belong to the romance of history. If diversity of fortune were an object to Carrara and his brother Signori, he must have been well satisfied with the results of these months. By the terms of his surrender he was pledged to go wherever Visconti might direct. He was ordered to Milan. There he began a double game. Nursing in his heart the hope of returning to Padua some day, he now gave all his attention to allaying Gian Galeazzo's suspicions. He, in appearance, devoted himself to pleasure, to dancing, to jousts; mixing freely with the gentlemen of Milan.* All was faithfully reported to Visconti; but one fox knew another, and the count of Virtù shrewdly remarked, "Ogni animale si domesticha eccetto la volpe." Novello went further in his efforts to conciliate Gian Galeazzo. He made a formal and voluntary surrender of all his rights over Padua and its territory. But in the middle of all this courtship, Carrara was planning the murder of Visconti. He proposed to surround him one day when out hunting and to despatch him. The lord of Milan, however, was not so easily caught; the plot was discovered, and Visconti, behaving in a truly Viscontean fashion, pretended that he did not believe in Carrara's complicity. He made him a present of the castle and territory of Cortusone, near Asti. This kindly deed was only, in fact, a more intricate, and therefore a preferable, way of securing Novello's murder; for the people of Asti were violently Ghibelline, and their minds were inflamed against Carrara as a Guelf. They were aware that to despatch him would be no crime in Visconti's eyes. But Novello's acuteness saved him. The moment he reached Cortusone he read the situation. With consummate address he called the peasants together, made a humorous speech † about his Guelfish leanings and Ghibelline birth, and ended

---

* "Diedesi ad un altro modo di vivere ed ad un' altra regola della vita sua, andando visitare le feste, le nozze, e davasi al danzare, ed alle giostre ed ad altri piaceri" (Gattari, *op. cit.*).

† He began by assuring them that "Io parlo come gentiluomo cacciato e non come Signore."

by remitting for ten years all taxes due to him as lord of Cortusone. He converted a fictitious hatred into a real gratitude. In return for such liberality, the peasants told Carrara that in almost every road and lane an ambush lay concealed against his life. It was clear that he must escape. He determined to make for Florence, where the hatred of Visconti, and the alarm caused by his attitude towards Tuscany, promised a welcome to any foes of his house. Novello announced that he was vowed to a pilgrimage at the shrine of St. Anthony of Vienne. He left Asti without giving the news time to reach Gian Galeazzo. Accompanied by his brave wife, Taddea d'Este—a woman of nearly inexhaustible fortitude, as her subsequent wanderings and sufferings proved—his two sons, and two servants, he crossed the Cenis in deep snow, for it was March, and made his way by Vienne to Avignon, where he was well received by the pope. From thence the whole family sailed down the Rhone to Marseilles, and there, with some difficulty, took ship for Genoa. But while they were off Hyères a violent storm swept down. Taddea, who was near her confinement, implored to be landed. The whole party disembarked, and, keeping along the shore in sight of their ship, they toiled on to Frejus. There the wind had fallen enough to allow them to go on board once more, but only to be tossed about with as much violence as ever. They were compelled to put in under Turbia, and spent the night in a ruined chapel, Taddea sleeping upon the broken altar. Next morning the sea had hardly moderated, yet they set out. At Ventimiglia they stayed for food;

but they were seen by some of the natives, who, recognizing their quality, told the governor. He sent soldiers to arrest them, and the party were forced to withdraw to a wood and defend themselves with stones. At length they were close pressed and in great danger of being killed, when Novello offered twenty ducats to the captain of the band, at the same time telling him that he was lord of Padua and a friend to the king of France. After some difficulty they were allowed to go. That night they spent on shore, not far from San Remo, and next morning, half starved for want of food, one of the sons, Ugolino, set off to forage. He came back with a kid, some bread, and a bottle of wine. The whole party went into an olive grove, lighted a fire, and roasted the kid. Two of their number kept watch on the tree-tops while the others eat. In the middle of their meal the watchers cried that some one was approaching. Novello and his sons drew their swords and waited. The alarm, however, proved to be false. The men who now entered the wood had been despatched in search of Carrara to tell him that Adorno, doge of Genoa, had sent a ship to bring the family on their way. The Carraresi were cheered by this welcome help, and, embarking once more, they purposed sailing straight to Genoa ; but again the storm bore down on them, and they were driven into Savona. There they found friends, the Florentine Donati and others, who prepared a supper for them, for it was now nightfall. The wanderers had not sat down to the food they needed so much, when a message came from Adorno telling them to leave

Savona at once, as Gian Galeazzo's emissaries were in Genoa, threatening instant war if the republic sheltered the Carraresi. Supperless, they went to sea again, and in the early morning put into Genoa disguised as hermits. They stayed in the city only a few hours, and then sailed away down that fairy coastland, past Nervi, Porto Fino, Santa Margherita, Rapallo, till they came to Porto Venere. There they landed and went to a small inn to procure some food. They had hardly tasted the meat, when Donati rushed in to say that Galeazzo Porro, a captain of Visconti, was coming with forty horse, on his way to Pisa in search for them. Nowhere could they escape the lord of Milan. The whole family rose in haste, and hid themselves in a neighbouring wood. The strain became almost more than Taddea could endure—she nearly succumbed; but, supported by Novello and her own high courage, they both pushed on to Pisa, where they confidently looked for help from their friend Gambacorta. It was evening when they came under the walls of the town. They found messengers from Gambacorta waiting them, to forbid them to enter Pisa on any account, as Porro was on the look-out for them. Almost crushed, they turned aside to a little hostelry; they found that full, and were obliged to make their lodging in the stables. Taddea went to sleep in the manger, while Novello and Donati divided the night into watches. It was near midnight, and Donati was on guard, when he heard the trampling of horses' feet; his alarm, however, was banished when the new-comer proved to be a servant of

K

Gambacorta, with horses and refreshments for the party. Next day they pushed on, avoiding Pisa, and reached Florence in safety at last.*

The hopes that Carrara had built on Florence and her aid were soon dispersed. He received a cold welcome and a hint that the Florentines would not be sorry if he would betake himself elsewhere, as they were now at peace with Visconti. But Novello knew that any peace in which Gian Galeazzo had a part must be a hollow affair, a *pace volpina*. Sooner or later he believed his chance would come, when Visconti attacked Tuscany. So for a season he bore the cold looks and obvious dislike of his hosts. And his patience met its reward. A change of feeling took place in Florence, and she began to arm. Carrara received the offer† of a company under Sir John Hawkwood; but he preferred to play his part nearer Padua, which was the sole object of his policy. He set out from Florence, intending to go to Bologna by way of Ancona and Ravenna, there to arrange an attack on the Milanese. But his evil star pursued him. The winds drove him past Ravenna to Chioggia, in Venetian waters, where he was recognized and forced to put to sea again, pursued all night by the Venetian galleys. He escaped, however, and reached Bologna safely; from thence he returned to Florence. There he found a state of things which

* The whole of this story is beautifully told by the Gattari, *loc. cit.* Francesco, languishing in prison at Como, whiled away the time by telling the tale in *terza rima*, which may still be read among Lami's " Delitiæ Eruditorum," tom. xiv.

† Gattari, *op. cit.*

delighted him. The Florentines were now eager for a league against Visconti, and Carrara was commissioned to start at once for Munich to persuade the elector of Bavaria to join the allies. He sailed from Leghorn to Monaco; from thence he passed through Geneva, Lausanne, Lucerne, and came to Zurich. There he made friends with his landlord's son, an Italian, young Massaferro, and from him he learned that the emissaries of the ubiquitous Visconti were even then in Zurich looking for him. He left in haste, crossed the Lake of Constance, and reached Munich. Novello found little difficulty in persuading the elector Stephen to join the league against Visconti; and he was soon able to send the news of the elector's adhesion to Florence. But Gian Galeazzo was always well informed of what was passing at foreign courts. When he learned that Bavaria had joined his enemies, he sent for the Florentine ambassadors, who were as yet ignorant of the fact, and who were at his court trying to arrange a peace. He apologized for keeping them waiting so long, consented to their terms, and expressed himself anxious to have the signatures at once. The courier of the embassy reached Florence before Novello's messenger, who conveyed the news of the elector's adherence, could arrive, and peace was signed. When Carrara's envoy from Germany reached the city, he was told that the Florentines were sorry for the trouble his master had taken, but that it was too late. This news was a serious blow to Novello, who was lying ill of a fever. It showed him how utterly unsupported he was, how little he could rely on anything but his own courage. But the shifty policy of Visconti again proved his best friend ; a rupture soon occurred between Florence and Milan. Novello left Segna in Dalmatia, whither he had gone to see his sister, to whom he was devotedly attached. He quitted Dalmatia with better hopes, for at Segna, under his sister's care, he had recovered from his fever. Moreover, he had paid a visit to a famous witch who lived in the wild, mountainous country above the Dalmatian coast, and from her he had received a prophecy of good omen. With that courage which never deserted him, he set out to recover his principality. He entered Friuli, thanks to the connivance of Venice, who was now thoroughly awake to the count of Virtù's unbounded ambition. At the head of a small army, recruited chiefly in Germany, but swelled by numbers of banished Paduans who flocked to his standard, he pushed straight for Padua. There was something fascinating in Novello himself, and still more so in this resolute attempt to regain his city with a handful of men— something attractive, which engaged the imagination of the people. His advance was a triumphal procession. The month was June, and in every town bands of boys and girls, crowned with roses, came out to meet him, and bid him welcome back and good speed in his effort for Padua. It was

> " Roses, roses, all the way
> And myrtle mixed in his path like mad."

The Paduans, thoroughly tired of Visconti rule, hailed Carrara with joy. The town was assaulted, help given from within, and to the cry of "Figliuoli, chi m'ama non m'abbandoni!" answered by shouts of "Carro, carro! Carne, carne!" Novello entered the city. He had fulfilled the witch's prophecy, given to him in the mountains above Trieste. "In the month of June he who went out by the gate came in over the wall." So, after two years' absence—two years of extraordinary adventure and wandering, of incessant plot and counterplot—the Carraresi returned to their own place (1390).*

The safety of the family became dependent once again on Venice; for this forcible occupation of Padua entailed a war with Visconti, and Novello alone was no match for the lord of Milan. But Venice was glad to see Carrara once more established as an outwork between herself and the count of Virtù, and she offered Novello abundant though secret support from the treasury of the republic. The league against Visconti progressed favourably as far as Carrara was concerned, and in 1391 his title to Padua was acknowledged by Gian Galeazzo, though at a rather large price—one hundred thousand florins. For the next few years the Carraresi enjoyed almost the only quiet they had ever known. Even so they were not without family mishaps. Novello sent for his wife from Florence; but Taddea seemed doomed to misfortunes on all the many voyages her fate compelled her to take. While on her way to Padua she fell into the hands of one of those robber chiefs who lived by the ransoms paid for their prizes. Taddea, however, reached Padua safely at last, and the family

* Gattari, *op. cit.;* Verci, *op. cit.*, lib. xx. ad ann. 1388-1390.

hoped to enjoy rest and the fruits of their labour. Novello seemed willing to adopt the right method to secure this peace. He turned his attention to the government of his city and to the encouragement of her trade. But, above all, he drew closer to Venice. He judged, and rightly, that her suspicions of Visconti were the guarantee for his own safety. Gian Galeazzo had ruined the Carraresi once; but the security of the family now depended largely on his existence, and the prosecution of his ambitious schemes to rule all Italy. Venice was compelled to protect every bulwark between herself and the count of Virtù. A clearer political insight would have warned Carrara to persevere in his present line of conduct, and to avoid all possibility of a rupture with the republic.

The next seven years witnessed the growth of the Visconti dominion, and the various transmutations of the league formed by the smaller princes of Lombardy against him. Visconti had made up his mind to absorb the lesser princes one by one. He began with Gonzaga, probably because he was a relation of the Visconti; he interfered in the Este succession; he showed a desire to attack Florence. Everywhere it was clear that he was preparing for a great stroke. One of his chief and most pressing objects was to break up the league in Lombardy, whose hostility tied his hands. For that purpose he endeavoured to win Carrara, the moving spirit of the league, to his side. He proposed a double matrimonial alliance, as a result of which Feltre, Belluno, Verona, and Vicenza should be ceded to the lord of Padua; he courted the young Carraresi who were sent to represent their father at Gian Galeazzo's coronation as duke of Milan ; he remitted part of the sum due to him by the peace of 1392. The bribe was enormously large. But Novello had learned by experience to mistrust the duke of Milan ; he had unpleasant memories connected with Visconti and Vicenza; above all, Venice was opposed to the alliance. Negotiations were broken off. Venice, and indeed all Italy, were now thoroughly alarmed by the advance of Gian Galeazzo. In the year 1399 Pisa, Perugia, Assisi, and Spoleto were in his hands, and he was drawing a cordon round Florence. The allies invited the emperor Robert to cross the Alps and crush the duke of Milan. Robert came, and with him the duke of Austria. The Lombard princes flocked to join him at Trent. But before Brescia Visconti routed the imperial army, which was saved from annihilation by the Carraresi alone. The duke of Austria was taken prisoner, and three days later he bought his liberty by a shameful promise that when he returned to the emperor's camp he would seize and send the two Carraresi to Galeazzo. The plot was found out, and Novello withdrew to Padua. The army melted away, leaving the emperor Robert standing alone and deserted, without men or money, a laughing-stock to all Italy.

The collapse of the emperor was a triumph for Visconti, and he at once made an advance upon Bologna. Jacopo and Francesco Carrara, the sons of Novello, were sent to help the besieged city. But the town fell, and the two young Carraresi were made prisoners. Their escape was one of the last episodes in the family history. Francesco was entrusted to the care of Gian Galeazzo's general, Facino Cane, to be brought to Milan. At Parma a Paduan living in that town told Francesco's barber of a secret way over the city walls. The same evening young Carrara slipped out of bed, and, putting on a blouse, sauntered out of the house whistling; he found the barber and the Paduan ready, and the three dropping from the wall escaped to a wood, and thence made their way to Paduan territory.* Jacopo, the other son, waited longer for his liberty. He was entrusted to the care of Gonzaga, lord of Mantua. While at Mantua he was in the habit of playing tennis under a wall, beyond which lay the lake; the balls frequently went over the wall, and one day, on going out to fetch them, Jacopo, who had been informed of the plan concerted for his escape by a letter sent to him in the belly of a fish he ate for dinner, found a boat ready and two faithful Paduans disguised as fishermen. They rowed him across the lake; horses were waiting on the other side, and he soon reached his native city.†

In the year 1402 the duke of Milan had matured his plans, and was ready to attack Tuscany, but death cut him short; he fell a victim to the plague in September. Though Italy breathed the freer, yet for Carrara the death of Visconti proved one of the greatest misfortunes that could have happened. As long as Gian Galeazzo lived, Venice was bound, whether she liked it or not, to maintain friendly

* Gattari, *op. cit.*

† See Vergerius, "Sapphics," for the return of Francesco and Jacopo Carrara, ap. Muratori, Rer. It. Scrip., tom. xvi.

relations with all the smaller princes of the mainland whose existence Visconti threatened. But now that he was dead, the republic was freed from that necessity; neither Carrara, nor Gonzaga, nor Este any longer held a pledge for her support. But more than that, the empire of Gian Galeazzo was not well cemented. It had been held together merely by the personal qualities of its creator; on his death it fell to pieces, and there followed a struggle for the fragments. The universal quickening of ambitious hopes which followed the death of Gian Galeazzo was perhaps the greatest misfortune which he inflicted on Italy. Every prince once again burned with a fatal desire to extend his territory; Venice felt the influence no less than Carrara and the other Signori.

The relief which Carrara and all Italy felt, when the count of Virtù was gone, made him forget that Venice still remained a potent factor in the problem of his existence. He believed that he might now with safety resume the ambitious policy of his father, and the opportunity to embark upon this fatal course was ready to his hand. He and his family were really foredoomed, escape was impossible; but it is part of their tragedy that they were compelled to be agents in their own destruction. Carrara accepted the offer of Feltre. Belluno, and Bassano made to him by the duchess regent of Milan, who desired, as Gian Galeazzo had desired, to weaken the league against the Visconti by seducing Novello to their side. More than that, Novello was believed by the Venetians to entertain designs on Ferrara, and was known to have gone there with an unnecessarily large troop of cavalry, to see the marquis, who was reported to be dying. Further, he allied himself with Guglielmo Scala; and by their joint efforts Verona was recovered from Milan. But Scala died a few days later, not without grave suspicions of poison administered by Carrara, his two sons were arrested and sent to Padua and Novello proclaimed himself lord of Verona.

The whole of this sudden expansion and success was fallacious. Novello stood on rotten ground. He had no real strength, and was unsupported by any alliance which could have justified him in offending Venice. Yet he hurried on, each new acquisition waking a deeper alarm in the mind of the republic. The duchess regent of Milan, whose government was weak and whose state was torn by internal quarrels, had long been endeavouring to win Venice to her cause against the league, and chiefly against Carrara.* Her first overtures were refused. She then raised the price offered by the addition of Verona and Vicenza. Venice hesitated ; not from any love for Carrara, but in deference to the opposition of her older politicians, who urgently dissuaded her from any course which would embark the republic upon a land empire. At last, after long debate, the proposals of the duchess were accepted and war agreed on. This was Novello's death-warrant. Affairs were precipitated in the following way. When Carrara seized Verona he claimed Vicenza also. But that city had always displayed an invincible repugnance to the Carraresi ;

* Romanin, vol. iv. bk. x. cap. i.

she now yielded herself to Venice in order to escape Novello. The republic accepted the dedication, and sent a herald to require Francesco Novello's son to raise the siege; in an access of fury, Carrara killed and mutilated the herald. The forces of Visconti and Venice invested Verona and Padua in 1404. But for a year and a half the Carraresi held out. Novello was indefatigable. He drilled a militia, and himself superintended the watches on the walls. No less vigorous and brave was Jacopo at Verona; but that city fell, Jacopo was sent a prisoner to Venice, while the troops liberated from the siege went to swell the numbers of those attacking Padua.

Novello's position was hopeless and terrible. He was deserted by his sole ally, the Marchese d'Este, betrayed by his general Barbiano, his life attempted by his kinsman, another Jacopo; the plague* raged in Padua, killing five or six hundred a day; the waters of the Bachiglione were diverted and the flour mills stopped. Still Novello refused to yield. Terms were constantly offered him by Venice—a large sum of money was promised for the town; but all efforts were in vain. The reasons for this obstinacy were, first, that Novello still entertained the hope of succour from Florence; false news from that quarter buoyed him up; further, he wished to give his secret schemes in Venice time to fructify. He never abandoned the expectation that some revolution inside that city might come to his aid; and he knew that if he were captured now, all his intricate and treacherous correspondence

* See Gattari for a graphic description of the plague.

with certain Venetian noblemen would come to light, in which case his chances of mercy were small. So he refused offer after offer ; each time the sum proposed as the price of the city growing ominously less, as the besiegers' mines and covered ways crept nearer to the walls and the prospect of taking the town by force increased. But at last the patience of the Paduans was exhausted ; they would endure no more. Novello's own hopes died away, and on the 23rd of November, 1405, he yielded Padua to the republic, and himself to Galeazzo Grumello, her general. He and his son, Francesco III., were sent to join his other son, Jacopo, in prison at Venice.

We have now reached the end. The tragic fate of the three Carraresi in the Venetian prisons excited much comment at the time, and has given rise to considerable dispute subsequently. As usual, there is a large mythical element in the popular story of their death. The secrecy and rapidity of the Venetian government lent itself to all who were anxious to make a mystery or horror out of the event, and this the Venetian people were eager to do. They hated the Carraresi, and received their prisoners with savage cries. They had not forgiven them the poisoned wells, and were only too willing to believe that the government inflicted tortures and agonies on its unhappy foes. What really happened seems to be as follows* :—Novello and Francesco were imprisoned in San Giorgio Maggiore until the Torresella dungeon in the ducal palace could be prepared for them. During this time they had an interview with

* Romanin, *op. cit.*, vol. iv. bk. x. cap. ii.

the doge, and the elder Carrara expressed his peni-
tence. The doge Steno replied that, if he wished to
show his contrition, he would induce Ubertino and
Marsiglio, two members of the family still at large, to
come to Venice: the republic was anxious to have the
whole of the race in their hands. The Council of Ten
proceeded to prepare the case against the Carraresi.
While thus engaged, two men came under their examination. The revelations which these men made as
to the information treacherously supplied to Carrara
by certain members of the government appeared
so grave, that the Ten asked for an addition to
their numbers, and sent to Padua for all Novello's
papers. Among these papers they seized his private
note-book, in which were registered the names of
those in his pay and an analysis of the informations he had received. These discoveries caused
a panic in the government. The Carraresi were
more closely imprisoned and treated with rigour,
only a prisoner being allowed to wait on Novello.*
The Ten asked for a further addition, and sat
day and night. The revelations, which continued,
grew graver and graver, and the alarm rose in proportion. Compromising papers were found in a boat

---

* " Et ad servendum eis deputetur unus de carceratis qui sit
confidens persona; et dominus Franciscus tercius filius suus
remaneat in carcere Orba cum uno ex suis pagis, illo qui ei pla-
cebit, et alter pagius licentietur."—Misti, "Cons. X.," p. 112, ap.
Romanin, *loc. cit.*, where we may read some curious instructions
as to the keys of the prisons. They were locked away in a box,
the key of which was enclosed again in another box, the key
of this last box being given to the doge every evening and
taken by him to his bedroom.

near San Basso, and several Venetian nobles became implicated in the treason. The trial of the Carraresi was postponed until the case of Pisani and Gradenigo had been disposed of. In January, 1406, sentence was pronounced on both. Pisani received five years' imprisonment; Gradenigo, three years of exclusion from all offices. The process against the Carrara family was resumed, and the Ten prepared the indictment on the charge of secret machinations against the state, which they and the whole court held to be proved by the papers before them. They delivered sentence as follows :—That all three Carraresi should be strangled in their prisons ; and the execution was carried out at once. Novello and Francesco are said to have resisted to the end, struggling fiercely with the executioners. Jacopo submitted quietly, only asking leave to write first to his wife.* Novello was

---

* Andrea Gattaro writes in tears over Jacopo. This is his description of the young Carrarese : "Era Messer Giacomo da Carrara di età d'anni 26. grande, e tutto bene formato, quanto altro cavaliere che avesse Lombardia, bianco come la Madre sapientissimo e grande amico di Dio, benigno, misericordioso ; il parlar suo dolce e mansueto, e l'aere suo Angelico, ardito ed animoso, fortissimo e virtuoso, che veramente se avesse avuto vita, sarebbe riuscito un altro Scipione Africano : ma pure così hebbe fine il corso della vita sua" (Gattari, *op. cit.*, p. 941). Here is his letter to his wife Belfiore : " L'infelice tuo sposo Jacopo da Carrara del qual so che avrai pietà, perche ti sempre sono stato grato ed amorevole, ed ora son privato di vita. Ti scrivo questa di mia propria mano, la quale quando avro scritta subito sarò morto. Sta sano, consolati, nè cesserai di pregar Dio per me che in questa vita più non mi potrai vedere, forsi mi potrai vedere tra li martiri candidati appresso Quello che regna in Cielo." I do not know whether this is

buried next day with great pomp in the Church of San Stefano.* The people endorsed the judgment of their government, and showed their own relief by crying, " Homo morto non fa guerra ! "

Undoubtedly the real reason for the execution of the whole family was the discoveries made after the fall of Padua. During the siege Venice had not been excessively harsh ; she had again and again offered terms which men in the position of Novello and his sons might have been glad to accept. They might have sold Padua for a large sum, and obtained permission to go where they chose, provided that they did not return to the Padovano. The repeated and apparently irrational refusal of these terms naturally exasperated Venice, who was at a loss to understand its motive until the damning papers came into her hands. We notice all through the proceedings a crescendo of terror on the part of the Venetians. The government were hurried into their severity by a panic. Nothing terrified Venice so much as intrigue among her own nobles, and here she found Pisani, Gradenigo, and Carlo Zeno all seriously implicated in treason. She had not forgotten either Tiepolo or Marino Faliero, and her alarm made her hasty and harsh. The policy pursued by Venice was so direct, showed so little

authentic, but it exists among the manuscripts of Count Robert Papafava, and is given as genuine by Cittadella, *op. cit.*, vol. ii. p. 586.

* For long his grave was supposed to be marked by a slab bearing the letters P. N. T., which were read as " Pro norma tyrannorum." But Cicogna has shown that they really are the initials of Paolo Nicolo Tinti, a merchant buried there. See Romanin, *op cit.*, vol. iv. p. 41 ; Sanuto, *op. cit.*

desire to finesse, that it startled the other Signori. With them it was a point to keep their enemies as prisoners ; their exact equivalent might appear in the market, in which case they could be exchanged ; while dead they were of use to no one. But Venice was not a Signore of the true type ; she had never hitherto desired to touch the complications of the mainland ; when she did, when she found herself forced into the midst of them, she was thorough. The republic was ready, where necessary, to adopt Machiavelli's maxim, that if compelled to kill a prince it is wisdom to destroy his whole race along with him. She was not brutal, but only cold ; with a constant desire for that quiet which was so imperatively demanded for her commercial prosperity.

The Carraresi died ; they had not the satisfaction of foreseeing the day of reckoning in store for Venice. But the enormous extension of territory which accrued to her on the fall of the Carrara family awoke in her that fatal greed for an empire on the mainland which turned every man's hand against her and brought her face to face with the League of Cambray. The Carraresi were extinguished. Their fate was typical of that which awaited almost all the other Signori, There is something pathetic in the terrible nemesis which pursued these men ; caught in the toils of a hopeless passion, dragged on whether they would or no. Theirs was a restless and unscrupulous ambition, compelled to move forward, but foredoomed to failure and death.

CARMAGNOLA, A SOLDIER OF FORTUNE.

THERE is an observation which is continually forced upon the student of Italian history. That country has experienced an almost insurmountable difficulty in achieving union. The fact that the difficulty is being now overcome only emphasizes the length and labour of the process. The history of Italy is the history of highly organized but conflicting particles. The episodes of her development depend upon the mutual destruction of these particles, no one of which possessed sufficient power to retain its own vitality while absorbing that of its neighbour. We may take this incapacity for unification as a sign that the major force of the Italian nature has been intellectual rather than practical; that Italy's grasp of understanding was complete, swift, and sure upon the centre of each situation; as the note of a character intellectually occupied by the problem of movement; of a temper interested in the formation of many types rather than in the selection of one; of a life always at the red heat of revolution, burning continually in the fires of destruction and re-creation. Her acumen perceived the antithesis too immediately upon the thesis to allow of any pause. This speed of vision con-

L

tributed to rescue the country from thorough conquest by any foreigner. The invader was dazzled, confused, and repulsed by the rapid changes. While he had just begun to recognize a direction, Italy, the land he supposed himself to be subduing and stamping, had, as it were, altered its identity—was no longer the same Italy; had measured all that the conqueror could do; had reached the furthest point of its helix, and had already commenced the backward sweep. But, though this quality helped to baffle those who attempted to master the country, it exposed her, inside her own borders, to unrest, to violent change, to warfare among her vital self-asserting members, to torture from her own too active self. She became a land of contradictions; refusing to dwell on any one moment because she saw that it was only a moment. Each statement instantly met its contradiction, based upon that point of falsity which is absolutely inseparable from all human exposition of truth. The very power that enabled the nation to posit the obverse compelled it to a consciousness of the reverse. It was condemned to a perpetual demonstration of instability, as the result of its too ardent desire to find the absolute stability. The dynamics of balance were always potent enough to destroy the statics. Therefore the people who had dogmatized faith for the whole of Europe were themselves deeply sceptical. Those who had formulated law presented a chaos of lawlessness. The Italian epic is no sooner created than it offers its own body as the food for parody and satire. Conviction and calm belief were impossible for Italy. She could formulate what the northern nations accepted with earnestness—

law, art, religion, the idea of freedom ; but the creator could not receive its own creation as an article of creed. Seldom before had a people devoted its whole energies, in every department of life, to the illustration of the Heraclitean doctrine that all is in flux.

Among the many particular curses entailed upon Italy by her fatal inability to unite, few were more widely or more bitterly felt than the curse of mercenary troops and wandering armies.* Philosophers and historians, Machiavelli and Villani, are agreed in lamentations over the decline of city militias and the supremacy of hired arms. These wandering bands were in their origin the children of disunion, and to the end they retained the marks of their parentage. They had their birth in that necessity which compelled the despots to use foreign troops in their various wars, either against their brother lords, or against their native town whose tyranny they were usurping. It was imperative that a tyrant's soldiers should be men of no party ; purely fighting men, and nothing more ; unfettered by any ties of politics or blood. Therefore the Signori called to their service Bretons, Gascons, English, Hungarians, and Germans. Their armies were composed of men and officers who spoke no Italian and whose sole glance was directed to the purse-strings of their employers. But these mercenary warriors, bound together by a common interest which was antagonistic to that of their employers, were not slow to perceive that, in order to make their own position entirely secure, they must choose their leader from among themselves ; that he

* See "Archivio Storico Italiano," vol. xv.

must be a man whose sympathies and aims were identical with their own; that their head must be structurally and vitally a portion of their organism. In obedience to this instinct, the mercenary army which Mastino della Scala was forced to disband in 1338, when it found itself without a master, elected Werner, duke of Wislingen, as its captain; and the Grand Company, the first fully developed company of mercenaries, was let loose on Italy.

Under Duke Werner the Grand Company learned self-discipline from the necessities of their case. Beyond the circle of their camp the world was all their enemy. But it was a world that had neither unity nor force enough to crush them. So long as the outermost line of their entrenchments remained unbroken, they were as united, as potent, as an undissipated poison germ floating in the blood of the nation. On every hand they were secure. If war failed them, the country lay open for them to pillage. The burghers were wealthy and timorous, the peasants unarmed. The soldier had only to put out his hand and take the harvests of the one and the gold of the other. In fact, the mercenaries discovered how to rifle their masters; and learned, moreover, that they could do so with impunity. After Duke Werner's death and the dispersion of the Grand Company, two other leaders, Fra Moriale, a Provençal, and Count Lando, a German, continued and developed the traditions of the foreign mercenaries. Fra Moriale especially was a born organizer. He attracted to his standard all the evil humours of Italy, the bankrupts in fortune or in fame. The nucleus of his band was foreign, it is true; but many of his soldiers and most of his camp followers were the ruined outcasts of Italian society. This is a fact of signal import- ance, for it bore directly on the development of the first company of native as distinguished from foreign mercenaries. Moriale's work was a work of con- solidation. His company was governed by one fundamental maxim—absolute liberty outside the camp, rigid discipline and justice within. The whole band was drawn closer together, and taught to look upon the camp as their city and their home. Through his action the mercenary army became self-sustaining, therefore more formidable and longer-lived. Moriale's work had been too thoroughly accomplished to be broken up at his death. The mercenaries elected as their new captain Count Lando, and their life of rapine and of plunder went on as before. They moved freely from territory to territory, sweeping the harvests from the fields, exacting what sums they chose from the prince or the republic whose lands they occupied, wearing the country barer and barer by their depre- dations. The burden became intolerable, the military occupation showed no signs of coming to an end, and Italy at length prepared to make an effort to suppress the mischief which was eating its way into her very vitals.

The pope, Florence, and Venice joined in a league against the adventurers. Though the curse of dis- union, of jealousy and conflicting interests, broke up the league and rendered it inefficient, yet out of this effort came the purely native company of Alberico da Barbiano, the first great Italian *condottiere*. Blessed by the pope and fired by St. Catherine of Siena, Alberico won the victory of Marino, and from that moment the nature of mercenary warfare in Italy was changed. The foreigners disappeared, and Italians took their place.

Italy, however, was not destined to escape the curse entailed by her own sloth. All she succeeded in achieving was the substitution of native adventurers for the foreigners she had expelled. The change in their aspect made little difference in their character; the one was the lineal descendant of the other, inheriting and continuing the same traditions of war. Italy had hoped to free herself from mercenary arms; but she failed. The triumph of the Guelfs and the insurgence of the communes had destroyed the aristocracy, the nucleus of the warlike element. The leading politicians now were merchants or bankers—men who clung to their money and believed that all was compassable by gold. From the ranks of these came the Signori; and they set themselves more or less deliberately to debauch the citizens and to render them effete. Their policy was only too successful. When the townsfolk preferred a tax on silver and on salt—silver for the rich and salt for the poor—to military service in defence of their liberty, of what use was it that Boiardo sang the praise of chivalry and arms? The country with its own voice declared itself a prey to the mercenaries. The essence of the soldier-spirit was gone. Italy turned willingly from the field to the counting-house. She shrank from the constant proof of her arms, and in the day of her need she was unable to bear them.

The native companies of adventure present two marked characteristics. They were united and solid upon the basis of their profession, opposed as soldiers to all other classes and professions in Italy; they were also mutually antagonistic and jealous of each other inside the limits of their profession. The previous existence of the Signori inevitably determined the aspect assumed by the native mercenaries. The minute partition of Italy among petty tyrants, swayed by various and conflicting aims, prepared the way for the minute divisions of the great army, and for the existence of the various *condottieri*, each serving his own selfish ends and standing in rivalry with his fellows, a rivalry which prevented them from ever becoming masters of Italy in any permanent sense. But, though cloven and broken among themselves, the mercenaries were solid and cohesive against the world outside them. The reason for this solidarity in their profession lay deep in the spirit of the race. The Italians never possessed the sense of nationality, except an ideal nationality in Rome. They were therefore able to experience within the borders of their own land the effect and the fascination of cosmopolitanism, together with its accompanying democratic tendency. An art or a profession, not a city or a country, became the bond of union. The true *patria* was a common enthusiasm for war, for painting, for scholarship, for religion. The bands of adventure are not a singular phenomenon. Side by side with them there rose the companies of religious fanatics, the school of John of Ravenna, the workshops of Squarcione and Verrocchio. Alberico's native company of St. George was the matrix of a hundred captains of adventure, "the Trojan horse of Italian warfare," from whose entrails a breed of soldiers was born, destined to cover Italy with their arms, to make her theirs for a time, to serve their purpose, and to pass away ; just as John of Ravenna's lecture-room was the Trojan horse of Italian scholarship, a hotbed for the growth of a hundred students, destined to seize and hold the world of lost classics, to recall Italy to Rome, to serve their purpose, and to pass away. And the action of the *condottieri* and of the Humanists is very similar. Both appear as interruptions—the one in the political, the other in the intellectual process. Both are solvents. Humanism proclaimed a doctrine of individual freedom ; adventure destroyed the political system, breaking down the despots and paving the way first for the conquest by Charles VIII., and then for the ultimate settlement of death under Charles V.

The result of Italy's effort to shake the foreign mercenaries from her throat was that Italians took the place of strangers. But the gain to the country was small. The chief difference between native and foreign commanders lay in the systematization of arms which the former effected. The Italians made an art of war, as they made an art of everything which they touched. Obeying a common impulse, the captains of adventure turned campaigning into a game. They laid down the rules and imposed the conditions under which it must be played ; and few would have ventured to violate these rules, for that would have been to renounce the *rôle* of artist and to outrage the national instinct for limitations and precision. In fact, war became an end in itself and not a means. The attention of commanders was directed not so much to victory as to a study and enjoyment of the moves by which they achieved success or suffered defeat. Under these conditions the art of war soon degenerated into a pedantry that admitted such an anomaly as a technical victory, and bore its fruits at Fornovo and at Agnadella. And the laws of this game, drawn up by professional soldiers, were framed to suit the soldier, not the prince who employed him. The interests of a general counselled him not to finish any campaign too rapidly; therefore no advantages were pressed to the full, no decisive blows struck. As a point of military etiquette, all prisoners were released immediately after an engagement. To prolong a campaign was to prolong the salaries of the commander and of all who served under him. Nor were the leaders unwilling to make service as light as possible for their men. By general agreement night attacks were abandoned and piquet and outpost duty might be dispensed with; quarter was invariably given. The life of the common soldier had no hardships after he had mastered his drill and the routine of service. The war he waged was not so much against the troopers of the hostile army as against the unarmed peasants of the place where he might be encamped. Wherever found, they were his prey, to work his will upon in any manner he chose. The democratic spirit of all true vagabonds, whether students, friars, soldiers, or artists, reigned in the camps. The soldier began life upon a strict equality, the sole title to distinction being excellence in his profession. Personal attachment helped to bind the men to one another in a union as fraternal as that of a monastery. Beyond the lines a soldier's freedom was unrestrained. "Liberty, Equality, Fraternity"—the watchwords of democracy, of revolution, of socialism—were the motto of the camp. But the democracy of arms, as it manifested itself in Italy, concealed nothing formative within its breast; it was chaos come again. The camp, therefore, attracted all the restless blood, the strong physical natures, the coarser-fibred appetites of Italy; just as the wandering religious companies attracted those of imaginative, vague, ecstatic, and ardent temperament.

Circumstances rendered the position of the *condottieri* powerful. The Signori were compelled, by the pressure of their neighbours, to use these mercenary captains; but they were costly weapons, and in using them the princes became bankrupt. On one condition only were the Signori able to retain the command of events. Their exchequer must be full. But it was only the wealthiest states, such as Venice or Milan, who could resist the drain of war. The moment the despot failed financially, the captains of adventure were masters of the situation; their ruined employer could not dismiss them unpaid, nor could he hire other arms against them. There was, however, a weakness in the position of the mercenaries. They were not at one among themselves; they could not agree to conquer and divide; they were ready to take the field against one another, not to destroy, but to supplant in the receipt of salary; they lacked width of ambition; they were, in fact, for the most part stupid. This weakness showed itself whenever the *condottieri* had to deal with solvent masters. A full purse could play them against each other, and store their labours for its own advantage. This was their real danger. Their perilous war was waged, not in the field against their brother captains, but in the cabinet against the princes who had escaped financial ruin. How dangerous this conflict might be received convincing proof in the tragic end of so many of these adventurers : Gabrino Fondulo in his iron cage ; Vignate executed at Milan ; Carmagnola beheaded at Venice ; these we must remember as counterbalances when we think of Michelotti lord of Perugia, or Sforza duke of Milan.

The story of Carmagnola illustrates these relations between the Signori and the captains of adventure. His career offers an example of the height to which a *condottiere* might aspire, of the mistake he might make, and of the fate that possibly lay in store for him. The problem presented to Filippo Visconti, the last of the Visconti dukes of Milan, when his brother's death left him sole prince, was how to recover the duchy, to which he had succeeded in name alone. On his father Gian Galeazzo's death, the dukedom had been partitioned among Galeazzo's generals, who had each seized the part that lay nearest to hand. Filippo determined to recover his lost patrimony. But he had many difficulties to contend with. He was without troops or generals, and his own peculiar temperament offered a serious obstacle. He suffered from a morbid timidity. A painful sensitiveness as to his personal appearance kept him in torture, and forced him to shrink from all publicity. He chose to live hidden away in the seclusion of his palace, surrounded by guards whom he distrusted, and over whose movements he set the watch of other and more secret guards, upon whom he himself kept a furtive and a timorous regard. He never escaped from the nightmare of murder. He daily changed his bedroom, and took his rest, as it were, with one eye open, fixed upon the *cubicularii** who protected his most private chamber. Filippo was possessed by the Visconti passion for intrigue, heightened almost to the pitch of insanity. In the recesses of his palace he spun from his restless brain a web of plot and counterplot ; the one forestalling, crossing, battling, defeating the other, till his own perception of the object in view was sometimes in danger of being lost in the maze. His mind presented a pandemonium of schemes, as though the regulative faculty had been paralyzed, leaving the designing powers alone in force. Nevertheless, Filippo applied himself to his task. His marriage with Beatrice di Tenda, widow of Facino Cane, brought him the nucleus of her husband's army. The duke turned to seek a general. His own timidity prevented him from taking the field in person, and his father's officers were now his enemies ; for each of them held some fragment of the duchy which Filippo intended to recover. At this time his eye fell upon Carmagnola as the man he was in search of. A man undistinguished as yet, and therefore likely to be subservient to his patron ; yet at the same time a soldier who had shown sufficient promise

* See Candido Decembrio, " Life of Visconti," cap. xlvi.

to warrant Filippo in placing him at the head of his troops.

Francesco Bussone was born of poor peasants, in 1390, at the village of Carmagnola, near Turin.* The natives of Carmagnola are still a strong and hardy-looking race, with thick necks and ruddy colours; as Francesco may have been when a boy, herding swine, before he went to camp. There is a portrait of him, painted as captain-general of St. Mark,† which shows us what he subsequently became towards the end of his career, when his profession had already stamped his character and determined his fate. A heavy face, with large and flabby cheeks, puffy and fat; coarse, thick lips and eyes, with a leer of lewdness and cunning in them; a pendulous nose, with no strong marking. Altogether a dulled, amorphous, and ignoble countenance, set upon an enormous, wrinkled neck. The face of a man lazy and self-indulgent, of appetites vulgar and cruel, with intellect of most indifferent power, yet inclined to believe his cunning to be wisdom. The face of a man doomed to fail through poverty of intelligence; incapable of surviving between the tortuous diplomacy of Visconti, and the thoroughness and cold determination of Venice.

Francesco left his swine-herding when only twelve years old, and went to camp under Facino Cane,‡ in the service of Duke Gian Galeazzo. He rose

---

* See "Ritratti ed. Elogj di Capitani Illustri" (Rome: 1635), p. 63; also Tenivelli, "Biog. Piedmont," Dec. iii. p. 149.

† I am indebted to Prof. Villari for the courtesy with which he sent me a photograph of this portrait.

‡ Ritratti, *loc. cit.*

rapidly, thanks to his great strength and bull-dog bravery, and before long obtained the command of a division. He was barely thirty when he came under the notice of Filippo and the last long act of his life began. Filippo set him the task of winning back the duchy of Milan from the usurping *condottieri*. With extraordinary rapidity, Carmagnola carried his work to a successful issue. Nor was his reward inadequate. He was allied by marriage to the ducal house,* and bore the Visconti arms upon his shield. His fiefs in Lombardy and Milan brought him a princely income, and he began to build a palace suitable to his sudden fortune. But Filippo had, in all his liberality, a further intention than that of merely satisfying his victorious general. The duke believed that he was binding Carmagnola to his service by ties which the soldier's cupidity would prevent him from breaking under any pressure of neglect or disgrace. Visconti did not desire to see this captain, whose value he had just discovered, take pay from any other master than himself; yet he was fully resolved that Carmagnola should never become so powerful as to be a serious danger to his own authority, or to play the part his father's general had played during his own minority. Such an issue seemed not improbable; for the rapidity of Carmagnola's success had won for him an Italian reputation. Filippo resolved to set him aside for a time, and to employ some of the many other officers whom his wealth placed at his disposal. He did not desire to alarm Carmagnola, but only to allow the warmth of

* He married Antonia Visconti, widow of Barbavara.

his celebrity to cool. Visconti sent his general to govern Genoa. Carmagnola's vanity soon opened his eyes to the fact that he was virtually cashiered. He refused to submit, even at the risk of losing his fortune, his palace, and his wife. After many fruitless appeals by letter to Filippo, Carmagnola determined to seek a personal audience of the duke. But what he sought could never be granted. Filippo rarely admitted his ministers to his presence; much more was he certain to shun an interview with an angry soldier. Carmagnola was told that the duke would not receive him. In a rage, and on the spur of the moment, he left the Milanese territory, and betook himself to the court of Savoy;* but meeting with a cold welcome from Duke Amadeo VIII., he set out for Venice, where he arrived on the 23rd of February, 1425. His reputation had preceded him, and his reception could not have been more flattering. He had taken one decided step towards independence, as he believed; towards destruction, as it really proved. His rupture with Visconti closes the first scene of this last act.

Carmagnola owed the warmth of his reception not solely to his fame as a general. The political conditions of Venice were such as to make his arrival peculiarly acceptable. The republic had already begun to take her place as a factor in Italian politics. She had lately acquired a large territory on the mainland, and appeared for the first time as one of the great Italian powers. She found herself now, however, conterminous with Milan, and there were not wanting

* Romanin, *op. cit.*, iv. 105; Tenivelli, *loc. cit.*

politicians who insisted upon the danger of the present direction. They pointed out that aggression on the mainland was a course that had no end, and that it exposed the Venetians to that dilemma—so fatal to the princes around them—of attacking or of being attacked; stability and peace would be impossible. And the attitude of Visconti seemed to confirm these warnings. The duke, like his father, cast his eyes towards Tuscany, and would certainly before long strike a blow for Verona, Padua, and the Lombard plain towards Venice and the east. The question before the republic was, should she assail Milan at once, or hold her hand and wait upon events? The doge, Mocenigo, led the conservative or anti-war party; and as long as he lived that party maintained its policy. But the section of Young Venice was all eager for military enterprise and a land empire. Their moving spirit was Francesco Foscari, still in the prime of a vigorous manhood, and so firmly seated in the affections of the younger nobility that no shadow of his tragic end could possibly have crossed his path. The party of war determined to secure, if possible, the election of their chief to the dukedom. Mocenigo was fully aware that the choice of his successor would be a critical point in the history of his country. On his death-bed he implored the senate and council to throw Foscari aside; but in vain. The elevation of Foscari to the dukedom virtually gave an affirmative answer to the question of war with Milan. The conservative party were still, however, of considerable weight; and the new doge was not sorry to find his hands strengthened by two events—the arrival of Carmagnola, and the presence of an embassy from Florence to propose an alliance of the two republics against the growing power of Visconti. Foscari and the Florentines were at once in accord, and the doge used all his influence to recommend the league. But negotiations were moving slowly when Carmagnola reached Venice, and Foscari gladly seized the new instrument which fortune had placed in his hand. He proposed that Carmagnola should at once be heard, in the Senate, on the position of the duke's affairs.

Carmagnola was under the influence of a blind fury against Filippo, and intent upon exacting some revenge for the slights he had suffered. His judgment was neither cool enough nor sufficiently intelligent to read the situation as it stood. The reception accorded him flattered his vanity, and induced him to believe that he had the power to mould the action of Venice. He did not see that the republic cared nothing for his private wrongs, but intended to use him for her own purposes if she were once convinced that he was the best man to give them effect. He failed to perceive that if Venice placed him at the head of her armies, she would not be content with such an injury done to the duke as might appease his own desire for vengeance; but rather that she would require from him nothing short of the destruction of Milan—her only object in this war; and any failure to satisfy her would be fatal to himself. Venice differed from the other Signori whom he and his brother mercenaries had served. She was rich, not bankrupt; firmly based, not shivering towards de-

M

struction at the slightest shock. Carmagnola made a fatal error in not perceiving the distinction. He could not hope to inspire her with dread; he might, with greater justice, have mistrusted himself when face to face with her cool diplomacy and determined purpose.

Carmagnola opened his speech before the Senate with a long and bitter tirade against the perfidy of the duke of Milan. Then, coming to matters of more practical moment, he depreciated the power of the duke, and insisted that the opportunity was favourable for an extension of Venetian territory. His speech had considerable weight with his audience; and when he had withdrawn, Foscari hastened to clinch the favourable impression. After dwelling on the crisis in Venetian affairs which the question of the Florentine league presented, he continued to enlarge on the necessity and the righteousness of the war, and concluded: "Carmagnola's speech has laid before you the power and the resources of Filippo. They are not so great as rumour has represented them. Nor should we be justified in looking for any other than a happy and prosperous conclusion to our enterprise under Carmagnola as the captain of our arms. For he is versed in war; nor can all Italy show his equal this day in bravery and proficiency in the military art. Under such a general is offered us, beyond all doubt, the certain hope of extending our borders. All these considerations urge us to undertake the war with a good courage; a war, I repeat, which is necessary; for our enemy is powerful, neighbour to us, and aspires to the sovereignty of Italy. Let us embark upon this war, then, and avenge our wrongs by trampling in the dust our common foe to the ever-lasting peace of Italy."* Foscari carried his audience with him. The last lingering suspicions about Carmagnolà's good faith, suspicions awakened by the recollection of the large stake he had left behind him in Lombardy—his fiefs, his palace, and his wife—were swept away on a wave of popular reaction when it was discovered that Visconti had tried to poison him at Treviso. The senate felt that the rupture was sincere; that Carmagnola might be trusted. In the spring of 1426 the Venetians formally appointed him captain-general of Saint Mark, and he received the baton from the doge before the high altar of the Basilica. In March he took the field against his old master, the duke of Milan.

Filippo had miscalculated the strength of the bonds by which he believed that he had bound Carmagnola to himself. He had set cupidity at too high a reading, and allowed too low a figure for vanity and pique. He had driven his ablest general into the arms of his foes. He had failed in an attempt to poison him. But Visconti was not a man to abandon his efforts to ruin his enemy. The difficulty merely enhanced the sweetness of success-ful revenge. Carmagnola, on the other hand, was now committed to a perilous course, with an exacting and uncompromising mistress to satisfy. One way of safety alone was open to him; he must be faithful to Venice. Success was his if he grasped this fact; failure and ruin if he missed it.

It is a tax upon the patience to follow the long-

* See Savina, cod. cxxxv. d. vii. alla marciana, p. 259.

drawn chronicles of Italian campaigning.* The slow movement of the armies, the result of the excessive preponderance of the cavalry and the difficulty of foddering the horses ; the indifference of commanders who had no desire to conclude the war ; the formal and technical openings of the game ; the marches and countermarches; the avoidance of pitched battles; the lengthened sieges—all form a wearisome labyrinth through which to toil. The interest of events lies chiefly in the curious contrast between the cabinet and the field; in the feverish impatience of the employers and the sluggish indifference of the employed. The rewards and bribes held out by the government to prick their generals to action were accepted and consumed by the mercenary with irritating imperturbability. It is only necessary to dwell on Carmagnola's campaigns in order to note the points which bear upon his final quarrel with Venice, and to mark the steps by which he unwittingly worked his own ruin.

The war opened with the siege of Brescia. But the honours of that siege and capture do not belong to Carmagnola. He almost immediately retired from before the city, leaving his chief engineer to carry on the works. After amusing himself for a few weeks with a plundering expedition on the shores of the Lake of Garda, he relinquished the field altogether, and withdrew to the Baths of Abano. He alleged that he was suffering from an old injury to his thigh, so painful as to render him unfit for active duties. The

* See Sanuto, "Vitæ Ducum," ap. Muratori, Rer. It. Script., xxii. p. 983 et seq.

Venetians had hitherto heard nothing of this injured thigh, and now they declined to consider this excuse as a real one. They were practically aware of the position in which they had placed themselves by employing a captain of adventure, and they looked upon Carmagnola's conduct merely as one of the usual hints to administer a *douceur.* Nor were they unwilling to obey such calls within reasonable limits. The Great Council created their captain a noble of Venice and Count of Castelnuovo.* They further offered him a principality in the Cremonese if he would quit Abano and push his arms across the Adda. But there were more serious features than the inactivity of their general in the case presented to the Venetian government. The duke of Milan had already begun that course of action whereby he intended to ruin Carmagnola. He had resolved to do all that lay in his power to make it appear that there existed an understanding between himself and his old commander-in-chief. His envoys were constantly arriving at the camp to seek interviews with Carmagnola. Filippo frequently proposed terms of peace to Venice, and on each occasion he named Carmagnola, the republic's own general, as his plenipotentiary. Carmagnola was flattered by this attitude of the duke, and by the rewards which Venice had already bestowed on him. He saw the two belligerents bidding for himself, and he easily believed that his services were essential to both; that he was the real centre of the situation; that from

* Sanuto, *loc. cit.;* Navagero, "Hist. Veneta," ap. Muratori, *op. cit.,* xxiii. p. 1088 et seq.

the Baths of Abano he might direct the destiny of Venice and of Milan.

The fall of Brescia compelled the duke to sign a peace, and put an end, for the present, to bribes and to suspicions alike. By a clause in this treaty of San Giorgio, the duke pledged himself to restore to Carmagnola all his property in Lombardy. The Venetians hoped in this way to sever all connection between Filippo and their general. But Visconti was far too wary to relinquish the advantage which he held. His breach of faith, on this and other points of the treaty, rendered war inevitable once more. In March, 1427, Carmagnola obeyed a summons to Venice, and again received the supreme command. This second campaign presents the same features as that of the preceding year—the same sluggishness on the side of the general; the same impatience, coupled with magnificent offers, on the part of Venice; the same intrigue and pretended intelligence on the part of the duke. It was rapidly becoming clear to the Venetians that they had mistaken the capacity of Carmagnola and the conditions of his temper; that they had not adequately reckoned the difficulty inseparable from the employment of a mercenary general. The duke, well pleased, saw that his enemies lost many opportunities of inflicting a loss upon him, while the man he hated was walking surely to destruction.

The campaign opened disastrously for the Venetians with the loss of Casal Maggiore, owing to the inactivity of Carmagnola, who allowed the place to fall without an effort to save it. At Venice the disgust was deepened by the news that an emissary from the duke had already found his way into the camp, and that he was the bearer of terms of peace, which the duke proposed, once more through the mediation of the Venetian general. Angry letters followed. But Carmagnola replied that he would dismiss the envoy, and pledged himself to recover Casal Maggiore in three days when the proper moment arrived. He redeemed his pledge. But the Venetians had little reason to rejoice at this success, for it brought them into direct collision with their general. Carmagnola wished to set his prisoners at liberty, in accordance with the custom of war. He informed the government of his intention and asked their consent. The republic cared nothing for the code of the mercenary captains ; she desired to win and keep every possible advantage, and saw, in the release of the prisoners, only a ruinous prolongation of the war. The reply was an order to retain the garrisons of the captured towns. Carmagnola was not prepared to disobey, and he submitted to what seemed to him a disgraceful breach of military honour. The friction of this episode increased the irritation at Venice, while at the same time it threw Carmagnola into the sulks. He allowed opportunity after opportunity to slip by. The duke of Milan at this moment was sorely pressed with war on both his borders ; Savoy attacking from the west, and Venice from the east. Yet Carmagnola, instead of pressing into the Milanese, wasted the campaigning months in idleness on Iseo. The complaints at Venice became loud voiced and popular ; loud enough to reach the general's ears. Carmagnola adopted a tone of indignation. He wrote to the

Senate accusing the republic of ingratitude, and demanding on what points they found his conduct amiss. Foscari had made himself in a measure responsible for Carmagnola; he did not now desire a rupture between Venice and her general, which would send him back to the duke of Milan charged with an intimate knowledge of Venetian resources. Foscari dictated the spirit of the answer which the Senate returned to Carmagnola. Its tone endeavoured to be soothing. The Venetians begged their general to believe the republic fully satisfied, and to be assured that the complaints, of which he had heard, represented no real feeling on the part of the government. A false statement of the case, and ruinous to Carmagnola, for it helped to blind his eyes and to make him think that Venice was in the same difficulty as the other Signori: that he was her master and might please himself in his conduct towards her; that he had only to hector and she would give way. In truth, Venice found herself on the horns of Machiavelli's dilemma, the fate of all who employ mercenary arms; she could not kindle her general to the glowing activity she desired to see in him, nor yet could she shake him off. Out of such a situation there was only one way of escape; but the season for taking it was not ripe yet.

From Lago Iseo Carmagnola returned to the Lombard plain, and met Visconti's army at Maclodio, where he fought the most important battle of this war and was entirely successful. But, mindful of the disgrace which had been forced upon him at Casal Maggiore, without so much as consulting the government he released the whole of his eight thousand prisoners the day after his victory. And the Venetians made no complaint; on the contrary, Foscari wrote a letter full of thanks to Carmagnola, and the Senate bestowed a palace upon their victorious general. The state was too thankful for this success to think of any recrimination. At length they were about to see the superiority of Carmagnola's military skill, and to reap the fruits of their expenses and their patience; for the battle of Maclodio had opened the way to Milan, and no army intervened between the troops of the republic and the capital of the duchy.

But they were bitterly disappointed. Carmagnola, instead of taking any vigorous steps to follow up his victory, closed the campaign on the plea that the season was late. And when the government urged him to take the field in the early spring of 1428, they were met by a request for leave to retire once more to the baths near Padua. Their disgust was intense. Negotiations for peace, however, were already on foot, and the Venetians yielded a grudging and ungracious consent. At Abano the general found, as he found wherever he went, an envoy from the duke already waiting him. The presence of these emissaries, constantly haunting his camp and dogging his footsteps, encouraged Carmagnola to believe that he might choose his own moment for returning to Milan; he did not surmise the peril that lay behind. Like a true *condottiere*, he was playing his own game, not fighting the battles of the republic. The interests of this game dictated that he should not press the duke too hard, but should rather, by a moderate use of his advantages, seek to lay Visconti under obligations on which he might base a claim, should he ever return to Filippo's service. And in all probability he did intend to return when this war should be concluded ; for at Milan he knew he would find a wealthy paymaster whose wars were continuous, and his half-finished palace still waited him.

Though Venice missed the full fruits of the victory at Maclodio, the duke of Milan acknowledged the weight of the blow, and peace was signed in April. Carmagnola made a triumphal entry into Venice, and the republic welcomed him with every circumstance of pomp. He received publicly, in the piazza, the investiture of Chiari, and his father, now an old man, came to see the honouring of his son. In less than forty years Carmagnola had risen from a peasant herd to be a knight and noble of one of the proudest states in Italy. The contrast of fortunes was great. Never, perhaps, has a career lain wider open to mediocre talent than in Italy of the fifteenth century. Days of pageantry followed, for Venice was liberal in her rewards ; and, though disappointed of her fullest hopes, yet a noble territory had been added to her empire, in the Bresciano and the Bergamasco which became hers by the peace of Ferrara.

A Visconti's peace, a *pace Volpina*, could not be long lived ; and before a year was over Venice saw that war was once more inevitable. The Venetians watched the crisis with complacency, under the impression that they were prepared and that they had secured the services of Carmagnola; for he had accepted the retaining fee usually offered to a general on the conclusion of a war. But at the very moment when hostilities seemed on the point of breaking out, Carmagnola sent in his resignation. The Senate met to consider this outrageous conduct, and declined to accept the proposal. The general then stated his terms with truly mercenary rapacity. He demanded a permanent salary of twelve thousand ducats, in peace or war. The position of the republic did not allow her to hesitate long. With Visconti ready to strike a blow, Carmagnola was her master for the time being. The government signed the new contract.* But Venice never forgot that for a single instant she had lost her grasp on circumstances, and that her general had held her at discretion. Jealousy and suspicion of her own nobility exposed her to this humiliation. We cannot help feeling how different would have been the issue of the war had a Venetian general, leading Venetian troops, been in the field. Such an army, however, was rendered impossible by the law which forbade a Venetian gentleman to command more than twenty-five lances.†

When war actually broke out in 1430, this third and last of Carmagnola's campaigns closely resembled its predecessors, save that the details are all exaggerated point by point, the conduct of each actor is more defined. The crisis of the drama approaches. There is a superfluity of sluggishness on Carmagnola's part; the duke of Milan redoubles the number of messages to the general, the Venetians show a steady crescendo of impatience, till the balance dips at length against

* Romanin, *loc. cit.*

† A lance was composed of three men. See Contarini, Della rep. d. Veneza."

their officer. The republic began by proposing the largest bribes yet offered. She promised Carmagnola a whole territory, or even the lordship of Milan, which he had actually asked for, if he would crush the duke and take his capital. Such offers were rapidly becoming a farce. Carmagnola refused to abandon his inactivity, and the progress of the war was marked only by a series of checks with long intervals of immobility between. All this while communications from the duke were unceasingly maintained. Filippo plied his messengers faster and faster as the climax drew near; each fresh arrival at Carmagnola's camp shook the fabric of his tottering fortunes and undermined his credit and security at Venice. Yet he never concealed a single event from the government. His frankness was insultingly perfect. Now he writes to the senate that such an one is with him from the duke; now he demands instructions how to treat another.* He took no warning from the answers he received, though they grew more and more sullen. He was not intriguing with Filippo, but he was trifling with Venice, and in his assurance he gave himself no pains to conceal the fact.

At Venice the animosity against Carmagnola showed signs of becoming malignant. In October, 1431, a motion had been made in the senate that they should institute a secret inquiry into the conduct of their general, "et non stare in his perpetuis laboribus et expensis." The proposal never came to the vote, but was deferred while the government had recourse once more to the old policy of bribes. Milan

---

* See Romanin, *loc. cit.*

was again offered to Carmagnola if he would act
with vigour and attack the duchy. Venice made
her ultimate appeal to the ambition and cupidity of
her general. She had no higher price to offer. Her
patience and her purse were at an end This final
pause was of no avail. Carmagnola did not move ;
the duke's envoys did not cease to haunt his camp,
but rather followed one another faster than before.
The endurance of Venice was exhausted, and Carmagnola's friends were forced to give way before the
cry for punishment.

On the 28th of March, 1432, the Ten took the
matter under consideration, and moved with their
accustomed rapidity and secrecy.* The same day the
council asked for the assistance of twenty assessors.
The court, therefore, which tried Carmagnola consisted
of thirty-seven members, including the doge, who
possessed only a casting vote. The court was bound
by oath to absolute silence on the matter outside the
council chamber. On the 29th a secretary was
despatched to Brescia with a letter inviting Carmagnola to Venice, as the government desired to
consult him regarding the conduct of the war. At
the same time, to allay all suspicion, the council
issued similar invitations to the other captains in
the service of the republic. The precaution was
unnecessary ; Carmagnola never showed the slightest
alarm. He obeyed the summons with the perfect
alacrity of a clear conscience, and reached Venice on
the 7th of April. A guard of honour met him at
Mestre, and conducted him with all ceremony to the

* See Cibrario, " Opuscoli Storici " (Milano : 1835).

ducal palace. In the Sala delle Quattro Porte they requested him to wait till the doge should be informed of his arrival. Meanwhile his suite, who had remained below, were ordered to go home, as the general would stay to dine with the doge. Upstairs, after a short interval, during which Carmagnola chatted to the senators about him, one of the council came with a message from Foscari, regretting that a sudden indisposition prevented him from receiving the count that day. Carmagnola turned to go down to his gondola ; as he passed along the lower arcade in order to reach the door upon the Molo, one of the gentlemen about him said, " This way, if you please, my lord count." " But that is not the way," replied Carmagnola. " Pardon ; it is the right way." At that moment he was surrounded and hurried to one of the prisons of the palace. As the door closed on him he cried, " I am a lost man." They tried to console him, but he answered, " No, no ! We do not cage the birds we mean to set at liberty again." For the first time in his life he saw his position truly. He knew now, when too late, that he had mistaken long-suffering for feebleness, and his own insolence for real power.

On the 9th of April the court appointed a committee of ten to draw up the charges against the count. The committee received authority to torture the prisoner and any other witnesses. Carmagnola underwent the question of the fire and of the cord. What confessions may have been wrung from him, or what evidence from others, we do not know, for the bill on which he was condemned no longer exists. Whatever the confessions may have been matters little. The Venetians were trying him for patent misconduct during his whole service, and were now resolved to close their account with an impracticable servant. Holy Week and the festivities of Easter came to interrupt the trial, and Carmagnola, tortured in body and despairing in heart, languished in prison while the city turned to its amusements. These came to an end on the 23rd of April, and the proceedings against the count were resumed. The committee sat day and night until the bill of attainder was ready to present to the court. On the 5th of May it was brought up to the council and read. Then, in accordance with the custom which governed the proceedings of the Ten, the vote to "proceed" was moved in these terms, "that after what we have heard and read we do now proceed against Count Francesco Carmagnola, once our captain-general, on the charge of injury wrought by him to our affairs and against the honour and well-being of our state." The votes fell: ayes, 25; noes, 1; for further consideration, 9. On the announcement of the majority, sentence was moved as follows:—"That the Count Francesco Carmagnola, public traitor to our state, shall to-day, in the evening at the usual hour, be led with a gag in his mouth, and his hands tied behind his back, as is customary, to the ordinary place of execution between the two columns on the piazza of Saint Mark, and there his head shall be struck off with a sword so that he die." The doge proved faithful to Carmagnola to the very last, and endeavoured to save his life by moving an amendment to substitute imprisonment for the capital sentence. Foscari's motion found only eight supporters, while for the original motion there were nineteen. The sentence of death was at once carried to the count. That same evening, about the hour of vespers, Carmagnola's guards led him to the piazza. He was dressed with great care and splendour in crimson velvet and a velvet cap *alla Carmagnola.* There, between the two square columns at the south-west corner of Saint Mark's, his head was severed from his body at the third blow. He was buried with considerable pomp in the Church of Santa Maria Gloriosa dei Frari; but shortly afterwards his body is supposed to have been removed to San Francesco in Milan.*

In less than six weeks Venice had taken a full revenge for more than six years of disappointment. The republic had opened the war against Milan with a distinct object in view, and a belief that she had found the man to carry it out. She made a mistake in relying upon the continuance of Carmagnola's first rage against the duke. She was baulked of her

---

* This church was destroyed in 1798 to make way for barracks; it is probable that the body of Carmagnola disappeared then. There was a tradition that the count's head was placed in an urn above the door leading to the cloisters of the Frari. In February, 1874, this urn was opened, and not only a head, but a whole body was found; but the vertebræ of the neck had not been severed, so that it could not be the body of Carmagnola. I am indebted for the above information to the courtesy of Sig. Guiseppe Rondani, secretary to the municipality of Carmagnola, who most kindly placed at my disposal the correspondence of that town with various societies in Milan and Venice, relating to their search for the remains of the count.

desire and placed in a dilemma, the inevitable result of employing mercenary arms. She freed herself by the only course open to her. Carmagnola, on the other hand, acted as a true captain of adventure, thinking chiefly of his own interests, holding his employers and their desires in small account; not openly and positively a traitor to them, but traitorous in so far that he cared but little for their success. He had the misfortune to be stupid and to have Venice for a mistress. He hardly knew his peril between the republic and the duke of Milan, who pursued and accomplished his ruin with a success that did not always wait upon his dark designs. Carmagnola, in short, took the chances of the perilous game of adventure. He came very near to winning the highest prize, but he forgot the one chance against him, the power and the solvency of Venice. For his mistake he paid the price with his head.

N

THE STATE ARCHIVES AND THE CONSTITUTION OF THE VENETIAN REPUBLIC.*

IN recent years a new tendency has been given to historical studies by the avidity with which scholars have investigated the masses of state documents accumulated almost untouched, through centuries, in the Record Offices of various nations. This tendency has been in the direction of minuteness and accuracy of detail. The finer shades of policy, the subtler turns in the game of nations, have been revealed by this intimate study of the documents which record them. Among the archives of Europe there is none superior, in historical value and richness of minutiæ, to the archives of the Venetian republic, preserved now in the convent of the Frari at Venice. The importance of these archives is due to three causes: the position of the republic in the history of Europe,

* In this essay I am much indebted to the following, among other works:—Baschet, " Les Archives de Venise" (Paris: 1870), and " Souvenirs d'une Mission" (Paris: 1857); "Il regio Archivio Generale di Venezia" (Venice: 1875); "Calendar of State Papers : Venice," vol. i.; Sir T. Duffus Hardy's Report on the Archives; Giannotti, " Della Rep. de Viniziani" (Firenze: 1850); St. Disdier, " La Ville et Rep. de Venise " (Paris: 1680): Amelot della Houssaye, " Histoire du Gouvernement de Venise" (Paris: 1667).

the fullness of the archives themselves, and the remarkable preservation and order which distinguishes them, in spite of the many dangers and vicissitudes through which they have passed.

Venice enjoyed a position, unique among the states of Europe, for two reasons. Until the discovery of the passage round the Cape of Good Hope, she was the mart of Europe in all commercial dealings with the East—a position secured to her by her supremacy in the Levant, and by the strength of her fleet; and, in the second place, the republic was the bulwark of Europe against the Turk. These are the two dominant features of Venice in general history; and under both aspects she came into perpetual contact with every European power. The universal importance of her position is faithfully reflected in the diplomatic documents contained in her archives. The republic maintained ambassadors and residents at every court. These men were among the most subtle and accomplished diplomatists of their time, and the government they served was exacting and critical to the highest degree. The result is that the despatches, news-letters, and reports of the Venetian diplomatic agents, form the most varied, brilliant, and singular gallery of portraits, whether of persons or of peoples, that exists. There is hardly a nation in Europe that will not find its history illustrated by the papers which belong to the Venetian department for foreign affairs. Nor are the papers which relate to the home government of the republic less copious and valuable. Each magistracy has its own series of documents, the daily record of its proceedings: in these we find the whole of that elaborate machinery of state laid bare before us in all its intricacy of detail ; and we are enabled to study the construction, the origin, development. and ossification, of one of the most rigid and enduring constitutions that the world has ever seen ; a constitution so strong in its component parts, so compact in its rib-work, that it sufficed to preserve a semblance of life in the body of the republic long after the heart and brain had ceased to beat.

Admirable as are the preservation and order of these masses of state papers, it is not to be expected that each series, each magisterial archive, should be complete. There are many broad lacunæ, especially in the earlier period, which must ever be a cause for regret: for Venice growing is a more attractive and profitable subject than Venice dying. During the nine hundred and eighty-seven years that the government of the republic held its seat in Venice, the state papers passed through many dangers from fire, revolution, neglect, or carelessness. When we recall the fires of 1230, 1479, 1574, and 1577, it is rather matter for congratulation that so much has escaped, than for surprise that so much has been destroyed. The losses would, undoubtedly, have been much more severe had all the papers and documents been preserved in one place, as they are now. But the Venetians stored the archives of the various magistracies either at the offices of those magistrates, or in some public building especially set apart for the purpose. The secret chancellery, which was always an object of great solicitude, containing as it did all the more private papers of the state, was deposited in a room on the second floor of the ducal palace. Many of the criminal records belonging to the Council of Ten were stored in the Piombi under the roof of the palace; and the famous adventurer Casanova relates how he beguiled some of his prison hours by reading the trial of a Venetian nobleman, which he found among other papers piled at the end of the corridor where he was allowed to take exercise. Soon after the fall of the republic, the following disposition of the papers was made. The political archive was stored at the Scuola di S. Teodoro; the judicial, at the convent of S. Giovanni Laterano; the financial, at S. Provolo. In the year 1815 the Austrian government resolved to collect and arrange all state papers in one place. The building chosen was the convent of the Frari; and the work was entrusted to Jacopo Chiodo, the first director of the archives. The scheme suggested by Chiodo has served as a basis for the arrangement that has been already carried out, or is still in hand.

Under the republic it was natural that access to important diplomatic papers and to secrets of state should be granted with reserve, and only to persons especially authorized to make research. The directors appointed by the Austrian government showed a disposition to maintain that precedent; and M. Baschet relates that it was only by a personal appeal to the emperor that he obtained access to the archives of the Ten. The Italian government allow nearly absolute liberty; and nothing can exceed the courtesy of the officials under their distinguished director, the Commendatore Cecchetti.

Any attempt to explain the archives of Venice and to display their contents, must be preceded by a statement of the main features of the constitution of the republic upon which the order and the arrangement of the archives is based. The constitution of Venice has frequently been likened to a pyramid, with the Great Council for its base and the doge for apex. The figure is more or less correct; but it is a pyramid that has been broken at its edges by time and by necessity. The political body was originally constructed in four groups, or tiers—if we are to preserve the pyramidal simile—one rising above the other. These four tiers were the Maggior Consiglio or Great Council, the Lower House; the Pregadi or Senate, the Upper House; the Collegio, or the Cabinet; and the doge. The famous Council of Ten and its equally famous commission, the three inquisitors of state, did not enter into the original scheme; they are an appendix to the state, an intrusion, a break in the symmetry of the pyramid. Later on we shall explain their construction and relation to the main body of government. For the present we leave them aside, and confine our attention to the four departments of the Venetian constitution above mentioned.

The Great Council, as is well known, did not assume its permanent form and place in the Venetian constitution till the year 1296. At that date the famous revolution, known as the closing of the Great Council, took place. By that act, which was only the final step in a revolution that had been for long in process, those citizens who were excluded from the

Great Council remained for ever outside the constitution; all functions of government were concentrated in the hands of those nobles who were included by the council; the constitution of the republic was stereotyped as a rigid oligarchy. Previous to the year 1296, a great council had existed, created first in the reign of Pietro Ziani (1172); but this council was really democratic in character, not oligarchic; it was elected each September, and its members were chosen from the whole body of the citizens. Earlier still than the reign of Ziani, the population used to meet tumultuously and express their opinion upon matters of public interest, such as the election of a doge or a declaration of war, first in the *Concione* under their tribunes, while Venetia was still a confederation of lagoon-islands; and then in the *Arengo* under their doge, when the confederation was centralized at Rialto. But of these assemblies the latter was disorderly and irregular, and the former was of doubtful authority. It is from the closing of the Great Council that we must date the positive establishment of the Venetian oligarchy, and the completion of that constitution which endured for five hundred years, from 1296 till the fall of the Republic in 1797.

The age at which the young nobles might take their seats in the council, that is to say, might enter upon public life, was fixed at twenty-five, except in the cases of the Barbarelli, or thirty nobles between the ages of twenty and twenty-five, who were elected by ballot on the fourth of each December, St. Barbara's Day; and in the case of those who, in return for money advanced to the state, obtained a special grace to take their seats before their twenty-fifth year.

The chief functions of the Great Council were the passing of laws and the election of magistrates. But in process of time the legislative duties of the council were almost entirely absorbed by the Senate; and the Maggior Consiglio only retained its great and distinguishing function, the election of almost every officer of state, from the doge downwards. The large number of these magistracies, and the various seasons of the year at which they fell vacant, engaged the Great Council in a perpetual series of elections. It is not our intention to explain in detail the elaborate process by which the Venetians carried out their political elections; such an explanation would carry us beyond our scope, which is to state the position and functions of each member in the constitution of the republic. But, briefly, the process was this. The law required either two or four competitors for every vacant magistracy, and the election to that magistracy was said to take place *a due* or *a quattro mani*, respectively. If the office to be filled required *quattro mani*, the whole body of the Great Council balloted for four groups of nine members each, who were chosen by drawing a golden ball from among the silver ones in the balloting urn. Each of these groups retired to a separate room, and there each group elected one candidate to go to the poll for the vacant office. The names of the four candidates were then presented to the council and balloted. The candidate who secured the largest number of votes, above the half of those present, was elected to the vacant office. Thus the election to a magistracy was a triple process; first, the election of the nominators, then the election of the candidates, and finally the election to the office.

The Great Council, as representing the whole republic, possessed certain judicial functions, which were used on rare occasions only, when the state believed itself placed in grave danger through the fault of its commanders. The famous case of Vettor Pisani, after his defeat at Pola, in 1379, and the case of Antonio Grimani, in the year 1499, were both sent to the grand council, who passed sentence on those generals. But, broadly speaking, the judicial functions of the Maggior Consiglio hardly existed, its legislative functions dwindled away, and were absorbed by the Senate, and its chief duty and prerogative lay in the election of almost every state official.

Coming now to the second tier in the pyramid of the constitution, the Senate, or Pregadi—the invited— we find that the Senate proper was composed of sixty members, elected in the Great Council, six at a time. The elections took place once a week, and were so arranged that they should be complete by the first of October in each year. In addition to the Senate proper, another body of sixty, called the *Zonta* or addition, was elected by the outgoing Senate at the close of its year of office; but it was necessary that the names of the *Zonta* should be approved by the Great Council before their election was valid. The Senate and the Zonta together formed one hundred and twenty members; and besides these, the doge, his six councillors, the Council of Ten, the supreme court of appeal, and many special magistrates, who presided over departments of finance, customs, and justice, belonged *ex officio* to the Senate, and brought the number of votes up to two hundred and forty-six. Further, fifty-one magistrates of minor departments also sat, with the right to debate, but without the right to vote.

The Senate was the real core of the administration. The presence, *ex officio*, of so many and such various officers of state sufficiently indicates the wide field which was covered by the authority of the Pregadi. The large number of the senatorial body, and the diversity of subjects with which it dealt, required that business should be carried on with parsimony of time and precision of method; and therefore private members were restricted to the right of debate. Only the doge, his councillors, the savii grandi, and the savii di terra ferma had the right to move the Senate; and their propositions related to peace, war, foreign affairs, instructions to ambassadors and representatives of foreign courts, to commercial treaties, finance, and home legislation. The various measures were spoken to by their proposers, and by the magistrates whose offices they affected. As in the case of the Great Council, the Senate also on rare occasions exercised judicial functions. It was in the discretion of the College to send a faulty commander for trial either to the Great Council or to the Senate; but in that case the charge must be one of negligence or misjudgment; if the charge implied treason, it was taken before the Council of Ten. A few of the higher officers of state were elected in the Senate, among them the savii grandi and the savii di terra ferma, and the admiral of the fleet. The functions of the Senate were legislative, judicial, and elective. But just as the Great Council was pre-eminently the elective body, so the Senate was pre-eminently the legislative body in the constitution of Venice.

The Collegio, or Cabinet of ministers, formed the third tier in the pyramid. The College was composed of the following members: the doge, his six councillors, and the three chiefs of the court of appeal; these ten persons formed the collegio minore, or serenissima signoria; in addition to these there were the six savii grandi, the five savii di terra ferma, and the five savii da mar; a body of twenty-six persons in all, forming the College. Beginning with the lowest in rank, the savii agli ordini, or da mar, were, as their name implies, a Board of Admiralty; but they acted in that capacity under the orders of the savii grandi, upon whom the naval affairs of the republic immediately depended. The savii agli ordini had a vote but no voice in the College; this post was given, for the most part, to young and promising politicians; it was a training school for statesmen: "Officio loro," says Giannotti, "è tacere ed ascoltare." The office lasted for six months only; and so there was a constant stream of young men passing through the political school, and becoming intimately acquainted with the affairs of the republic and the methods of government. How excellent that school must have been will become apparent as we proceed to note the functions of the College, of which the savii agli ordini formed a silent part.

Next in order above the savii agli ordini came the savii di terra ferma. This board was composed of five members; the savio alla scrittura, or minister for war; the savio cassier, or chancellor of the exchequer; the savio alle ordinanze, or minister for the native militia in the cities on the mainland; the savio ai da mò, or minister for the execution of all measures voted urgent; the savio ai ceremoniali, or minister for ceremonies of state. These savii di terra ferma, like the savii agli ordini, held office for six months only.

The six savii grandi, who came above the savii di terra ferma, superintended the actions of the two boards below them, and, if necessary, issued orders which would override those of the other ministers. They were. in fact, the responsible directors of the state. The savii grandi were required to prepare all business to be laid before the College. where it was first discussed and arranged before being submitted to the Senate for approval. To facilitate this labour of preparation, each of the savii grandi took a week in turn, and the savio of the week was in fact prime minister of Venice. It was he who read despatches, granted audiences to ambassadors, and prepared official replies. The doge presided in the College, it is true, but it was the savio of the week who opened the business, and suggested the various measures to be adopted.

Besides these boards of savii, the College included the ducal councillors, and the three chiefs of the court of appeal. We shall speak of these latter when we come to the judicial department of the constitution.

The office of ducal councillor was, perhaps, the most venerable in Venice. These six men held, as it were, the ducal honours and functions in commission ; they embodied the authority of the doge to such an extent, that without their presence he could not act; he became a nonentity unless supported by four at least of his council ; while, on the other hand, the absence of the doge in no way diminished the authority of the ducal councillors. For example, the doge without his council could not preside, neither in the Maggior Consiglio, nor in the Senate, nor in the College ; but four ducal councillors had the power to preside without the doge. The doge might not open despatches except in the presence of his council, but his council might open despatches in the absence of the doge. Yet, great as were the external honours of the ducal councillors, the office was rather ornamental than important. It was the savii grandi who were the directing spirit through all the multitudinous affairs of the College. As we have seen, those affairs embraced the whole field of government, except the field of justice. The College had no judicial functions, nor did it legislate. As the Maggior Consiglio was the elective member, and the Senate the legislative, so the College was the initiative and executive member in the state. The College proposed measures which became law in the Senate ; and the execution of those laws was entrusted to the College, which had the machinery of state at its disposal. It is this right of initiating which distinguishes the College ; and it is just upon this point that the ducal councillors appear to have a slight pre-eminence ; for the doge, his council, and the savii alone had the right to initiate in the Senate; the doge, his council, and the chiefs of the Ten alone had the right to initiate in the Council of Ten; the doge and his council alone had the right to initiate in the Maggior Consiglio. The doge and his council alone move through all departments of government, presiding and initiating, and embodying the spirit of the republic; and yet in no case is their power great; for the savii had more influence in the Senate, the chiefs of the Ten in the Council of Ten; and the Great Council, where the doge and his councillors had the field to themselves, was of little importance in the direction of affairs.

At the apex of the constitutional pyramid we find the doge.* The doge also had his distinctive functions in the state; his duties were ornamental rather than administrative. Though all the acts of the Government were executed in his name, laws passed, despatches sent, treaties made, and war declared, yet it is not in these departments that the doge stands pre-eminent; it is throughout the pomp and display of the republic that he is supreme; and the archive wherein his glory shows most brightly is the *Ceremoniali.*

The doge was elected for life. When a doge died, the eldest ducal councillor filled the office of vice-doge until the election of the new prince. The remains of the deceased doge were laid out in the chamber of the Pioveghi, on the first floor of the ducal palace, dressed in robes of state, the mantle of cloth of gold, and the ducal biretta. Twenty Venetian

* See Checchetti, "Il Doge di Venezia" (Venezia : 1864).

noblemen were appointed to attend in the *chapelle ardente*. On the third day the doge was buried; and the Great Council on the same day elected the officers who were to revise the coronation oath, and to render its provisions more stringent if the conduct of the deceased had revealed any point where a future doge could exercise even the smallest independence in constitutional matters. At the same time the council elected another body of officers, who were required to examine the conduct of the late doge, and, if he had violated his coronation oath, his heirs paid the penalty by a fine. Immediately after the appointment of these officers, the Maggior Consiglio proceeded to create the forty-one electors to the dukedom. The process of election was long and intricate, and occupied five days at the least; for there was a quintuple series of ballots and votings to be concluded before the forty-one were finally chosen. When the forty-one noblemen had been appointed, they were taken to a chamber specially prepared for them, where, as in the case of a papal election, they were obliged to stay until they had determined upon the new doge. They were bound by oath never to reveal what took place inside this election chamber. But that oath was not always observed in the spirit; and memoranda of certain proceedings of the forty-one are still preserved in the private archives of the Marcello family. The first step was to elect three priors, or presidents, and two secretaries. The presidents took their seats at a table on which stood a ballot-box and an urn. The secretaries gave to every elector a slip of paper, upon which each one wrote the name of the man whom he proposed as doge. The forty-one slips of paper were then placed in the urn, and one was drawn out at hazard. If the noble, whose name was written upon the slip, chanced to be an elector, he was required to withdraw. Then each of the electors was at liberty to attack the candidate, to point out defects and recall misdeeds.* These hostile criticisms, which covered the whole of a candidate's private life, his physical qualities and his public conduct, were written down by the secretaries, and the candidate was recalled. The objections urged against him were read over to the aspirant, without the names of the urgers appearing, and he was invited to defend himself. Attack and defence continued till no further criticisms were offered, and then the name of the candidate was balloted before the priors. If it received twenty-five favourable votes, its owner was declared doge ; if less than twenty-five, a fresh name was drawn from the urn, and the whole process was repeated until some candidate secured the necessary five and twenty votes. As soon as this issue was reached, the Signoria was informed of the result, and the new doge, attended by the electors, descended to Saint Mark's, where, from the pulpit on the left side of the choir, the prince was shown to the people, and where, before the high altar, he took the coronation oath and received the standard of Saint Mark. The great doors of the Basilica were then thrown open, and the doge passed in procession round the piazza and returned to the Porta della Carta. At the top of the Giants' Stair the eldest ducal councillor placed

* See the Marcello MS.

the biretta on his head, and he was brought to the Sala dei Pioveghi, where the late doge had lain in state, and where he too would one day come. Then the doge retired to his private apartment, and the ceremony of election closed.

As we have already observed, the position of the doge in the republic of Venice was almost purely ornamental. The doge presided, either in person or by commission through his councillors, at every council of state; he presided, however, not as a guiding and deliberating chief, but as a symbol of the majesty of Venice. He is there not as an individual, a personality, but as the outward and visible sign of an idea, the idea of the Venetian oligarchy. The history of the personal authority of the doge falls into three periods. A period of great vigour and almost despotic power dates from the foundation of the dukedom, in the year 697, down to the reign of Pietro Ziani in 1172. During this first period, the ducal authority showed a tendency to become concentrated, and almost hereditary in the hands of one or two powerful families. For example, we have seven doges of the Partecipazio house, five doges of the Candiani, and three of the Orseoli. But the rivalry and balanced power of these great families eventually exhausted one another, and preserved the dukedom of Venice from ever becoming a kingdom. A second period extends from the year 1172 down to 1457, and is marked by the emergence of the great commercial houses, and the development of the oligarchy upon the basis of a Great Council. The aristocracy during this period were engaged in ex-

o

cluding the people from any share in the government, and in curbing and finally crushing the authority of the doge. The steps in this process are indicated by the closing of the Great Council, the revolution of Tiepolo, the trials of Marino Faliero, Lorenzo Celsi, and the Foscari. The third period covers what remains of the republic, from 1457 down to 1797. During this period the doge was little other than the figurehead of the republic; the point of least weight and greatest splendour; the brilliant apex to the pyramid of the Venetian constitution.

So far, then, we have examined the four tiers in the original structure of the constitution, the doge, the College, the Senate, and the Great Council; and we have seen that, broadly speaking, these were, respectively, ornamental, initiative and executive, legislative and elective. But this pyramid of the constitution was not perfectly symmetrical; its edges were broken. This interruption of outline was caused by the Council of Ten. The exact position in the Venetian constitution occupied by this famous council, and its relations to the other members of the government, have proved a constant source of difficulty and error to students of Venetian history. Leaving aside the obscure problem of the origin of the Ten, it is still possible for us to indicate the constitutional necessity which called that council into existence. As we have pointed out, the College could not act on its own responsibility without the Senate; the Senate could not initiate without the College, for the preparation of all affairs passed through the hands of the College. To establish connection between these two branches of the administration was a process that required some time; it could not be done swiftly and secretly. In all crises of political importance, whether home or foreign, some instrument, more expeditious than the Senate, was required to sanction the propositions of the College. That instrument, acting swiftly and secretly, with a speed and secrecy impossible in so large a body as the Senate, was created with the Council of Ten. The Ten were an extraordinary magistracy, devised to meet unexpected pressure upon the ordinary machine of government. The history of the emergence of the Ten proves this view. Without determining whether the council existed previous to the year 1310, we may take that year as the date of its first appearance as a potent element in the state. The rebellion of Tiepolo and Querini, an aristocratic revolt against the growing power of the new commercial nobility, paralyzed the ordinary machinery of state, and revealed the danger inherent in a large and slow-moving body of rulers. The Ten were called to power by the Venetians, just as the Romans created the dictatorship, in order to save the state in a dangerous crisis.

The place of the Ten in the constitutional structure is below the College and parallel with the Senate. Below the College the administration bifurcates; the ordinary course of business flows through the Senate, the extraordinary through the Ten. The Ten possessed an authority equal to that of the Senate; the choice of which instrument should be used rested with the College. The Ten appear to be of more importance than the Senate, solely because they were used upon more critical and dramatic occasions. Wherever the machinery of the College and Senate moves too slowly, we find the swifter machinery of the College and the Ten in motion. And so not only in political affairs, home and foreign, but also in affairs financial and judicial, the Council of Ten takes its part. The Ten, as being the readier instrument to the hands of the College, gradually absorbed more and more of the functions which originally belonged to the Senate. This process of absorption, and the extension of the province of the Ten, is marked by the establishment of its sub-commissions, which took their place in every department side by side with the delegations of the Senate and the ordinary magistrates. In politics and foreign affairs there is the famous office of the three inquisitors of state. In the region of justice all cases of treason and coining, and certain cases of outrage on public morals, came before the Ten; and it was always open to the College to remove a case from the ordinary courts to the Ten, when state reasons rendered it expedient to do so. In the police department the Esecutori contro la Bestemmia, and in finance the Camerlenghi, were officers of that council. In the War Office the artillery was under their control; and in the arsenal certain galleys, marked C.X., were always at their disposal.

These five great members of the state, four regular and one irregular, formed the political and legislative departments of the Venetian government. It remains now to give a brief account of the judicial machinery of the republic before proceeding to examine the papers which belong to these various departments.

In the administration of justice all cases, criminal as well as civil, were broadly divided into cases arising in the city itself, *di dentro*, and cases arising on the mainland or elsewhere throughout the Dominion, known as cases *di fuori*. In Dalmatia, the Levant, and on the mainland, justice was administered, in the first instance, by officers who bore most frequently the title of rector. In Venice cases were tried, in the first instance, before various special courts, each having jurisdiction in certain cases only. Among these courts we may mention the police courts of the signori di notte and the cinque alla pace; the court of the Pioveghi, which decided cases of contract; the Sanitary court, the Jews' court, the Strangers' court. From all these courts of first instance, in the Dominion as well as in Venice, there was an appeal to the supreme courts. The courts of appeal were four in number; the quarantia criminale, the quarantia vecchia civile, the quarantia nuova civile, and the collegio delle biade. To begin with the lowest in authority; the collegio delle biade was a court composed of twenty-two judges, whose duty was to try civil cases on appeal, both *di dentro* and *di fuori*, in which the value at stake stood between fifty and three hundred ducats. The cases *di dentro* and the cases *di fuori* were heard by this court in alternate months. As the court was composed of twenty-two members, it might be equally divided; in that case the cause was sent up to the appeal courts above; to the quarantia vecchia, if it were an appeal *di dentro*; to the quarantia nuova, if it were an appeal *di fuori*.

The quarantia vecchia civile and the quarantia nuova civile were two courts, composed of forty judges each, whose duties were to try appeal cases where the stake stood above the value of three hundred ducats. Cases *di dentro* went before the old court, cases *di fuori* were heard in the new court. The forty judges of the quarantia nuova were elected in the Great Council ; they were required to be above the age of thirty. These forty judges served eight months in the quarantia nuova, and then moved on to the quarantia vecchia, where they served a second eight months; they then passed into the quarantia criminale for a third period of eight months. The Great Council elected a new quarantia nuova every eight months; and a nobleman's term of judicial service lasted for twenty-four months, in all ; after which he was ineligible for re-election till eight months had elapsed. If the new court were equally divided on a case of appeal, the cause passed into the old court, and *vice versa ;* if the courts, upon this second hearing, were still equally divided, the case was sent up to the Senate, upon a motion made in the Great Council.

The quarantia criminale tried all criminal cases of appeal, both *di dentro* and *di fuori ;* but whereas the two other quarantie were purely courts of appeal, the quarantia criminale had the power to cite criminal cases before it in the first instance. The criminal appeal court was the most ancient and honourable court in Venice ; its three presidents sat *ex officio* in the Collegio, and were members of the Signoria, accompanying the doge whenever he presided at any council, and embodying and representing the spirit of Justice in the Venetian constitution. The three presidents of the criminal court held their seats in the Signoria for two months at a time, and were then succeeded by other three. During their absence from their own court their place was taken by three ducal councillors, called the consiglieri da basso, who represented the doge by the side of Justice, as the presidents represented Justice by the side of the doge.

Each of the three quarantie had three officials permanently attached to the court for the purpose of preparing and explaining the case to be submitted to the forty judges. The officers of the criminal court were called the avvogadori di commun; those of the old civil court were called auditori vecchi; those of the new civil court were called auditori nuovi. If a suitor wished to appeal against the decision of a rector in a civil suit, he came to Venice and saw the auditori nuovi. They cited both parties before them, and heard the case exactly as it had been pleaded before the rector. If one or more of the auditori held that the appeal ought to lie, then, supposing the value in dispute to be below fifty ducats, the auditori themselves heard the case; but if the value was above fifty and under three hundred ducats, the case was sent to the collegio delle biade; if the value exceeded three hundred ducats, the case went before the quarantia nuova. The appellant caused the clerk of the court to enter his case on the list in pursuance of an order from the auditori; and the cases were taken in order of date, except cases between members of a family, or cases affecting a ward or perishable goods, and these had the precedence. The presidents were bound to yield the court to the appellant as soon as possible; and when the case had been called on, it might not occupy more than three days. The auditori who had allowed the appeal were bound to defend it before the court, and to show reason why they had permitted the court to be moved. No advocate might speak for more than an hour and a half measured by a sand glass; but that hour and a half did not include the time occupied in reading papers. When the pleadings were closed, the court arrived at its judgment by vote. Three kinds of vote were possible: the vote *tagliare*, to quash the judgment of the court below; the vote *lodare*, to confirm that judgment; or the vote *non sinceri*, undecided. If the votes *tagliare* exceeded the votes *lodare* and *non sinceri* taken together, the case was sent down again to the original court. If the votes *lodare* exceeded the votes *tagliare* and *non sinceri*, the judgment of the court was confirmed. But if neither of these results were reached, the court heard the case again, minus the *non sinceri* voters. This same method of procedure was observed in the other quarantie; but if the quarantia criminale quashed a judgment, the case was not sent down to the original court; the quarantia itself passed the final sentence.

In many cases appeal, which implied a journey to Venice, was too expensive for the poor of the distant provinces. To meet this difficulty the auditori nuovi were obliged to go circuit every two years through the mainland towns, and three sindici da mar through the towns of Dalmatia, Greece, and the

Levant, hearing appeals and citing them to Venice when necessary.

The arrangements for the pay of justice were both simple and efficient. The members of the criminal forty received two-thirds of a ducat, and the members of the other forties received one-third of a ducat each every time they sat. The avvogadori, who had charge of the criminal cases, were paid a fixed sum yearly out of fines and confiscations. In civil cases the plaintiff paid to the judge of first instance a certain amount per cent. on the value at issue. If he appealed, he paid the same amount again to the auditori. If he won his appeal, he recovered from the judge of first instance, who was therefore paid for sound judgments only; if he lost his appeal, he recovered from the auditori, who were thus refused payment for sending a case before the court which the forty judges ignored; and this regulation served to protect the court of appeal from abuse; for frivolous appeals brought no pay to the auditori, and were sure to be disallowed by them at the outset.

One of the most remarkable features in the Venetian constitution is the infinite subdivision of government, and the number of offices to be filled. Nobles alone were eligible for the majority of these offices, and if we consider how small a body the Great Council really was, it is clear that the larger number of Venetian noblemen must have been employed in the service of the state at some time in their lives. The great political and administrative activity which reigned inside the comparatively small body that formed the ruling caste, as compared with the absolute stagnation and quiet which marked the life of the ordinary citizen, is one of the most noteworthy points in the history of Venice. Every noble above the age of twenty-five was a member of the Maggior Consiglio; every week that council was engaged in filling up some office of state, had some new candidate before it. The tenure of all offices, except the dukedom and the pro-curatorship of St. Mark, was so brief, rarely exceed-ing a year or sixteen months, that the fret and activity of elections must have been nearly incessant. This constant unrest bore its fruit in perpetual intrigues, and censors were appointed to check the rampant corruption and bribery. But the main point which is impressed upon us is the universality of political training to which all the nobles of Venice were subjected. No matter how frivolous a young patri-cian might be, he was obliged to sit in the Great Council; he would be called upon to assist in electing the Ten, whose omniscience and severity he had every reason to dread; he might even find himself named to fill some minor post. It was impossible, under these circumstances, that he should fail to be educated politically, or that he should ever lose the keenest interest in every movement of the state. It is to this political activity that we must look for one of the reasons which conduced to that extraordinary long-evity which the constitution of Venice displayed.

Each of the government offices, many as they were, possessed its own collection of papers. These are either still in loose sheets, just as they left the office, or bound in volumes. They are indicated by the name of the government department, the subject dealt with, and the date. The papers are of three kinds; first, there are the files or *filze*, the original minutes of the board, written down in actual council by the secretaries, and with the *filze* are the despatches or other documents upon which the council took measures. In many of the more important departments, such as the Senate, the Ten, or the College, these *filze* were epitomized; the substance of each day's business was written out in large volumes known as " Registri ; " each entry. was signed by the secretary who had made the digest, and was accepted as authentic for all purposes of reference. These registers are, in many cases, of the greatest value where the files have been destroyed or lost. They were more constantly in use, and therefore more carefully preserved; and now they frequently form our sole authority for certain periods. As a rule the registers are very full and good ; they contain all that is of importance in the files ; but in making research upon any point it is never safe to ignore the files where they exist. In some cases the secretaries made a further digest of the registers in volumes known as " Rubrics," which contain in brief the headings of all materials to be found in the registers. As the registers sometimes supply the place of lost files. so the rubrics are occasionally our only authority where registers and file are both missing. The rubrics are often of the highest value. As an instance, we may cite the twenty volumes of rubrics to the despatches from England between the years 1603 and 1748. The method of research, therefore, where all three kinds of documents exist is this : to examine first the rubrics, then the registers, and then the files. But the infinite subdivisions of the government offices in Venice render the task of research somewhat bewildering; and a student cannot be certain that he has exhausted all the information on his subject. until he has examined a large number of these minor offices. He will probably find some notice of the point he is examining in the papers of the Senate or of the Ten. and if it be a matter of home affairs, he can trace it thence through the various magistracies under whose cognizance it would come ; or if it be a matter of foreign policy, he will find further information in the papers of the College.

Under the republic these collections of state papers were not known as archives, but as chancelleries. The collections of highest interest, the papers to which the student is most likely to turn his attention, are those relating to the ceremony. to the home, and to the foreign policy of Venice. These three groups are contained in the ducal, the secret, and the inferior chancelleries. The three chancelleries were committed to the charge of the grand chancellor and his staff of secretaries, who received, arranged, and registered the official papers as they issued from the various councils of state. The grand chancellor was not a patrician ; he was chosen from that upper class of commoners known as *cittadini originarii.* an inferior order of nobility, ranking below the governing caste, but bearing coat armour. The office of grand chancellor was of great dignity and antiquity, and was held for life. The chancellor was head and representative of the people, as the doge was head and representative of the patricians; and, when the nobility began to exclude the people from all share in the government, the grand chancellor was allowed to be present at all sessions of the Great Council and of the Senate as the silent witness of the people, confirming the acts of the government, and bridging, though by the finest thread, the gulf that otherwise separated the governed from the governing. The part which the grand chancellor took in the business of the Maggior Consiglio and of the Senate was a constant and an active part. It was his duty to superintend the arrangements for every election, to direct the secretaries in attendance, to announce the names of the candidates for office, and to proclaim the successful competitor. His seat in the Great Council hall was on the left-hand of the doge's dais, and his secretaries sat below him. But the custody of the state papers was by far the most important function which the grand chancellor had to perform. To assist him in these labours he was placed at the head of a large college of secretaries, trained in a school especially established to fit them for their duties. In the year 1443 a decree of the Great Council required the doge and the Signoria to elect each year twelve lads to be taught Latin, rhetoric, and philosophy, and the number of the pupils was gradually increased. From this school they passed out by examination, and became first extraordinaries and ordinaries, called notaries ducal, then secretaries to the Senate, and finally secretaries to the Ten. The post of secretary was one which required much diligence and discretion. The secretaries were in constant attendance on the various councils of state, and thus became intimately acquainted with all the secret affairs of the republic. They were frequently sent on delicate missions. It was a secretary of the Ten who brought Carmagnola to Venice to stand his trial; and, as we shall presently relate, it was a secretary of the Senate who announced to Thomas Killigrew, the English minister, his dismissal from Venice. The secretaries were sometimes accredited as residents to foreign courts, though they were not eligible for the post of ambassador. Inside the chancellery the secretaries were entirely at the disposal of the grand chancellor, and their duties were to study, to invent, and to read cipher; to transcribe the registers and rubrics; to keep the annals of the Council of Ten, and to enter the laws in the statute book.

We may now turn our attention to the principal series of state papers which issued from the five great members of the constitution, the Maggior Consiglio, the Senate, the Ten, the College, and the doge, and show how these papers were arranged under the three chancelleries of which we have spoken.

The cancelleria inferiore was preserved in one large room near the head of the Giants' Staircase in the ducal palace, and was entrusted to the care of the notaries ducal, the lowest order of secretaries. The documents in this chancellery related chiefly to the doge; his rights, his official possessions, his restrictions, and his state. Among these papers, accordingly, we find the coronation oaths, the reports of the commissioners appointed to examine those oaths, and the reports of the commissioners appointed to review the life of each doge deceased. This series is valuable as revealing the steps by which the aristocracy slowly curtailed the personal authority of the doge, and bound his office about with iron fetters, and crushed his power. In addition to these papers the inferior chancellery contained the documents relating to the dignitaries of Saint Mark's in its capacity as ducal chapel; the order and ceremony of the ducal household; the expenditure of the civil list; and the archives of the procurators of Saint Mark, which contained the wills, trusts, and bequests of private citizens.

The ducal chancellery, which the Council of the Ten once called "*cor nostri status*," was preserved on the upper floor of the palace, and was reached by the Scala d'oro. The papers were arranged in a number of cupboards surmounted by the arms of the various grand chancellors who had presided in that office. The documents of the ducal chancellery are of far higher importance than those contained in the cancelleria inferiore; they consist of political papers which it was not necessary to keep secret. Among the many interesting series of documents which fell to the ducal chancellory, the most valuable are the "compilazione delle Leggi," or statute-books distinguished by the various colours of their bindings— gold, roan, and green—to mark the statutes which relate to the Maggior Consiglio, the Senate, and the College respectively; the "secretario alle voci," or record of all elections in the Great Council; the "libri gratiarum," or special privileges. But most important of all is the great series of documents which include the whole legislation of the Senate relating to Venetian affairs on sea and land. Of this vast series, those marked *Terra* contain 3128 volumes of files, 411 volumes of registers, and 7 volumes of rubrics; those marked *Mar* number 1286 volumes of files, 247 volumes of registers, and 7 volumes of rubrics. It will easily be seen how important the ducal chancellery is, both for the verification of dates, and also as displaying so large a tract of the Venetian home administration.

But important as the ducal chancellery undoubtedly is, it cannot vie in interest with the cancelleria secreta, which might, with every justice. have been called "*cor nostri status*," for it is in the papers of that chancellery that the long history of the growth, splendour, and decline of the republic is to be traced in all its manifold details and complicated relations. The secret chancellery was established by a decree of the Great Council in the year 1402. Its object was to preserve those papers of highest state importance from the publicity to which the ducal chancellery was exposed. The regulation of the secret chancellery was undertaken by the Council of Ten, and the rigorous orders which they issued from time to time abundantly prove the difficulty they experienced in securing the secrecy which they desired. The secret chancellery became the depository of all state papers of great moment; and if we take the chief members of the constitution in order, and note the documents issuing from them which fell to the custody of the *secreta*, we shall see how the great flow of Venetian history is to be followed here rather than in any other department of the archives.

To begin with the Maggior Consiglio, we have the long series of registers containing the deliberations of the council from the year 1232 down to the fall of the republic in 1797, occupying forty-two volumes, and distinguished, at first, by such capricious names as "Capricornus," "Pilosus," "Presbiter," and "Fronesis;" and later on by the names of the secretaries who prepared them, "Ottobonus primus," "Ottobonus filius," "Busenellus," and "Vianolus." In the special archive of the avvogadori di commun, a contemporary series of registers is to be found; it covers from 1232 to 1547, and should be consulted together with the first series, for it is more voluminous and minute. The first reference to England that occurs in the Venetian archives is in the volume "Fronesis" (1318–1385). This, and all other documents relating to Great Britain, have been collected and rendered accessible in the splendid and monumental series of the "Calendar of State Papers," edited with such diligence and care by the late Mr. Rawdon Brown.

The Senate supplied a far larger number of papers to the secret chancellery than that yielded by the Great Council. This was to be expected, owing to the central position of the Senate in the constitution, and its prominent place in the management of Venetian policy, home and foreign. The oldest documents in the archives of Venice belong to the Senate. They are contained in the volumes of pacts or treaties, seven in number, without including the

P

volume " Albus," which is devoted to treaties between
the republic and the Eastern Empire, or the volume
" Blancus," which contains the treaties between Venice
and the Emperors of the West. The thirty-three
volumes of "Commemoriali" formed a sort of com-
monplace book for the use of statesmen; in them
were registered briefly the most important events
and abstracts of principal documents which passed
through the hands of the government. The "Commemoriali" cover the years 1293 to 1797; but after
the middle of the sixteenth century they were neglected, and they are chiefly valuable down to that date
only. After the "Patti" and "Commemoriali" we
begin the record of the regular proceedings in the
Senate. This series contains papers relating to home
government, foreign policy, the dominions of Venice
on the mainland, in Dalmatia and the Levant, ecclesiastical matters, relations with Rome, instructions to
ambassadors, and reports from governors. So widely
spread and so varied were the attributes of the Senate,
that the analysis of a single day's proceedings in that
house would prove most instructive to the student of
the Venetian constitution, and would, in all probability,
bring him into contact with a large number of the
leading magistracies of the republic. The series of
senatorial papers proceeds in almost unbroken completeness from the year 1293 down to the close of
the republic; and, counting files, registers, and rubrics,
numbers 1599 volumes. This main series is known
by different names at different periods, and shows
signs of that tendency to subdivision which charac-
terizes all Venetian government offices. The volumes

which run from the year 1293 to 1440 were known as "Registri misti;" those covering from 1491 to 1630 were called "Registri secreti." After the year 1630 the papers of the Senate are divided into those known as "Corti," relating to foreign powers; and those known as "Rettori," relating to the government of the Venetian dominion.

Besides this great series of "Deliberazioni," containing the general movement of business in the Senate, there is another voluminous series of documents, equally important, and even more interesting to the student of general history—the despatches received from Venetian representatives at foreign courts, and the "Relazioni," or reports which ambassadors read before the Senate upon their return from abroad. Nothing can exceed the brilliancy of this series; and the value of the "Relazioni" at least has been fully recognized. Yet it should be borne in mind that the "Relazioni" are only a part of the series, and that, taken alone and isolated from the despatches, they lose much of their value. For we must not forget that the "Relazioni" were drawn up on more or less conventional lines; the headings, under which the report was to fall, were indicated by the government, and were invariable; and, further, the home-coming ambassador handed his report to his successor, who frequently used it as a basis in drawing up his own. The result is that, except in the descriptions of court life, and in the sketches of prominent characters, the "Relazioni" are apt to repeat themselves. But, taken with the despatches, which arrived almost daily, they form the most varied, brilliant, and minute gallery of national portraits that the world possesses. The reports and despatches were made by men whose whole political training had rendered them the acutest of observers, and they were presented to critics who were filled with the keenest curiosity, and were accustomed to demand full and precise information. Not a detail is omitted as unimportant; the diurnal gossip of the court, the daily movements of the sovereign and his favourites, are all recorded with impartial and unerring observation. The relation of the "Dispacci" to the "Relazioni" is the relation of the study to the picture. The "Relazioni" are the large canvas upon which the whole nation is broadly depicted, the "Dispacci" are the patient and minute studies upon which the excellence of the picture depends. The majority of the Venetian "Relazioni" between the years 1492 and 1699 have been published; the earlier part by Signor Alberi, and the later by Signori Barozzi and Berchet. The eighteenth century still remains to be worked out. In the series of "Relazioni" and "Dispacci," Great Britain occupies a comparatively small space. While France, Germany, and Constantinople, each give five volumes of reports, England gives one only, dating from 1531 to 1773. Of despatches from England there are 139 volumes in all; while from Constantinople we have 242, from France 276, from Milan 230, and from Germany 202.

Previous to the year 1603, when the regular series of despatches from England begins, there had been intermittent relations between the republic and the English court. Sebastian Giustiniani was Venetian ambassador in London in the reign of Henry VIII. (1515-1519); and in the reign of Mary, Giovanni Michiel represented the republic for four years—from 1554 to 1558. The Protestant reign of Elizabeth caused a long break, during which the republic received its information about the affairs of England from its ambassadors in France and Spain. Permanent relations were not resumed between the two powers till the accession of James I., one of whose earliest acts was to send Sir Henry Wotton to Venice as his ambassador. The appointment of Sir Henry Wotton was a movement of gratitude on the part of the king; and the cause of it cannot be better told than in the words of Sir Henry's biographer, who thus describes this "notable accident:"

"Immediately after Sir Henry Wotton's return from Rome to Florence—which was about a year before the death of Queen Elizabeth—Ferdinand the Great, duke of Tuscany, had intercepted certain letters, that discovered a design to take away the life of James, the then king of Scots. The duke abhorring this fact, and resolving to endeavour a prevention of it, advised with his secretary Vietta, by what means a caution might be best given to that king; and after consideration it was resolved to be done by Sir Henry Wotton, whom Vietta first commended to the duke, and the duke had noted and approved of above all the English that frequented his court.

"Sir Henry was gladly called by his friend Vietta to the duke, who despatched him into Scotland with letters to the king, and with those letters such Italian antidotes against poison as the Scots till then had been strangers to.

"Having parted from the duke, he took up the name and language of an Italian; and thinking it best to avoid the line of English intelligence and danger, he posted into Norway, and through that country towards Scotland, where he found the king at Stirling. Being there, he used means, by Bernard Lindsey, one of the king's bed-chamber, to procure him a speedy and private conference with his Majesty.

"This being by Bernard Lindsey made known to the king, the king required his name—which was said to be Octavio Baldi—and appointed him to be heard privately at a fixed hour that evening.

"When Octavio Baldi came to the presence-chamber door, he was requested to lay aside his long rapier,—which, Italian-like, he then wore;—and being entered the chamber, he found there with the king three or four Scotch lords standing distant in several corners of the chamber; at the sight of whom he made a stand; which the king observing, bade him be bold and deliver his message; for he would undertake for the secrecy of all that were present. Then did Octavio Baldi deliver his letters and message to the king in Italian; which when the king had graciously received, after a little pause, Octavio Baldi steps to the table, and whispers to the king in his own language, that he was an Englishman, beseeching him for a more private conference with his Majesty, and that he might be concealed during his stay in that nation; which was promised and really performed by the king, during all his abode there, which was about three months. All which time was spent with much pleasantness to the king, and with as much to Octavio Baldi himself as that country could afford; from which he departed as true an Italian as he came thither."

The presence of Sir Henry in Venice, where he was a *persona gratissima*, both on account of his love for Italy and his knowledge of the language, did much to strengthen the new relations between England and the republic. The feeling between Venice and the Stuart kings became extremely cordial; but on the outbreak of the Civil War, in 1642, the republic suspended the commission of Vincenzo Contarini, who had been appointed to succeed Giovanni Giustinian as ambassador to England. The secretary Girolamo Agostino, however, continued to discharge Venetian affairs till the year 1645; and his despatches contain minute particulars concerning the progress of the Civil War. In the year 1645, Agostino was recalled, and the interests of Venice in England were entrusted to Salvetti, the Florentine resident. Agostino left behind him in England a secret agent, with instructions to forward a weekly report on the progress of affairs to the Venetian ambassador in France, among whose despatches we find these news-letters from London. After the death of Charles I. it is not likely that the republic would have been represented at the court of Cromwell, towards whom the feeling of Venice was not cordial, had she not been in great straits for help against the Turk. But in the year 1652 she resolved to dismiss the representative of

Charles II., then in Venice ; and, at the same time, the government instructed the ambassador at Paris to send his secretary, Lorenzo Pauluzzi, to London to open negotiations with Cromwell. With Pauluzzi the series of despatches from London recommences ; but these despatches are to be found among the communications from the Venetian ambassador in Paris, by whom they were forwarded to the Senate. The despatches of Pauluzzi are of great importance, and give us a vivid though hostile picture of Cromwell and his surroundings. In 1655 the negotiations between England and Venice had advanced so far that the republic had determined to send an ambassador extraordinary to the Protector's court. Giovanni Sagredo, ambassador at Paris, was chosen. The result of Sagredo's mission is contained in the long and brilliant *relazione* which he read in the Senate on his return to Venice in 1656. In this splendid specimen of a Venetian report, to which we shall return in a subsequent essay, Sagredo gives, with singular lucidity and grasp, a brief sketch of the condition of Great Britain ; of the causes of the Civil War ; of Cromwell's rise to power ; of his foreign relations ; and closes with a portrait of the Protector which confirms Pauluzzi's unfavourable view, and draws a terrible picture of that restlessness and dread which clouded Cromwell's last days —" più temuto che amato . . . vive con sempiterno sospetto." When Sagredo returned to Venice, his secretary, Francesco Giavarnia, was left behind in England, as Venetian resident, and continued to hold that post till the Restoration, sending despatches every week direct to Venice, detailing the close of the Protectorate, and the return of Charles II., whom he was the first to welcome at Canterbury the day after his landing. In 1661 the republic gladly reopened full relations with the Stuarts. Giavarnia was superseded by two ambassadors extraordinary, who conveyed to Charles two gondolas for the water in St. James's Park, and from that date onwards the diplomatic connection between England and the republic followed the ordinary course.

We come now to the papers of the Council of Ten; all of these were committed to the custody of the secret chancellery. We have already seen that the Council of Ten was an extraordinary office, used upon extraordinary occasions, where secrecy and speed were required. Its chief occupations may be summed up under three heads—safety of the state, protection of citizens, and public morals. That being the case, the number and interest of its documents is very great — greater than that of any other council of state; but this interest is confined, for the most part, to matters affecting the home policy of the republic; foreign affairs find comparatively little illustration among the papers of the Ten. The series of documents, containing the ordinary business of the Ten, dates from the year 1315 to the close of the republic. The documents are arranged according to the matter they deal with; that is to say, political matter, *parti communi* and *secreti*, or criminal matter, *parti crimminali*. The immense importance and interest attaching to the papers of the Ten will be illustrated by the statement that there we find the cases of Marino Faliero, of the

Carraresi, of Carmagnola, of Foscari, of Caterina Cornaro, and of Foscarini.

Among the papers of the Collegio we find ourselves once more in the general current of foreign politics. The ordinary proceedings of the College, the papers containing the arrangement and discussion of affairs to be presented to the Senate, are included in the volumes of files and registers, known as the "Notatorii del Collegio." The College was entrusted, as we have said, to receive all the representatives of foreign powers and to open all letters and despatches addressed to the government. It is in the three series known as "Lettere Principi," "Esposizioni Principi," and "Ceremoniali," that we obtain the fullest information about the action of the agents from foreign courts resident in Venice. The series called "Lettere Principi," letters from royal personages, covers the years between 1500 and 1797, and is contained in fifty-four volumes of *filze*. England is represented by two of these, beginning with the year 1570, and ending with 1796, entitled "Collegio, Secreta, Lettere. Rè e Regina d'Inghilterra." These volumes contain one hundred and seventy-one letters, thus distributed among the various sovereigns: there are thirteen in the reign of Elizabeth; forty in that of James I.; four in that of Charles I.; three from Oliver Cromwell; one from Richard Cromwell; one from Speaker Lenthal; ten during the reign of Charles II.; five during that of his brother; three during the reign of William, including one from the Chevalier; seven in the reign of Anne; eight in that of George I.; twenty-one from George II.; and fifty-five from George III.

These letters are concerned with formal announcements and the exchange of courtesies, the credentials of ambassadors, and notices of royal births, marriages, and deaths. Their historical importance is very slight. The long series of George III. is almost entirely occupied by noting the yearly increase of his family. The autographs of the ministers who countersigned the letters form their greatest attraction. The late Mr. Rawdon Brown has published facsimiles of these autographs down to the year 1659; but after that date we find such interesting endorsements as those of Lauderdale, Arlington, Bolingbroke, Carteret, Pitt, Halifax, Henry Conway, Shelburne, and Charles James Fox. On a loose parchment among these letters is one very curious document. It is dated Bologna, 21st February, 1671, and begins "Carlo Dudley per la gratia di Dio duca di Northumbria et del Sacro Romano Impero, conte di Woruih e di Licester, et Pari d'Ingliterra." The document goes on to state that Charles Dudley, duke of Northumberland, in consideration of the affection and partiality always shown towards his person and house, grants to Ottavio Dionisio, noble of Verona, the title of marquis to him and to his eldest son, to his younger sons and to his brothers and their sons, the title of count, in perpetuity; and this in virtue of the declaration and authority of his Holiness Pope Urban VIII., which conferred on Charles Dudley and his eldest born the right to exercise all the privileges of an independent prince. At the date which this document bears, 1671, there was no duke of Northumberland; that title had lately been bestowed by Charles II. on an illegitimate son, and had perished with him. This Charles Dudley was probably some pretender to the honours of the Dudley family who once held the dukedom of Northumberland. The document is curious, for the noble family on whom Charles Dudley conferred this title of marquis still exists, and we do not know that any British subject, either before or after, has ever claimed to be a fountain of honour. But Charles Dudley is not the only English pretender who figures among the papers at the Frari. *Filza* 8 of the loose papers, titled "Miscellanea Diversi Manoscritti," contains the marriage certificate and will of James Henry de Boveri Rossano Stuart, natural son of Charles II., and seven letters from his son James Stuart, dated Milan, Gemona, and Padua, 1722 to 1728. The majority of these letters are addressed to Cardinal Panighetti, from whom this "povero principe Stuardo," as he calls himself, hoped to receive money and support in some imaginary claims on the Crown of England. The letters are full of a certain pathos—the pathos which cannot fail to attach itself to fallen royalty. The handwriting is that of an uneducated man ; and James Stuart, in these letters, certainly shows no signs of the ability required to meet so trying a situation. He appeals to the cardinal first on the grounds of his creed. It is "for the faith that he finds himself in the miserable little town " of Gemona. Failing upon this line, James Stuart abandons himself to astrology, in the hope that the stars may give an answer favourable to his hopes. But to all his appeals the cardinal replies with cold reserve, and when he hears of astrology, he adds a sharp and crushing reprimand.

Leaving the " Lettere Principi " we come to the last two series of state papers of which we shall speak, the "Esposizioni Principi," or record of all audiences granted to ambassadors and of the communications made by them in the name of the power they represented; and the "Libri Ceremoniali," or record of the great functions of state, the coronations and funerals of the doges, the elections of the grand chancellors, the reception accorded to ambassadors, princes, and distinguished travellers. The republic of Venice was as punctilious as any court of Europe upon the points of precedence, ceremony, and etiquette. The reader will not have forgotten the amusing account, given by the elder Disraeli, of the long struggle between the master of the ceremonies and the Venetian ambassador at the court of St. James. The government required from its representatives a minute account of every detail of etiquette observed towards them, and replied in kind in their treatment of foreign ministers in Venice. The republic was punctilious abroad, and no less so at home. Every stage in the public entry, first audience, and *congé* of foreign ambassadors was carefully regulated and based upon precedent. The ambassadors of Spain and France had each a special volume devoted to the ceremonies and etiquette which the republic observed towards them. M. Baschet describes at length the receptions of the French ambassadors, for whom he claims the highest rank among the representatives of foreign powers at Venice Great Britain sent fifty-eight embassies, in all, to the republic, between the years 1340 and 1797. Of these ambassadors, Sir Gregory Cassalis filled the office twice, Sir Henry Wotton thrice, the earl of Manchester twice, and Elizeus Burgess twice. The ceremony to which the ambassador was entitled may be gathered from the accounts of these embassies preserved in the " Esposizioni Principi" and the " Ceremoniali."

The reception of Lord Northampton in the year 1762 will afford us the most detailed view of the ceremony, for on that occasion some questions of precedent arose, and the Cavaliere Ruzzini, who was entrusted with the conduct of the affair, presented a long report to the Senate on the subject. The ambassador was not officially recognized by the government until he had made his public entry, and presented his credentials at his first audience in the College. Until that had taken place, he remained incognito, and was in fact supposed not to be in Venice. Before the ambassador arrived, the English consul was expected to hire a palace for his use. There was no fixed embassy in Venice; Thomas Killigrew lodged at San Cassano, Lord Holdernesse at San Benedetto, Lord Manchester at San Stae. John Udny, who was consul at the time of Lord Northampton's embassy, rented the Palazzo Grimani at Canaregio for the ambassador whenever his appointment was announced, and an amusing and characteristic story attaches to this affair. The palace belonged to a Contessa Grimani, and was in bad repair; but the owner promised to restore and fit it up for the ambassador. When the consul went to see the palace, shortly before the ambassador's arrival, he found that nothing had been done to it, and moreover that a gondolier and his wife occupied the ground-floor and refused to move. He wrote at once to the contessa requesting her to move the gondolier, to which he received for answer that the gondolier's wife had been nurse to one of the countess's boys, and the Grimanis had promised her twenty ducats a year; if the ambassador liked to pay that amount, the gondolier would turn out; if not, they must manage to share the palace between them. The consul appealed to the English resident, John Murray, who wrote an angry letter to the government, complaining of this treatment; "La carità della nobile donna," he says, "verso la moglie del gondoliere merita senza dubbio gran lode, ma il sottoscritto s'imagina che l'avvocato più scaltro si troverebbe bene intrigato di produrre una legge o esempio per incaricare l'Ambasciatore Inglese di questa carità."

The matter was probably arranged, for on the 22nd of October Lord Northampton arrived, incognito of course, with all his suite, and took up his residence. Lord Northampton was ill, and it was not till the beginning of the next year that he took the necessary step to make his entry and to secure his first audience. The etiquette observed upon such occasions required that the ambassador should send his secretary to leave copies of his credentials at the door of the College, and to ask on what day the doge would receive him. The College reply through one of their secretaries that an answer will be sent. The doge was then consulted what day would suit him, and he answers by putting himself at the disposal of the College. The Senate is then informed of the ambassador's arrival, and sixty senators, under the direction of a leader, are appointed to attend the ambassador until the ceremonies of his reception shall be completed. The days selected for Lord Northampton's reception were the 29th and 30th of May, 1763; and the Cavaliere Ruzzini was named as head of the sixty senators who were to attend the ambassador. Ruzzini informed Lord Northampton of these arrangements, and at the same time sent him a programme of the ceremony, which was based upon that observed towards Lord Holdernesse, and was identical with that which the republic offered to the ambassador of the king of Sardinia. Before his public entry, the ambassador and his suite went to the island of San Spirito, in the lagoon towards Malamocco. The fiction of the ceremony supposed all ambassadors to be lodged there until they had presented their credentials. San Spirito was chosen as the point of departure for the ambassadorial procession, because the distance between that island and Venice was supposed to correspond exactly with the distance between London and Greenwich, whence the Venetian ambassador was wont to begin his progress. Sir Henry Wotton's second embassy forms a rare exception to this rule, for the Venetians were so fond of that charming and accomplished poet, that they allowed him to make his entry from San Giorgio Maggiore, which is much nearer the city and more convenient. After midday on the 29th, Ruzzini and his sixty senators, each in his gondola, arrived at

San Spirito, and found the household of the ambassador drawn up along the landing-place *en grande tenue.* Lord Northampton was informed of Ruzzini's arrival, and came to meet him on the staircase. After exchanging the prescribed compliments, Ruzzini, with the ambassador on his right hand, descended, and both entered the cavaliere's gondola. The whole procession left San Spirito, and proceeded by the Grand Canal to the ambassador's lodging at San Girolamo, accompanied, as Ruzzini says, by "un immenso popolo spettatore del nostro viaggio;" for these official entries were among the most popular of the Venetian spectacles, and the whole city went out to witness them. At the palace fresh speeches and compliments followed. Lord Northampton was suffering acutely from an illness of which he died that same year, but Ruzzini reports with obvious satisfaction that he did not spare him a single ceremony, "adempi ad ogni parte del consueto ceremoniale." The next day Ruzzini and the sixty senators again attended at the ambassador's palace to conduct him to his audience in the College. Lord Northampton was worse than he had been the day before; but Ruzzini was implacable. It cost the ambassador three-quarters of an hour to ascend the Giant's Stair. When at last he reached the door of the Collegio, the doge and all the College rose; the ambassador uncovered and made three bows, and, leaving his suite behind him, he mounted the daïs and took his seat on the right hand of the doge. The ambassador then covered his head, and simultaneously one of each order of the savii did the same. The ambas-

Q

sador handed his credentials to the doge, and remained uncovered while they were being read. The doge made a brief and formal reply welcoming the ambassador to Venice, and each time the king's name occurred, the ambassador raised his cap. After repeating his three bows, the ambassador retired, and was accompanied to his palace by the sixty senators who had waited for him at the doors of the Collegio. This closed the ceremony of entry.

The English ambassador extraordinary enjoyed certain privileges, which were established on the precedent of the embassy of Lord Falconberg, Cromwell's son-in-law. Among these privileges was the right to lodging and maintenance at the cost of the republic, a right which the ambassador usually compounded for the sum of five or six hundred ducats; a box at each theatre in Venice was placed at his disposal, and when he took his *congé* the Senate voted him a gold chain and medal of the value of two thousand scudi. The ambassadors ordinary enjoyed certain exemptions from customs dues. These exemptions were frequently abused, and were the cause of constant friction between the government and the representatives of foreign powers. In the year 1763 Mr. John Murray's Istrian wine was seized, and he only recovered it after expressing himself *ben mortificato.* Mr. Murray was constantly in trouble on this subject. The year before he had addressed an indignant letter to the government because "a certain official of the custom-house had accused him of allowing his servants to sell wine and flour at the door of the residency. It is but a poor satisfaction after so long a period of suspicion to know that that official is bankrupt and no proof of the accusation is forthcoming." But by far the most curious episode of this nature was that which befell Tom Killigrew, the poet, grandfather of the Mrs. Anne Killigrew of Dryden's famous ode and a friend of Pepys, who recalls him as "a merry droll, but a gentleman of great esteem with the king, who told us many merry stories," this, perhaps, among the number. Killigrew was sent to represent Charles II. at Venice in 1649, just after the execution of Charles I., and while his son was *a ramingo*, or knocking about, as the Venetian ambassador politely puts it. Killigrew was received in the usual way on February 10, 1650, and made his address *in lingua cattiva*, as the report affirms. But the republic tired of its alliance with an exiled king, and resolved to dismiss Killigrew as soon as possible. Killigrew was poor, and his master had little or nothing to give him, so he hit upon the expedient of keeping a butcher's shop, where he could sell meat cheaper than any one else in Venice, by availing himself of his exemptions from *octroi.* The Senate resolved to fasten upon this illicit traffic as a pretext for dismissing Killigrew; and on the 22nd of June, 1652, they sent their secretary, Busenello, to tell Killigrew, *vivâ voce*, that he must go. Busenello went to San Fantin, and there found one of Killigrew's butchers, who told him that the resident only kept his shop there, but lived himself at San Cassano. At San Cassano Busenello was told that Killigrew was dining at Murano, and would not be home till evening; but very sooı after he saw the resident at his window, and insisted on being announced. He explained "with all possible delicacy," as he says, the order of the Senate ; but Killigrew received the message with every sign of anger and pain. With tears in his eyes he declared that it was the other ambassadors who robbed the customs, while he had all the blame. It was true that he did keep "a little bit of a butcher's shop to support himself," but that could not hurt the revenue ; and he added that, under any circumstance, he should leave Venice, for he had received his letters of recall from France, four days previously. The Senate no more than their secretary believed in the existence of this letter of recall ; but Killigrew really had the letter, dated March 14th, and it was sent into the College, along with a brief exculpatory epistle from the resident, on the 27th of June. Killigrew left Venice the same day, as he was bound to do by ambassadorial etiquette; and Charles had not another recognized agent to the republic until his restoration ; for the Venetians definitely adopted the policy of courting Cromwell, in the vain hope that he would assist them against the Turk.

With the papers of the College we close this notice of the political documents in the archives at the Frari. The other departments of the government had each their own series of papers, equally copious and valuable. The heraldic and genealogical archives of the Avvogadori di Commun, for example, the charters of the German and Turkish exchanges, and the records of the mint and the public banks, offer a wide and a rich field for study ; and in spite of the profound and extensive labours of such scholars as Thomas, Checchetti, Barozzi, Berchet, Fulin, Lamansky, Mas Latrie, and Rawdon Brown, it will be long before the materials in the vast storehouse of the Frari are exhausted or even adequately displayed.

CARDINAL CONTARINI AND HIS FRIENDS.

THE general impression that the influence of the Renaissance culture upon Italian society was corrupt is, on the whole, a just one. That influence began to show itself distinctly at the opening of the sixteenth century. The period of humanistic study and acquisition had passed ; the period of application had begun. And Rome was the focus of the application, as Florence had been the seat of the earlier efforts to acquire. At Rome society gathered round the court of the Vatican and the head of the Church. But it was a Church in which Aretino might aspire to the purple ; in which Bandello was a bishop and La Casa Inquisitor and compiler of the first " Index Expurgatorius." The society was corrupt, but eminently refined, displaying a finish and a charm which captivated the gentler temper of men like Erasmus and made them cry that only the floods of Lethe could drown for them the memory of Rome, though in the sterner nature of Luther this refinement merely added disgust to indignation. It is needless here to dwell at any length upon this point, for the whole subject has lately received ample and eloquent treatment by an English historian. But it is well to bear the fact in mind when we turn to the pleasanter contemplation of a portion of this society which was refined and not corrupt. The nature of men like Contarini, Pole, Sadoleto, Giberti, and their friends stands out with additional sweetness and lustre when we remember the dark setting of intrigue, of dissoluteness, and of ruin which surrounded them. They were a company of noble men animated by noble objects of ambition, and bound together by the closest bonds of friendship. We come across them with a feeling of pure pleasure; they shine like good deeds in an evil world. It does not matter that they failed in their ecclesiastical policy; that the *via media* which they espoused between the youthful vigour of Protestantism and the corruption of the Roman Church was never adopted; that it exposed them only to suspicion from the Lutherans and to charges of heresy from Farnese and Caraffa; that they foundered between the two great and divergent lines of Reform and counter-Reformation. Their object was a noble one, and it ennobled lives singularly adapted to take the lustre of nobility.

To understand the place of these men in the ecclesiastical policy of the Reformation, it is needful to look a little more closely at the conditions which surrounded them. The aims of the papacy had become secularized in the hands of such mundane and warlike popes as Sixtus, Alexander, and Julius. The desire to found a reigning house and to realize that ever-present, ever-vanishing dream of the Church, a temporal kingdom, determined the policy of these pontiffs, and the Venetian ambassador thus summed up Julius in a despatch to his government: "The pope," he said, "wishes to be the lord and master in this world's game." As the head was so was the body. The bishops endeavoured to make their Sees heritable property—the basis on which to establish a family. The secularization of aim resulted in a secularization of manner. The pope who aspired to be a prince adopted the manners of a prince. The bishops who contemplated founding a house adopted the bearing which became the head of a house. Mundane aspirations induced mundane habits, splendour of life, of dress, of retinue, of board. And again, a Venetian summed up Leo as a pendant to Julius. Julius desired to be lord and master of this life's game. Leo "desired to live." Beyond the immediate region of the Church the Italians had been engaged in breaking open the treasure-house of the dead languages, and the perfume invaded the country. The secularized manners of the churchmen came in contact with a wavering ethical standard, the outcome of humanism and the free play of intellect that recognized nothing superior to itself. The result of this contact was twofold, a deterioration in the manners, habits, and thoughts of society, and a confirmation of the secular tendency among the clergy. For humanism brought with it scepticism as to the foundations of Christianity, and with this scepticism there arose a doubt whether the Church had any rights other than secular. In Rome this twofold result soon disclosed itself in a brilliant and intellectual atmosphere that was at the same time corrupt. Poets and scholars and accomplished women crowded to the court of the Vatican or to the palaces of cardinals, princes, and ambassadors.

Each great house had its clique, its coterie of parasites enjoying the refined sunshine and speculating on the prizes that lay in store should their patron attain to the papacy. To the charm of life was added the zest of a hazard, and the adventurer who sought the favour of this or that prince of the Church secretly prayed that his cardinal might draw the winning number. But at the very moment when the Italians had so prepared life as to be able to enjoy the papacy, should God give it to them, the cup of pleasure slipped from their hands. The refinement and brightening of intelligence which rendered the papacy enjoyable, the secularization of its aims which added a further colour to life's game, were preparing beyond the Alps the very means by which the papacy was to be robbed of all enjoyment, were paving the way for Luther's advent and the sack of Rome. The expansion of intelligence, the discovery of intellectual muscles, and the pleasure experienced in their play, which resulted from these years of humanistic study and training, opened for the ancient and organized people of Italy the door of delightful existence. But the quickening element passed beyond the borders of Italy itself. On the other side of the Alps it found a different nidus, harder and more vigorous, in which to germinate. And so among the Teutonic people the revival took the character of religious earnestness; let us reform the Church, they cried. In Italy it had taken the aspect of cynical pliability; let us enjoy the Church, said the Italians. The result was Luther's advent with all its compulsive power over the papacy. The schism north of the Alps put into the hands of two great princes, the king of England and the emperor of Germany, a weapon for mastering the papacy so powerful that Clement could not stand against it. At any hostile movement on his part Charles threatened to release Luther; on the first refusal to obey, Henry declared the secession of England. The screw was too powerful, and had bitten only too well. Escape was impossible. It remained to be seen what compliance could do; to test the appeasing efficacy of compromise and reform.

But before reform had become a necessity publicly acknowledged by the Church, there existed inside the Church itself a party of men who had begun to recognize the need, and who turned their thoughts to the question. These men used to meet together for discussion at the Church of SS. Dorothy and Silvester, in the Trastevere, and under the presidency of Padre Dato, its parish priest. In the midst of corrupt and indifferent Rome, of Rome that was enjoying the Church, this handful of earnest men had caught an echo of the elemental movement that was in progress beyond the Alps. Reform and not enjoyment was the subject of their thoughts. This company, which met in the gardens of SS. Dorothy and Silvester, called itself "The Oratory of Divine Love." It was composed of men drawn together from various parts of Italy; from Venice, Modena, Vicenza, and Naples; all of them distinguished, but for whom the future reserved widely differing issues. There was John Peter Caraffa, the lean and impetuous Neapolitan, with the fierceness of the Inquisition in his heart, destined to become Paul IV., to wage a hopeless war against Spain, to be forced by circumstances he could not control into the arms of this power he hated, to die deceived by his nephews and detested by the Church. There was Gaetano Thiene, founder of an order of nobles, enthusiastic in zeal, but of gentler mould and fascinated by the impetuosity of the fiery Neapolitan. There, too, were Contarini and Sadoleto, fast friends through life, working for the same object and sharing the same hopes, a possible compromise with Protestantism and a reunion of the Church under her ancient chief, the pope. In fact, the Oratory of Divine Love contained in miniature the future of the Roman Church. Its tendencies were there, as yet undeveloped. The two lines it might possibly adopt were expressed in the temper of the Oratorians—the line of absolute defiance to Protestantism, of uncompromising and haughty antagonism, of fire and blood and inquisition tortures ; and the other line of toleration, of patience, of hope that the lost sheep might yet be won back to the fold. But in the gardens by the Tiber the companions were still undivided, unconscious of the heart-burnings and the cruelty at one another's hands which lay in store for them ; no Luther had yet come among them with a sword of separation. It is only by the light of subsequent history that we see how they met later on, when the divergence of their natures had become marked under the pressure of the growing schism ; how that fierce monk Caraffa, drinking his thick black wine, his "champ-the-battle," as he called it, turned in fury on his former friends ; how he thwarted Contarini at Ratisbon ; how Sadoleto's Commentary was placed upon the "Index;" how Pole was deprived of his office of legate in England ; how even their humble followers were pursued; how Priuli lost the bishopric of Brescia. We do not, however, desire to follow all the members of the Oratory to the close of their divergent ways, but only that party among them which gathered round Contarini, the party of moderation and compromise, the party also of failure. Nor is it in their public life and their ecclesiastical policy that we wish to look closely at these men; that belongs to the general history of the counter-Reformation. It is rather to their inner lives that we would turn and note, if possible, the manner of men these friends appear among themselves.

It would be a difficult, and almost a hopeless task, to extract the essence of these men, had not both Pole and Sadoleto left a copious correspondence behind them. In their letters, through the obscurity of a foreign tongue, we see themselves and their friends taking shape, acting, and reacting on one another, growing nearer together as the years pass by. "I seem to hear your voice speaking to me out of your last letter," writes Sadoleto to Pole. "My letters to you have apparently miscarried. They reached you either later than they should have done, or else not at all. But whatever betide the letters, it is not in paper and ink that our love resides, but rather in the hearts of both of us; and not merely written there, but inburnt, so that it can never be obliterated." And these phrases of affection pass current among them all. They were, in sympathy, one at heart. The common trials and dangers which beset them bound them closely together. Each one of them suffered misfortune. Contarini saw his country barely escaping from the ruin of Cambray. Pole was an exile with a price upon his head. Sadoleto experienced the fluctuations of court favour and disgrace. Not one of them avoided the imputation of heresy. And it was inevitable that it should be so. The intellectual aspect of Luther's reform, the distinctly rational assertion of free judgment, could not fail to appeal to the cultivated Italians brought up on Aristotle at the feet of Pomponazzo. It was only the narrowest margin which distinguished Contarini and his friends from Castelvetri, the excommunicated outlaw, driven to the mountains to save his life, and dying at length in exile at Chiavenna. And when Sadoleto made his last effort on Castelvetri's behalf he, though a cardinal, appeals to the heretic as a man of letters first, as a good churchman last. "I love you on every score, and cannot believe that you hold any opinion unworthy of a man of letters and a good Christian." The reasons which kept these men just inside the Church were twofold. They were already high in the office of that Church, and the wish of their hearts was not to pass outside themselves, but to bring the wanderers in. Another and profounder reason held them where they were. The economy of the Church, so complete in its details, so precise in its gradations of rank and of duties, could not fail to exercise a strong fascination over the Italian temper, which desires form above everything. And now this satisfying symmetry was threatened with destruction ; its very crown and apex was in danger ; a many-headed Church appeared to be no Church at all. It was Henry's declaration of himself as chief of the English Church which compelled

Pole to choose exile rather than obedience. With the theological and philosophical doctrines, however, of the reformers these friends showed a deep sympathy which continually made itself felt in their writings. And this common attitude towards the great question of their day, an impossible attitude and doomed to failure just because it appreciated too accurately the good and the evil on either side, formed the groundwork upon which the affection of these men was based. This is the sphere within which they exercised their finest qualities, their warm friendship and loyalty, their intellectual keenness, their devotion to high and noble studies. Within this region they differed, as even the best friends must differ, in cast of character; each of them displayed his individual temperament; but within this region also they were sure of one another's sympathy, and stood together as a party.

It is round Contarini that the party gathers; he is the most active and the most distinguished of their number. Born in 1483 of noble Venetian parents, an October child, when eighteen years of age he went to the University of Padua. With characteristic impetuosity of temper he attacked both practical and speculative studies—mathematics, engineering, and philosophy; and gave solid proofs of his ability to use them all. On his return to Venice he was employed by the government to regulate the river courses throughout the difficult country of Bassano. It is said that when he was in Spain, representing Venice at the court of Charles, Magellan's ship, the *Victory*, came home after her voyage round the world, laden with cloves gathered in the Spice Islands. The

Victory arrived a day later than her log-book showed, and Contarini alone was found able to explain what had become of the missing day. The temper of his mind, the Venetian mind, was chiefly practical; and the larger part of his life was spent in active political duties, for Venice first, and then for the Church. Writing to a friend, he says his letters are not intended for circulation : "They are scribbled in haste by a busy man."

But Contarini never lost his interest in philosophy, nor the passion for Aristotle, which consumed him when he first went to Padua. His friends used to say that if the whole works of the Stagyrite were lost Contarini could supply them all again from memory. And it may well have been so, for his biographer and constant friend, Beccadello, tells us that he was in the habit of reading Aristotle for seven continuous years three or four hours a day, and then during his afternoon walk he "ruminated" on the subject of his morning's study, reconstructing the whole chain of argument until it was indelibly impressed upon his mind. And philosophy remained for him a constant source of relaxation and delight after the more pressing engagements of his political career. "You ask me," he writes to a friend, "for my opinion on the relation between the mind and the understanding. Till now I have been too deeply occupied by my duties in the Council of Ten. But to-night, Christmas Eve, I am free, and shall take some recreation and no small pleasure in discussing the point with you. Moreover, meditation on this subject is by no means unsuited to the solemn nature of the day." Then he passes on to the topic, and loses himself in a lofty flight which closes in the nature of the Divine. He forgets the Ten and his political duties in the eternal consolations of a philosophy based on faith, in the happiness of a man whose hopes and whose reason are not divorced. Study and writing were the rare pleasures and not the constant occupation of Contarini's life, and he valued them more highly for their rarity. "I know no better means for whiling away a summer's afternoon than listening to the music of some mighty poet." Poetry and philosophical discussion were a relief and a delight, but writing was a veritable passion with the man. He lost his appetite and his sleep; he wandered about restless and alone, while planning a work in his head. His friends could always tell when the labour was upon him and he was about to produce. After he had once seen and grasped his subject he wrote with the greatest fury and rapidity, as much as six pages in an hour, so hurriedly, indeed, that "many words remained in his pen." Having thus discharged his mind, he handed the whole work over to a secretary, to polish, rewrite, and find the missing words. He absolutely refused to touch his thoughts again, partly, no doubt, from lack of time, partly from indifference to the graces of style and from preoccupation with the matter of his work, partly also owing to a slight impatience with the laboured polish of his contemporaries Sadoleto and Bembo. His style suffered from this haste, but his health suffered more owing to this addiction to the passionate pleasure of writing. He became subject to insomnia; sleeping but little, and never after he had wakened from his first sleep. These night vigils were devoted to the study of St. Augustine, or to the solution of some problem in ethics. "Here I am," he writes, "awake in one of these long winter nights, as so often happens to me; and I turn my thoughts to the consideration of your question, which are the nobler, the speculative or the moral qualities?"

With a temper keen and impetuous, we should expect to find that Contarini possessed a certain amount of fearlessness and the courage of his opinions. And, indeed, he always did display a frankness of manner and directness of speech little in accordance with the courtly habits of the Vatican. Though choleric, he never allowed his temper to pass beyond his control; and his real gentleness of nature, and his unswerving loyalty to his friends, bound them to him in the closest attachment. Pole consulted him about his private affairs in England. "Keep a good heart," answers Contarini, "and do not doubt that the day will come when we shall sing the psalm, 'Glad were we for the days in which we saw evil, for the years wherein Thou hast humiliated us.' . . . I have no time to write except to say, keep well and come back soon to the man who loves you more than any other." It was not his friends only who knew the worth of the man; that was only natural. But perhaps no one in that age of difficult and crooked policy had a greater power of inspiring confidence than Contarini. The Venetians knew very well what they were about when they sent him as their ambassador to the court of Charles, with whom their

R

relations were strained and hostile. And Contarini immediately won the regard of the emperor and retained it. Charles took Contarini with him when he made his hurried visit to England, and had not forgotten him when they met once more at Bologna, at Nice, and at Ratisbon. The mixture of frankness, goodness, and grace which characterized Contarini, made him a singularly lovable man; one to whom people turned with a sense of confidence and rest; and his modesty and simplicity in no way lessened his charm. There is a pretty story told of how he met Margaret, the queen of Navarre, at Nice when the pope and Francis and Charles were trying to arrange their differences. Contarini went, as in duty bound, to pay his respects to Margaret. The queen came from her rooms towards the head of the stairs to meet him, and the cardinal was about to kneel and kiss her hand, when the lady ran forward laughing, and crying, "No, no, not to me," took him by both his hands and kissed him on the cheek. Contarini stood blushing like a boy, and all confused, till one of the bystanders told him with a laugh that such was the *dolce costume* of Navarre.

It was from his own countrymen, however, and early in life that his worth received the highest tribute of praise. Contarini was in Venice, actively engaged in the business of the republic. He had just returned from an embassy to Rome, and was looking forward to a long life in the secular service of his native city, when Paul III. determined to raise him to the cardinalate and to summon him to Rome in order to initiate those reforms of the Church which the progress of Luther made imperative. Contarini, unaware of the honour in store for him, was at his place in the Great Council when the pope's messenger arrived on Sunday morning and requested to see him. This, while the council was in session, could not be allowed; but a secretary took the despatches and, opening them, suddenly announced to Contarini that he had been raised to the purple. The counsellors rose in a body and pressed forward to congratulate their colleague. But one of them, Alvise Mocenigo, was not so easily pleased; he could not rise from his seat with the others, as he was suffering from the gout, but above the buzz and patter of congratulation he cried, "These priests have robbed us of the best gentleman this city has." Old Mocenigo's growl was fully justified; Venice was struggling to repair the mischief wrought by the League of Cambray, and nothing could have been more useful to her than the tact, the firmness, and the popularity of Contarini. But she lost him; and that activity which might have been employed to good purpose in the service of Venice was transferred, with no result but failure, to the service of the Church.

Contarini was no sluggard, the change of climate did not change his temper. He no sooner reached Rome than he began to form his party, clearly understanding the objects for which he had been summoned thither. He had made the acquaintance of Pole in Venice. He now called Pole, Sadoleto, Giberti, Aleandro and Cortese to his aid; and, in spite of bitter opposition and jealousy inside the Sacred College, he pressed the proposals for reform. The college endeavoured to crush the new-comer with scorn. "Had Contarini come from the Senate of Venice to reform the cardinals whose very names he did not know?" That was true. Contarini did not know their names, but he had been beyond the Alps and knew better than any of them the strength of Luther's party and the imperative need for purification inside the Church. Yet his enemies were able to poison the ear, though not the mind, of the pope against Contarini. "I know how it is," said Paul to the cardinal while the latter was remonstrating with him on some of his recent creations; "it is in the very nature of cardinals to be jealous lest others should be made their equals in consideration." "Pardon me," replied Contarini, "your Holiness cannot with justice bring this charge against me, for I have suggested the appointment of many who have proved good servants to your Holiness and the Church. And indeed I do not count my hat my chiefest honour. . . . If your Holiness would make the Church fair to see, publish no more decrees; there are enough; but rather set forth living books who shall give voice and expression to these decrees." This was Contarini's appeal that his hands might be strengthened by the admission of his friends to the Sacred College. To the credit of Paul, he did not take umbrage at a frankness so unwonted in the court of St. Peter, but read the earnest sincerity of the man. He commissioned Contarini and his friends to draw up a scheme of reform; and the result of their meetings was the famous "Advice of the Select Cardinals," which Sadoleto latined in such vigorous style. This document is the most singular monument to Contarini's courage. He struck fearlessly at the root of the evil; at the college itself, at the boy bishops, at the absentee and pluralist cardinals, and at the monastic orders whose entire suppression he advocated. But all his zeal was in vain. The "Advice" was read and shelved; the hydra of abuse did not lose a single head. And in the midst of these absorbing public occupations Contarini was ceaselessly engaged in literary correspondence with his friends; in reading, emending, and annotating the work submitted to him by Bembo, Sadoleto, or Pole. Busy, too, with treatises of his own on Free-will, Justification, Predestination, the authority of the pope, written with such outspoken frankness and with such deep sympathy for the Lutheran point of view, that it is a marvel how they escaped the "Index Expurgatorius." Nor did all this engagement make him bate one jot of his activity on his friends' behalf. He hears that Pole is in want of cash; by the next post his friend learns that the pope will increase his salary. For Sadoleto's sake he undertakes the cause of the poor peasants at Carpentras against the Jews. But if he willingly expends himself for his friends' behoof, he claims that they, too, shall not be dilatory nor self-indulgent. His letters calling them to Rome and the service of the Church shook Pole and Sadoleto in their peaceful study at Carpentras. Both felt and obeyed the compulsion of this vigorous and loving man.

The failure of Contarini's hopes of reform and the collapse of the "Advice" did not extinguish his activity. And when Charles proposed the Diet of Ratisbon, and asked the pope to send Contarini as legate, the cardinal, though fifty-eight years old, gladly embraced the opportunity of attempting once more the task of reconciliation and compromise. At the end of January he left Rome, and, to the horror of his attendants, he pressed straight on across the Apennines above Bologna, though they lay deep in snow. "We arrived here," writes one of his retinue from Bologna, "all of us pierced through with cold, which accompanied us the whole way, and will not leave us yet awhile. The Padre Beccadello, though smothered in a mountain of furs, looked as if he would have perished of the frost." But Contarini never complained. His eyes were fixed on Ratisbon, and his thoughts were occupied by a vision of the Church made one again through his endeavours. Pole had followed the same road two years before on his way to Spain, but with fainter hopes and a feebler courage. "The fine weather," he wrote to Contarini, "has allowed us to cross the Apennines, but the cold on the mountains actually burned us. The passage would have been impossible had there been rain or snow." Contarini would not admit such an impossible, but he did not know the greater difficulties that waited him in Ratisbon, difficulties which defied even his powers of gentleness and zeal to overcome. When the work of the Diet was once begun he made rapid progress towards a reconciliation with the Protestants, and differences seemed to be vanishing under the charm of his treatment. But every step in that direction only rendered the consummation of his desire more hopeless. Luther suspected such a facile agreement; Charles dreaded a Germany united and catholic once more through the labours of the pope; at Rome Caraffa inveighed against compromise, and accused Contarini of heresy; the treacherous offers of Francis to the one party and the other induced both Protestant and Roman to hope that concession might be avoided. The legate's task was an impossible one. Inspired by Caraffa, Cardinal Farnese wrote a long despatch to Contarini, in which the latter could not fail to read the ruin of his prospects. "Bear yourself cautiously, and do not be drawn to assent to any proposition through the hope of accord. In the exposition of doctrine let us have no ambiguity. And finally, if you will allow me to sum up all in a word, do not conduct yourself so frankly as to run the risk of being gulled by our enemies." Such was the temper of Rome, and this despatch was the warrant of Contarini's failure. He returned to Italy and found his acquaintances cold towards him. "What are these monstrous articles which you have subscribed at the bidding of the Lutherans?" said one. "That is only some squib of Pasquin; do not believe it." "Pardon, this is no squib. I read it in a letter from a great cardinal." So the Church which he had tried to serve refused to acknowledge his efforts. Only his friends drew closer to his side, and their letters came faster and fuller of affection as the end approached. Contarini was sent as legate to Bologna in 1542, the year after the Diet of Ratisbon. The summer heats began to rage with great fierceness, and he retired to S. M.

del Monte above the town. In the monastery there was a *loggia* looking northwards across the Lombard fields towards the Alps, which were just visible in the distance, a fine and serrated line of snow above the tropical shimmer and haze of the plain. Here Contarini loved to sit and talk and feel the cooler breeze. But the keen wind gave him a chill and threw him into a fever. He knew at once that he was dying. Beccadello, his faithful attendant, tried to cheer him. " Do not think of this ; let the doctors see to it; only get well and we will set out on our mission to the emperor." " Before another and a greater Emperor I must present myself this day." He was, as always, only too wise, says his biographer; he died that same evening, fifty-nine years old.

If Contarini proved himself vigorous in the political life which he adopted, his friend Sadoleto was hardly less so in his own particular way. It is part of the charm of this company of Contarini that each member displays his own distinctive features clearly marked ; though all are bound together by affection and sympathy. Sadoleto is first and foremost a man of letters. He cannot help regarding Rome from the humanist point of view; he is one with Erasmus in the colour of his indignation at the sack of the Eternal City. "O barbariem inauditam ! Quæ fuit unquam tanta Scytharum, Quadorum, Wandalorum, Hunnorum, Gothorum, immanitas?" Sadoleto wished to contemplate Rome from a distance ; to focus it through the line of its classical history; to see it through the emotional atmosphere of all the ages and of all learning. To be compelled to deal with Rome as the seat of the Sacred College, as the home of the pontiff at war with Luther, destroyed the illusion. Therefore Sadoleto escaped from Rome whenever he saw his opportunity. He escaped to plunge himself among his books in his See of Carpentras; to lose himself in the region that he loved, the study of the classics and the conversation of his friends. Not that he was cold-hearted to the Church; he was willing to labour for her; but she did not fill and brim his whole sphere of vision as was the case with Contarini. When his friend Pole failed in his legation to France, Sadoleto wrote to him with hardly concealed in-difference. "I was sorry to learn that your mission has failed, but I take it the less to heart, as I always foresaw the issue. Only come back safe and sound to us." He was a scholar and a good friend, but hardly a politician or a churchman. He knew that politics were not his region; and when, under the pressure of Contarini, he did mix in affairs he chose the pen, the weapon that came the readiest to his hand. But we never can read far in his epistles before we find him abandoning the discussion of events to cry, "Veniamus ad litteras." The criticism, the correction, and the composition of books were the main passion of life for Sadoleto; for Contarini they were luxuries to be enjoyed but sparingly. Yet the gravity and weight of Sadoleto's style fully justified his choice. And this engine of vigorous diction which he perfected, he devoted almost entirely to the service of the Church. Within his chosen sphere of literature he was a diligent servant. But as he grew older this literary temper and its claim upon him grew stronger. "I wish to devote the rest of my life to study," he writes to Farnese. "I therefore think of giving up my diocese; I only long for peace and quiet anywhere. I renounce Carpentras and my gardens; only give me quiet, be it where you will." This quiet for which he prayed was employed in no ignoble manner. It was then the custom to pass books in manuscript from hand to hand among the friends of the author. Criticism and correction were invited, and this led to a continual correspondence upon literary topics. Sadoleto's study in his *villa suburbana* at Carpentras was one of the centres of this activity, one of the fires of the literary forge. And he was happiest when he was thus employed in company with some congenial spirit. He caught Pole once on his return from one of his many embassies, and we can see from their correspondence how happy they were together. Sadoleto preludes to Pole : "I have not written before because I know that you are in receipt of all our news. My love for you, however, requires the verification of no letters. Only come back safe and sound to me." Then Pole follows to Contarini : "I am here in Carpentras, living in a monastery, a place solitary and devout; moreover, quite close to the gardens of Sadoleto, whither I go at least once a week to spend the whole day;" and again : "These politics prevent me from enjoying to the full the delightful and tranquil company of Sadoleto. Here, however, is an admirable solitude; and were it not for the letters from Rome we should have no news at all."

Pole, the most feminine spirit of the three, was continually swayed between the stronger characters of his friends Contarini and Sadoleto. On this occasion Contarini broke in upon their peace with cries and claims of duty. Pole had to face the French legation, and the happiest months of his life, those spent with Sadoleto at Carpentras, came to an end. But it was not literary work solely which occupied Sadoleto's days in his bishopric. He was a man capable of the strongest personal attachments when the object was brought within his immediate reach. All that lay beyond his direct perception, and which yet commanded his regard, he transferred to a region of emotion other than personal, into an atmosphere that was artistic or intellectual. But his personal feelings were rendered all the stronger for this concentration. His affections are the affections of an artist accustomed to deal with the whole sphere of emotion as the matter of his art, and who suddenly finds his familiarity with passion translated into terms of himself and overmastering. But it is just in these burning moments of his heart that the true nobility and gentleness of Sadoleto most appear. He has left one love-letter behind him, through which the deep current of a genuine affection flows unmistakably. It does not appear to whom it was addressed; but he says, "I have never ceased to love you. Yet, since it is the wont of lovers to be ever anxious on behalf of those they love, I wish to enjoin on you one thing which both my love and your youth recommend; strive, without any appearance of vain glory, but in wisdom and modesty, to approve yourself among your company. I, as beseems my love for you, and my ever-constant wish in all that affects you, promise and dedicate to you, to your well-being and adornment, whatever belongs to me ; my every effort, forethought, influence, authority, diligence, all, in short, that nature or fortune has bestowed on me, however trifling it may be, is yours for all time ; not only on my word as an honourable man, but on the faith and evidence of this letter wherewith, as by a solemn pact, I desire to be bound to you." With such a well of affection in his nature, Sadoleto could not miss the warm attachment of his friends. But his lot was cast in troublous times for a scholar and a recluse. He experienced the changes and caprices of favour and disgrace, and was forced to undertake no less than five journeys between Rome and Carpentras. Thanks to one of these, he escaped, by twenty days, the sack of Rome and all the horrors it brought upon his learned friends. But these long and dangerous expeditions broke in upon his leisure and seriously embarrassed his affairs, and towards the close of his life he found himself in extreme poverty. "I am so utterly poor," he writes, "that I cannot make even a four days' journey in a manner becoming to a cardinal. Horses or mules I have none." But his poverty could not purchase him seclusion. He lived to see his friends die away one by one ; to hear that his Commentary on St. Paul was condemned and placed upon the "Index ;" to be torn from his study by an imperious summons to Rome, where he died in his house by San Pietro in Vincola, seventy years of age.

The third of this trio of friends, Reginald Pole, "the gentle cardinal," the *spirito angelico*, "my Saint Pole," as Sadoleto calls him, was at once the least powerful and the most femininely attractive of the three. It is not only his gentleness—a gentleness which led him to shelter the man who tried to assassinate him—nor yet his misfortunes, his own exile, and his mother's execution that engage our sympathy. It is the sweetness and sprightliness of his character which are so attractive; for Pole, the Englishman, is the only one of the three friends who shows a grain of humour. Cast among strangers whom he had to make his friends, whom he desired above all to have as his friends, it is touching to watch him struggling with the barrier of language between them. In his early letters he sometimes attempts Italian. He halts along for a sentence or so, and then reverts to the more formal but more familiar Latin. Gradually, however, the barrier was broken down, and Pole learned to use Italian freely. Before the disgrace of himself and the ruin of his whole family, Pole had come to study at Padua, after leaving Oxford. He had an income of nine hundred pounds a year, and lived as became a nobleman and a relation of the king of England. On his return home the question of the king's divorce placed him on the horns of a dilemma—obedience to the king and rupture with the Church, or exile. Pole chose the latter alternative, and remembering his days of study in the Venetian city, he made his way to Padua once more. It was upon this second visit that he formed an intimacy with his friends Contarini and Priuli, and also with the man who afterwards proved his foe, Caraffa the Neapolitan. Contarini at once established an ascendency of affection over the gentle Englishman; and it was between the political impulse of Contarini and the literary impulse of Sadoleto that Pole spent the greater part of his life in Italy. When Contarini was summoned to Rome to undertake the work of reform, he called Pole, among other friends, to his aid; and Pole appears as "the English cardinal" among the signatories of the "Advice." Pole had never enjoyed robust health, and the strain of work in Rome made him glad to escape whenever possible. Contarini was well aware of his friend's delicate constitution, and anxiously urged him to pay more heed to his physical condition, and to keep himself efficient for the service of the Church. And thereupon followed a humorous correspondence. Contarini recommends a fish diet, and above all attention to the advice of Priuli and his Italian friends, who understand the climate. Pole replies, "You have now commissioned Priuli to act as a keeper of my health and arbiter of my goings; but he began to use his authority after so cavalier a fashion that my horse, which he had borrowed, guessed my feelings towards him and gave him a fall; since then I find him much milder. But, joking apart, travelling tries me severely. The wind and open air, to which I have not been accustomed for some months, give me a fever; and that attacks me chiefly at night." This same Priuli is the man who, of all others, was most deeply attached to Pole. From the time when they first met in Venice Priuli never left his friend. His villa near Treviso was always open to Pole; and thither Pole retired when in need of rest, or, as in the middle of the Council of Trent, in search of health. Priuli was with him on his many legations; with him too at his palace of Lambeth during the two years that Pole was archbishop of Canterbury; and when Pole died. "Alvise Priuli, for twenty years my tried friend," was left his heir and executor. In spite of the joke about the horse, and his unwillingness to be drilled, Pole had the good sense to listen to Priuli's recommendations, and from his next letter, written to Contarini from Piacenza, it is clear that he has profited. "Again! another letter on the same subject! Do you think you have no weight with me that you must follow up the first by a second? But from this I learn how anxious all love must needs be. I cannot deny that my strength has greatly benefited by listening to your advice, and I am not only well, but even in robust health. We stop here a whole day, a thing I have never done before upon the journey. I am left alone in the house, as my people have all gone out to see the town. So I take up my pen once more that I may spend the time with you." It was partly his delicate health, partly his poverty—for all his English fortune had been confiscated—partly, too, a constitutional shyness and shrinking from publicity, which made Pole dislike and avoid these official journeys. He came only too willingly to the lure of Sadoleto's gardens at Carpentras, and loudly bewailed the hardship which compelled him to quit them for a journey into France. And, later on, he writes as legate from Viterbo to Contarini, explaining how he likes to live: " I use my morning hours in study, and am therefore very jealous of them. Business comes after dinner, and the rest of the day is devoted to the company of Messer Carnesechi and Antonio Flaminio. If only you were here this place would be a paradise on earth. Your absence is the sole drawback to my complete satisfaction. But were I to judge from my past experience of the way in which God has ordered my goings, I should have reason to doubt whether this full measure of quiet could be mine for long." It is only in the company of a friend or of a friend's volume that he can forget the tedium of the road. "Your book," he writes to Sadoleto, "was carriage, and springs, and companion to me, so much did it ease my journey." Pole never could see a monastery without wishing to seek rest inside its walls; he constantly speaks of himself as though he were a hunted deer running for the shelter of a cloister, be it at Dilingen, at Carpentras, or at Maguzano on the Lake of Garda. He is happy when he escapes from Rome to the country; he is happy at Viterbo in the company of Flaminio, the poet of the country; or at Rovellena, among the Euganean hills, "our paradise, as I can truly call this place, both because of the charm of its situation amid these delicious hills, and also and much more because of the friends whose society I here enjoy;" happy, too, at Dandolo's villa, "ubi jucunde et hilare epulati sumus." Pole was made for the frank enjoyment and companionship of his friends in all the quiet and refined conditions of life, but not for the bustle and self-assertion of the great world. Whether it was the poverty of his health, or that the tragedy of his house was ever present to his memory, this instinctive shrinking accompanied him through life. It showed itself in his refusal of the cardinalate, a refusal which compelled the pope to take him, as it were, by surprise, first appearing to consent, and then, on the morning of the Consistory, causing him to be tonsured, consecrated, and declared a cardinal before he well knew what had happened to him. It showed itself later on, when he declined to urge his candidature for the tiara; and in the indifference with which he learned that he had missed it by a single vote, an indifference that irritated a member of the Sacred College into calling him *un pezzo di legno* to his face. But Pole was not wooden in insensibility; he had his objects of desire. He longed, as most men do, for what he never did possess, quiet and the enjoyment of his friends. Caraffa pursued him as he pursued all who belonged to Contarini and the party of conciliation. Pole missed the pain of seeing England break with his Church once more. He and Queen Mary died in 1548, on the same day; but Pole closed his career under a cloud of suspicion at Rome, deprived of his office as legate, and threatened in his See; the youngest, the gentlest, and the most unfortunate in this trio of Contarini and his friends.

These three men differed widely from one another; though chance threw them together in a close and beautiful intimacy. The happiest of Pole's days were passed in Italy. There, in contact with the friends he had made, his character is at its brightest and its best. Pole's Italian sojourn, however, is no more than an episode in his story. His real life centres in Eng-

land.   There he experienced the misfortunes of his
youth ; and there the dark story of the persecutions
from Canterbury gathers about his last years.   In England he was called on to face the crucial trials of his
career.   Sadoleto's life could hardly have had a
different issue.   He was a scholar and a recluse by
nature, and the difficulties of the times made his high
station a certain source of unhappiness.   Yet among
these three friends Sadoleto's character presents the
greatest harmony and completeness.   For Contarini
the problem was rather different.   He was endowed
with a burning activity of temper, and a natural bias
in two directions, towards philosophical study and
towards politics.   The fact that he was a Venetian
determined him rather as a man of action than as a
speculator.   But, having adopted the career of politics,
his philosophical bias avenged itself and compelled
him to pursue a line of compromise.   Such a line was an
impossible one, and doomed to failure between Luther,
Caraffa, Charles, and Francis.   Had he not been a
philosopher Contarini might have been a politician of
the type of Caraffa ; had he been less of a politician
he might have been a speculator in the school of Pomponazzo, and a possible precursor of Bruno.   Through
his intellectual sympathies he felt the tumult and the
doubt of this period of change, and his sleepless
nights are witness to the questionings of his soul.
The interest of his life and the pathos of his failure
lay in this, that he was at once something more and
something less than a politician or a philosopher.   He
reflected faithfully the period of transition and the
complexity of his own day.

MARCANTONIO BRAGADIN, A SIX-TEENTH-CENTURY CAGLIOSTRO.

I.

ONE of the most curious and permanent features in the history of the human spirit is the perennial expectation that the impossible may be realized. The human spirit, like a child with its toys, seems to grow weary of that which it possesses, and to reach out its hands to that which it has not. The very improbability of attaining an object throws a fascination around it, and renders it more attractive than that which lies under our hand. Mankind never ceases to hope—often in secret—that the picture of his imagination may become actual for him in some way or other. The form which this expectation assumes continually varies. Now its result is a credence in oracles; now a conviction that the millennium is imminent; now the philosopher's stone or El Dorado attracts desire; now it is the prospect of classifying ghosts or of reading the secret behind the veil. But, however various the manifestations of this reaching towards the unrealized may be, each age, and especially each age of any remarkable vitality, has shown itself aoristic, undefined, and formless in some direction.

It is to this dubious point that the curiosity, dissatisfaction, and outgoings of mankind have always rushed. Here, at this flaw in the solidity of the human intellect. at this breach in the fortress of fact, this breach that lets infinity flow in upon mankind, we find assembled the strange and restless spirits of their time—the magician, the prophet, the philosopher. The qualities of these men differ widely from one generation to another as the object of their hopes differed. Sometimes it was a noble expectation which drew them to the gates of the infinite ; a hope of Christ's second coming, or a belief in universal equality and brotherhood. Sometimes the expectation was mean and tainted ; such as the belief in the power of alchemy to create gold, or a hope of inexhaustible pleasure to be purchased by a compact with the devil. But, noble or mean in its extravagant aspirations, each age shows us the human spirit occupied, in part at least, with a hope that the impossible may become possible, that the limitless may be grasped.

Each epoch, then, will have its Cagliostros, trading, with more or less of conscious duplicity and villany, upon the governing appetites and expectations of the men about them. These charlatans, in spite of their iniquity and their certain failure, are seldom utterly uninteresting—the possibility and the peril of self-deception touch mankind too nearly. And, moreover, these charlatans possess the power of bringing to the surface the salient qualities of the men with whom they are implicated, and their career throws into high relief the leading characteristics of their age. The close of the sixteenth century was a period of extreme ferment and corruption throughout Europe. The air was charged with expectation. Men's minds were on the alert for something startling and new; old landmarks had been swept away, old faiths called in question. Machiavelli and the Reformation had riven Europe and shaken thrones. Court and camp were in a condition of morbid activity. Princes and sovereigns moved restlessly, impelled by an insatiable desire for change. Their palaces abounded in adventurers, ready to propose and attempt impossible schemes of political aggrandizement. In the world of politics the bounds of sanity were overstepped, and in the social world the same process was at work. It was one of those periods when the moral conscience seems to have fallen asleep and to have relaxed its bracing and binding power. In every department of life charlatans were abroad, preying upon the cupidity, the folly, or the appetites of society. Our sixteenth-century Cagliostro, Marcantonio Bragadin, was only one among a hundred others of similar temper; but we have selected him for several reasons. In the first place, his career led him to cross the paths of many people of importance : * of Henry IV. of France and the dukes of Bavaria and Mantua; of Popes Sixtus V. and Gregory XIV.; and, finally and principally, he came in contact with the republic of Venice. He occupies two volumes of official letters, reports and resolutions, which exist now in the archives of the Frari.† In these manuscripts we are able to follow

---

* Doglioni, " Hist. Venet.," lib. xviii.; Daru, " Hist. de Venise," lib. xxviii.

† See also Cicogna Codice, No. 80.

a part of his life with a minuteness that accounts for almost every day, and in the process a vivid picture of a charlatan's career, his successes, and his failure, is unfolded before us; while at the same time we receive a singular demonstration of the patient accuracy and the thorough method which distinguished the Venetian government, even when dealing with a subject apparently so unimportant as the movements of a reputed alchemist.

II. IN NUBIBUS.

Marco Bragadin, of Cyprus, as he called himself, would seem to have belonged to the noble Venetian house whose name he bore. How that may be we cannot say for certain. His birth, his boyhood, and early youth are lost in obscurity; and Cyprus is the only fact upon which we can rely. In Cyprus he was born, somewhere about 1540, of a father who practised alchemy and medicine with considerable success. Between Cyprus in 1540, and Venice in 1574, we catch only one fleeting and doubtful glimpse of Marco as court fool and disreputable attendant in the train of Bianca Capello, grand duchess of Tuscany.* The next we hear of him is in Venice, with his brother Hector, staying in the house of a friend—he had already begun to make friends and followers— a certain Caldogno, of Vicenza. There is nothing as yet about alchemy or mystery of any sort, only friendship, and that *pura fascinatione*, the sheer fascination which one of his victims subsequently

---

* See Celio Malespini, "Novelle," tom. ii. Nov. xc.

recognized as a characteristic of the man. At this time Venice was in a ferment of revelry for the advent of Henry III. of France. The lavish expenditure, the riot, and the licence of these few days' pageantry turned most heads ; and it occurred to the two Bragadins that they would like to go to France in Henry's train, seeing the number of adventurers who swarmed about the king, and scenting the right man for their prey, if they could come at him. Money for the journey was not easily to be had ; but, thanks to Marco's "sheer fascination," the Caldogno family advanced fifty ducats and a bill of exchange for four hundred more ; and, thus provided, the Bragadins set out. At this point they disappear once more behind their cloud, and what happened in France is obscure to us. But it would seem that Marco began his practice of alchemy or "philosophy," as it was called by its professors, in that country, where the famous Nostradamus was little more than dead, and that he left something of a reputation behind him, enough at least to secure for him repeated invitations to return. Whatever reputation Marco may have gained, this visit to France did not prove financially successful ; and we find him back again in Venice, all the four hundred and fifty ducats gone, himself in great straits, overwhelmed with debts, pursued by creditors, and with no ostensible means of livelihood. In this pass he took a step which hampered him all his life, and from the consequences of this act he never struggled free. He resolved to enter a monastery of the Capuchins. Before he assumed the cowl, the Father Superior obtained for his novice an accommodation with his creditors, and Marco joined the order of St. Francis a free man, as he believed, but, in reality, he had fastened such a halter round his neck as was not to be loosed except by his death. Bragadin had taken this step merely as a temporary measure and under the great pressure of his debts. A cloister life had few attractions and offered no scope to a man of his temper. He was not long in making his escape and finding his way back to France. And it was after this second visit to France that he emerged into clear light, and began to attract the attention of the Venetian government.

III. BRAGADIN EMERGES.

Hitherto Bragadin's course has lain chiefly *in nubibus;* there have been few indications of the man's nature or powers; we have heard little as yet of transmutation of metals, and nothing of the *anima d'oro.* Only in Cyprus, Florence, Venice, and France, has the veil lifted a moment to show us Marco in no very reputable or hopeful circumstances. Now, however, he emerges into lucidity, and the vigilant eye of Venice is turned upon his career.* In September, 1588, Bragadin was established in a small village of the Bresciano, at the foot of the Alps, not far from Bergamo. He had just returned from France, where his second visit had proved no more lucrative than the first. For he was living in a very poor way, "in miserable rags," with one companion, a Flemish gun-smith skilled at mending arquebuses. Here, at

* Cod. No. 80.

Torbiato, he might have remained undisturbed and unnoticed, but that the officers of the Inquisition got wind of his whereabouts, and were in search of him as an apostate and runaway monk. So Bragadin was forced to change his quarters; and the next we hear of him is from Lovere, on the Lago d'Iseo, with the police close at his heels. One night he was roused by a hammering at the door, and looking out to see who knocked, he found the house surrounded, and the chief constable of Bergamo come to arrest him. " Alone and undressed, he flung himself out of a high window, and so escaped," but not without a deep wound under his chin, the scar of which he bore long afterwards. Considering the height of the window, and his narrow escape from capture, he decided that a miracle had been performed on his behalf, and asserted it with such confidence that he persuaded some of his friends to believe the same.

A miracle alone, however, is not a source of income; and, as yet, Bragadin's prospects did not seem very bright. But presently he is back again at Lovere, and an extraordinary change has come over his manner of life. At Torbiato he was poor, alone, and pursued; at Lovere he is rich and surrounded by servants. The governors of Brescia report thus of him in October, 1589 : " He entertains in his house, now twenty, now thirty nobles and other citizens of Brescia. His expenses are so great that no private individual could support them. Rumour says that during these last four or five months he has disbursed twenty thousand scudi; and just now he has one hundred mouths to feed, and one hundred horses in his stables." Truly a surprising change from the "miserable rags" of Torbiato just a year ago. And the way in which Bragadin had wrought this transformation gives him rank as a charlatan. His method was that of the professional impostor and scamp. He began by whispering to his neighbours of Torbiato that God had committed to his keeping a secret whose value was inestimable, but not for worlds must they divulge this to another; he told it them solely because they had taken pity upon his rags and poverty. And what was the secret? Then Bragadin produced a fine powder, wrapped in a paper, and said that here was the *anima d'oro*, the spirit of gold, by whose potency he could convert quicksilver into the precious metal, and reap a profit of five hundred per cent. Unlimited prospect of gold! It was more than human imagination could resist, and all to be had by simple belief in this precious man; no other price asked; for Bragadin began by refusing presents from these lesser folk, meaning to fly at far higher game. Events followed the course he expected. Such a light could not long lie hidden under a bushel. The rumour spread that at Lovere lived a man who owned the spirit of gold; and presently there arrived a certain Alfonso Piccolomini, gentleman and soldier in the service of the duke of Mantua, and shortly after the duke himself, to see whether the *anima d'oro* might not be carried off to Mantua, locked away, and so make his Highness rich forever. Money was not wanting now, for Bragadin had doubtless represented to Piccolomini that the labourer is worthy of his hire even before he has laboured. And so the duke "stayed to dine and sup, and treated Bragadin with more respect than he shows to our government"—so report the governors of Brescia. "He made great offers to Bragadin if he would go to Mantua. With these, however, Bragadin merely played, and gave no promise." A few days later, the duke is back again to supper; "a great feast, with fish, flesh, *confetti* from Genoa and Spain; all at the cost of seven hundred scudi, not including an arquebus which Bragadin presented to the duke, and which was worth six hundred more;" and after supper Bragadin did himself the honour to refuse a diamond ring "worth some million"—a singular moderation, considering that it was the duke's pocket which had furnished the feast.

In this distinguished company the humbler friends of Torbiato are forgotten and thrust aside. But they do not forget their quickened hopes, their visions of perennial gold; and, resenting Bragadin's conduct, they report ill of him to the authorities in Brescia. These visits of the duke of Mantua required consideration. The governors referred for orders to Venice, and received instructions to furnish "the fullest information regarding the life, habits, expenses, servants, friends, and intentions of Bragadin." In this way the alchemist came under the notice of the Venetian government, and the series of daily reports begins.

IV. ANIMA D'ORO.

Hitherto Bragadin's illustrious friends had heard only promises and glowing accounts of the inexhaustible resources of *anima d'oro.* Tangible proof as yet there was none. And they became impatient. But Bragadin was now aware that Venice had began to show some interest in his movements. This was just what he desired. The more bidders for him and for his precious "medicine,"* as he called it, the better terms he would be able to make; so at least he thought. He was ready to give proof, but was resolved to do so only in the presence of some Venetian of authority whose report would impress his government. He chose his man well. Count Marcantonio Martinengo, of Villa Chiara, was a noble of the republic, a distinguished general who had represented Venice at the courts of Rome and France, a man valued for his straightforward honesty and simplicity. At that time he was recovering from illness at a country house near Brescia. Bragadin begged Piccolomini, as a friend of Martinengo, to invite the count to be present at the operation of making gold from quicksilver which he now intended to perform. Martinengo gladly accepted the invitation, for he had heard the rumours about Bragadin and was curious. But first he consulted the authorities of Brescia, and obtained their consent to his action on the understanding that he should send them a detailed report of all that occurred.† This is Martinengo's report : "Sig. Marco Bragadin, as a most faithful and loving subject of this serene republic, wishing to demonstrate the reality of the gift committed to him by the Divine Majesty, chose and summoned me as a

---

* See Ben Jonson's "Alchemist." Subtle might almost have been studied from Bragadin.

† "Rivista Vienese," xii. 1840.

tried friend and servant and vassal of his Serenity, that I might bear true testimony to the facts. He made me take a pound of quicksilver, which I had ordered my servant to buy, and put it in a crucible upon a fire of live coals. He left it there as long as one might take to say a *Pater noster* and an *Ave Maria.* Then he made me take some orange-coloured powder which he values very highly, about as much as a grain of millet ground into meal; and this he made me mix with a red wax, that the powder, which is very fine, might not fly away. Then he made me take another small grain of some material between green and black. This he declared was of no value at all, and in proof he flung some of it out of the window; but at the same time he said that it was absolutely necessary for the operation, which could not be performed without it. This stuff with my own hand I mixed in wax, and then threw both the pellets into the crucible where the quicksilver was already boiling. Then we heaped on more coals, so that the fire was blazing all round, and left it about a quarter of an hour; at the end of which, I, by his order, took the crucible, glowing hot, and put it in a vase of liquid, like water in consistency but of a pale blue colour. And when the crucible was cooled, we turned out of it a lump weighing a pound, which I have forwarded to you, that it may be sent to Venice, and tested with the usual tests for gold of twenty-four carats." The lump was sent to Venice and tested. We shall hear more of it later on.

This was a good day's work for Bragadin. He roused all the curiosity and cupidity of the Venetian officials by his lump of seeming gold, which reached them through the governors of Brescia. But more than that, he had attached to himself Count Martinengo by a faith that no subsequent exposure was able to shake. Martinengo was a plain, honest man. He had seen the gold made; that was enough for him. From that day forward he believed in the God-gifted Marco Bragadin, and was completely subdued by the "sheer fascination" of the man and his work. In all future proceedings he acts for Bragadin; defends him; watches his interest; counts it his greatest honour to know this sage favoured of heaven, this man "with a singular devotion to goodness." Nothing could have been more fortunate for Sig. Marco. For, on the other hand, the Venetian government, who cared little about the source of his gift, be it from heaven or hell, who were not at all impressed by his "singular devotion to goodness," and indifferent as to his character "more than middling," had been touched in a place where they were highly susceptible. This Brescian nugget wakened in them the vision of an inexhaustible treasury. Their one anxiety now was that Bragadin should be brought to Venice as soon as possible; their greatest fear lest the duke of Mantua or some other prince should carry off this golden prize. In their negotiations with the alchemist they found no fitter intermediary than the Count Martinengo, the man of Bragadin's own choice; and so, as plenipotentiary between himself and the Venetian government, Bragadin secured a man wholly devoted to himself, the humble slave of his "sheer fascination."

V. "HIS NATURAL PRINCE."

The negotiations for bringing Bragadin to Venice required some delicacy in handling. France, Rome, Mantua, and Venice were all bidding for the honour of his presence. Venice was unwilling to arrest him and carry him off by force, though at the same time she was fully resolved that he should not escape. Bragadin was aware of this resolve; and the knowledge that he was virtually caught irritated him into making a show of freedom by playing with other princes, and by loudly declaring that he would take no other road than that which "God should inspire him to choose." Though he had desired to number Venice among the claimants for his person, he was now more than half afraid of his own action, dreading the results of the notoriety he had created and feeling that he had touched a power he was unable to control. The Venetian government did not wish to alarm him, and preferred that he should come to Venice seemingly of his own accord. At the request of Martinengo they sent a safe-conduct for Bragadin, his powders, jars, and retorts, and ordered the governors of Brescia to invite him to dine and to show him every attention. On the other hand, Piccolomini, as a soldier of adventure in command of his own troop, was plying Bragadin with wild offers— to seize Orvieto and make it over to Bragadin, if he would consent to manufacture gold in that city. The duke of Mantua, too, was at work in person. Late one evening he arrived incognito at Brescia, in a hired carriage with three attendants. He at once called on Bragadin, and was admitted, by a secret stair, to the room where the alchemist was, he threw his arms round Bragadin's neck, implored him to be his friend, made him shake hands on it, assured him of his immutable regard. Bragadin replied in the same strain, and ended by saying, "When I am at Venice I shall be with a prince who is so entirely my friend that I can promise you all good offices through my mediation." Then the two passed the evening over a splendid supper, and next day the duke sent to his host a collar, a jewelled watch, and robes with golden buttons.

But the pressure from outside, from the governors of Brescia, from Martinengo, from Contarini and Dolfin, two commissioners sent on purpose to hasten Bragadin's departure, was rapidly becoming more than he could resist. As a matter of fact, one course only was open to him ; and on the 8th of November he announced that, "inspired by God to refuse all other offers, he was now resolved to serve his natural prince," the doge. The conditions which he asked were modest enough ; for his game now was to establish himself well at Venice, and secure the confidence of the government and the great nobles. "I do not seek," he says, "nay, I do not desire either dignity, or honour. I am content with the pleasure I feel in serving others. I bring to Venice my treasure, and in Venice will my heart also be. I only entreat your Serenity to leave me perfectly free to act as God shall inspire. This operation of making gold requires much time, and ninety months of undisturbed labour will be needed to perfect and to multiply the *anima d'oro* which I now possess, so that I may be able to make a suitable gift to your Serenity. The medicine I have with me is capable of producing one hundred thousand ducats; but in order to create five millions, as I desire to do, I require thirty months for boiling a certain water in dung under ground. One only favour I have to ask; that is, that your Serenity should use your influence to secure my absolution at Rome and release from my monastic vows."

But, though everything had been arranged, Bragadin still delayed his departure. The duke of Mantua still continued to ply him with presents and letters beginning, " The lover to the beloved ; " and the governors of Brescia had such grave suspicions that the duke intended to waylay and carry off Bragadin, that they deemed it necessary to have the whole country scoured, and to double the guards at the gates. At length, on the 20th of November, Bragadin, Martinengo, and a large escort set out for Peschiera, Verona, Padua, and Venice. The journey was arranged to look as like a triumph as possible. The authorities in each of the towns received Bragadin at the public palace, feasted and entertained him, consulted his wishes as to the details of his route, and supplied him with an escort suitable to a prince— "for the greater honour of his person," they always said. But in reality Bragadin was a prisoner and he knew it. At Padua he made one effort to shake off his guards. He announced that he would go to Venice down the Brenta by water, and one boat could not accommodate all his retinue. He chose this route because he knew that Piccolomini was lying in wait near Dolo, to carry him off to Mantua or elsewhere. But the scheme failed ; for the governor assured him that a personage so dear to the republic could not be allowed to reach the lagoons unattended. Upon the 26th of November Bragadin entered Venice, and found himself safe under the protection of "his natural prince."

VI. THE JAR IN THE TEN.

Venice was in a state of expectation at the arrival of the famous Marco Bragadin Mamugnà—"Mammon Bragadin," as the people immediately nicknamed him. The Venetian government was always remarkable for the rapidity of its action, when it had once adopted a course ; and in this case they did not belie their reputation. Bragadin arrived on the 26th, and on the 28th, by the advice of Contarini and Dolfin, two of his well-wishers and high state officers, he sent Martinengo to the Council of Ten, to convey a letter addressed by himself to the doge, and to offer two jars of *anima d'oro*, as an earnest of his good faith, upon the condition that these jars should be placed in a cupboard In the mint, and the keys of the cupboard handed over to Bragadin, so that he might take from the jars the "medicine" as he required it for his work. Martinengo was introduced to the council, and the two jars placed beside him on the floor. He reported at length on his relations with Bragadin, and then demanded the answer of the Ten as regarded the offer of his friend. The gift of the *anima d'oro* was accepted, and likewise

Bragadin's conditions. The two jars were ordered to the mint, and were carried out in solemn procession by Pietro Marcello, governor of the mint, accompanied by the heads of the Ten and Martinengo, who saw the precious powders stowed away, and himself carried the keys of the cupboard to the alchemist.

The government suspended judgment, but pursued their usual method of swiftly and silently securing everything in their own hands before proceeding to decisive action. They held Bragadin safe in Venice, and now they had his *anima d'oro*, his *pièce justificative*, under lock and key. Bragadin had the keys, it is true, but he could not touch his medicine without their knowledge and consent. From Bragadin's point of view, this present of the *anima d'oro* was intended to inspire confidence, and to justify any delays for which he might apply ; and to make assurance doubly sure on this head, he took a further step. On the 23rd of December Marcello, master of the mint, reports to the Ten : "This morning I went to the mint. Bragadin came, accompanied by Martinengo, Contarini, and Dolfin. They were brought into the mint by the Riva. We all went to the cupboard where the jars were placed a few days ago, and, having opened the cupboard with the keys Bragadin had brought with him, we placed therein a packet, sealed with four seals of Spanish wax on the strings, three on one side and one on the other. These seals, Bragadin tells me, are his own and one of Count Martinengo's. He further adds that this packet contains his secret and his Will. After that we all separated and went our ways." The government could hardly look for any greater marks of honesty. They now possessed Bragadin's "spirit of gold," and the receipt for making it, sealed with his own *intaglio* showing the figures of Philosophy and Truth.

But in the mean time, the good effects of this apparent candour ran a serious danger of being destroyed. The Brescian nugget had been tested, and found to be silver, coloured with bronze. This discovery might have put an end for ever to Bragadin and his secret, but that rumours of it reached his ears, and he made a countermove to efface its injurious results. A few days after hearing the report of the assayers in the mint, the Council of Ten received from several of its own members an account of certain events which had taken place in the house of Contarini, where Bragadin had volunteered a demonstration of his powers. He had gone through his usual performance with his crucible, his orange and black powders, his wax and coloured water, and at the close he had made this speech, holding the contents of the crucible in his hand: "Gentlemen," he said, " take the gold ; bear true witness to what you have seen ; test it at your leisure. I hear that the piece which I made in the presence of Count Martinengo has been tested in your mint, and is said not to be pure gold. I affirm that they mistake ; it is pure gold. I will take a bit of this to test it" (and with that he cut off a piece with his knife), " and then we shall see who is wrong. I have come here of my own free will, to serve my natural prince. I rely upon his safe-conduct, and I assure you that I make no pretensions, nor desire aught but to live and die

Marco Bragadin the Cipriot." Twice during his career on Venetian territory, Bragadin had performed his operation of projection ; both times reluctantly and at a pinch. On both occasions it had served his purpose for a time, and allayed a growing suspicion. But this was a bank upon which he could not draw for ever. One more draft and his account will be run out, his cheque dishonoured and himself undone.

After hearing the report of their members, the council hesitated again ; they thought the matter worth further consideration ; and on the 13th of December the Senate appointed a committee of the governors of the mint, " to deal with this affair as quickly, dexterously, and prudently as possible, that we may find out the very truth upon the matter ; persuading Bragadin with friendly exhortations to give us satisfaction on the point." So Bragadin was on his last trial—was face to face with the moment crucial for his prospects in Venice.

VII. ON THE GUIDECCA.

Hitherto we have followed Bragadin's career from the inside only. To the outer world, however, his position appeared very different. There were no signs of immediate collapse, no appearance of a rotten core, no indication of doubtful foothold. To Venice he had come as the great Marco Bragadin, philosopher and alchemist, creator and dispenser of gold, world-famous and holy man, to whom the government showed all honour and regard. The great nobles, greedy for wealth. gave him a ready welcome, and supplied him with funds on which they hoped to gain an honest cent. per cent. The people, ready to adopt the fashion of the moment, believed in the Divine origin of his gift, and were ready to stone those who should utter a doubt. Even before his arrival Bragadin had secured many wealthy and powerful connections ; the families of Contarini, Dolfin, Dandolo, and Cornaro claimed friendship with him, and so his arrival in Venice was, in appearance, a triumphant success. He hired the beautiful palace of the Dandoli on the Guidecca,* with its gardens, *cortili*, fountains, and *loggie* looking over the lagoon, and there he established himself with an immense retinue of servants, actors, and musicians, and entertained his noble friends at masques and balls and banquets of regal magnificence. In fact, the *pura fascinatione* of Signor Marco and his golden reputation reigned supreme in Venice for a while. He possessed many gifts which attracted people, talking well and playing several instruments ; while, to support his character as alchemist and intimate of the secret world, he was followed wherever he went by two enormous black dogs with gold collars round their necks ; and it did not take the people long to determine that these two hounds were his familiar spirits. Gold there evidently was in the house on the Guidecca, but as yet it had come chiefly from the pockets of others, and not from Marco's laboratory. But, for all that, the *éclat* was brilliant, and the fame of Bragadin and his golden secret spread far beyond Venice. This is the account which a learned con-

* Sansovino, " Venezia, Città nobilissima e Singolare," *in vita* " Cicogna."

temporary sends to a friend. "It is true," he writes, "that I have been to Venice to gain some information about this famous Mamugnà. They say that he really is able to transmute metals, and therefore many nobles run after him in the hope of having their debts paid. They court and almost adore him, and the least title they give him is that of 'most illustrious.' Presents pour in from all sides, even from princes. The price of coal, philosophers' cloaks, and crucibles has gone up. Every one professes mammonry. If you want my opinion, I don't believe a word of it. *Species rerum transmutari non possunt.*" *

Bragadin's success was certainly great. But underneath this blaze of notoriety there lay the ominous order of the Senate, calling his case for immediate judgment, with its rigid and uncompromising demand to know "the truth of these matters." And his admirers, his noble and needy friends, were growing impatient, and reiterated their desire *di subito veder oro*—to see gold straightway. This caused much uneasiness to Bragadin ; for, as he carefully explained, gold could not be seen in this sudden and summary way ; a philosopher requires, above all things, time and a "serene mind." But explanations were hardly acceptable while debts remained to be paid and promises fulfilled. In fact, the gale of public fame and private impatience was driving the alchemist's bark further and faster than he desired, and in the background hung the order of the Senate, waiting to be discharged.

* Giovanni Bonifacio, "Lettere," No. 78 (Rovigo : 1627).

VIII. "TILL GOD INSPIRES."

The resolution of the Senate was communicated to Bragadin two days after Christmas. He had calculated on rousing cupidity, securing confidence, and then delaying all action from month to month upon the plea of requiring leisure, while he lived upon the credulity and the gold of others. But the rapidity of the government upset his scheme. Reluctantly, "*renitente volontà*," with shrinking will, he turned to give battle to a power he could not hope to control. In answer to the request of the committee, he forwarded a letter to the doge *—an interminable windy letter, whose core and meaning is reached only after much difficulty and wading through pages of bitter complaint that the proofs of his power which he has already given have not secured him credence. He assures the doge "that it is his nature to act spontaneously, and not when he is forced. For this power is a great gift from God, and he would leave God to make use of him as he pleases." He concludes—some instinct that excuses would not avail compelling him —by an appeal to the cupidity of the government: "I do not desire to deceive you in aught, and if compelled I can, in a very short time, convert my powder into purest gold. But I warn you that if I act thus we shall lose the notable advantage to be derived from allowing the powder to multiply, which I can cause it to do at the rate of three hundred per cent. This would take a long time, but at the end I could, with

---

* "Revista Vienese," *ut sup.*

part of this multiplied powder, produce a sum sufficient to allow you to taste the benefit of my skill, while the rest I would put to breed again. Your Serenity, then, must choose whether you will at once see that gold which my powder can now make—it will be a comparatively insignificant amount—or will you let me put it to multiply? Finally, I beg that in any case I may not be disturbed during these holy days of Christmas; that I may have leisure to attend to my soul's health, the repose of my body, the soothing of my tormented spirit, and, in short, that I may prepare myself for the service of your Serenity."

Bragadin's friends were for taking him at his own time and waiting till the inspiration came to him. But the committee, with the imperative order of the Senate upon them, refused to delay. They continued to urge Bragadin, while he floundered deeper and deeper into the mire, from which he knew that there was no escape compatible with success. On the 29th of December he sent a formal communication to the committee. He "begged to be left alone that week, as he was attending to his soul; he had confessed, and hoped to take the sacrament, and so receive a holy joy. But next week he would comply with their demands." The answer came back that his request was reasonable, that he might take his own time, but must appoint a day in the following week. The day agreed on was the 6th of January, Epiphany.

IX. AT THE PALACE.[*]

"On the 6th of January," so runs the report, "Bragadin and Martinengo came to visit the doge. They asked if he would like to see the operation performed, and a proof made of Bragadin's power. The doge replied in the affirmative, and a servant was despatched to buy a pound of quicksilver and a crucible; while the privy councillors, the heads of the law court, and the masters of the mint were summoned to attend. A fire of coal was prepared in the doge's private chamber; and when the servant returned with the quicksilver and the crucible, Signor Marco took the crucible in his hand and said that it was too large for the quantity of silver, and that he would have required a fire twice as large. Then he explained to all that by reason of its high edges the crucible was of no use, and took another smaller one which he had with him. This he handed round to the company, that they might see whether there was anything in it or no; and all saw that it was clean and free from suspicion. Then he took the quicksilver and folded it in the handkerchief of Pasquale Cicogna, the doge's nephew, and pressed it out into a plate of white metal; and because it had not all come out of the handkerchief, he squeezed it again, and made the rest pass through, and flung away some dirt that remained in the handkerchief. Then he took the plate and handed it to Galeazzo Secco, the doge's chancellor, and wished him to pour the silver into

[*] " Cod. Cicogna," *ut sup*.

the crucible; but the chancellor was afraid of spilling it, so Signor Bragadin himself poured it out. Then he took a small folded paper, which he opened, and inside was seen a very fine orange-coloured powder. Then, turning to the illustrious Alexander Zorzi, Bragadin said, 'Do you recognize it? Look at it well; is it some of my medicine from the mint?' Then he took a little on the point of a knife and threw it on the quicksilver in the crucible. After this he opened another paper containing some black stuff in small pieces, and threw one of the pieces into the crucible, saying that it was of no value; and to prove it threw the rest, paper and all, into the fire. Then he took a piece of red wax and placed it in the crucible on the top of the silver. One of the council said, 'If that stuff is of no importance why do you put it into the crucible?' and Marco replied, 'I don't intend you to know why I put it there; I mean to keep that secret to myself.' Then, when he was about to take up the crucible, he said, 'I must shake the sleeves of my cloak well, so that no one may say that I have slipped gold into the crucible.' So he shook them well, twice over. Then, taking the crucible, he said, 'If you do not all of you presently acknowledge that this stuff is gold, I am ready to be branded a scoundrel.' Then he called Quirini and Zorzi to see him put the crucible on the fire, and to witness the operation; and, turning to the doge, he said, 'Serene prince, will it please your Serenity to come nearer, for this operation is performed on your behalf.' So his Serenity rose and came to look on, while Quirini sat down on a bench near the fire.

Then Signor Marco put the crucible on the coals, and began to blow, and made the others help him. And presently one heard the stuff beginning to boil, and making a noise as though one had thrown salt on the fire; and this went on some little while. Then Priuli, the councillor, rising to see what was going forward, said, "One would think they were frizzling pitch by the noise it makes.' After a bit Signor Marco. raising the lid so that we could see the quicksilver boiling, cried, 'You see how it boils. All this will soon be gold;' and he put the lid on again, and covered it over with live coal, and set to blowing once more. And when the boiling and frizzling had ceased somewhat, he called for a pitcher of water, and taking the crucible off the fire, he put it in the pitcher, plunging it well in. Then he drew it out immediately, and, placing the crucible on the window-sill, he took out a lump of gold of the shape of the crucible, and handed it round for all to see and examine. The councillor Donado alone kept always in the distance, without caring to see anything."

So for the third time Bragadin had made his famous operation in the hope of delaying exposure. But this was his last attempt to draw upon an exhausted account. Two days after the scene at the palace, the assayers of the mint handed in their report: "Glory to God. Test made of a lump of metal committed to us by the masters of the mint, which is found by us, testers in the mint, to contain four carats of silver and four carats of bronze." With this brief and final document Bragadin's career and prospects in Venice are closed for ever. Some few of his acquaintances still clung to him, inspired by cupidity that could not believe itself baulked, or, as in the case of Martinengo, by a real belief in Bragadin that rose superior to all failure. But the tide of popularity ebbed more rapidly than it had flowed; and for the Carnival of 1590 Paolo Sarpi invented the masquerade of Bragadin, the Mammon God.* The people hooted him openly in the streets; and, after enduring the contumely for a month or more, he escaped to Padua, where the Cornari offered him a house and protection.

X. FLIGHT.

Little more remains to be told; but that little lies outside Venice. It was not the Venetians who were to score off and close for ever Bragadin's reckoning with the world. The pressure of his debts, the pursuit of his creditors, who had already secured the sequestration of his goods, and his proximity to Venice, made Padua by no means a safe or pleasant home for Bragadin. Moreover, the Senate had considered a proposal to arrest and punish the man who had fooled it. The motion was rejected solely on the ground that such action would compromise the dignity of the state, and publish the fact that the Venetians had been gulled. Worse than all, Bragadin could not trust his host Cornaro, who still pretended to believe in his gift, and continued to clamour for gold.

* Bianchi-Giovani, "Biog. di Frà Paolo Sarpi," i. 110, 111. See Cicogna, "Miscel.," 1919, where a popular song on Bragadin may be found.

These circumstances alarmed Bragadin so much that he resolved to quit Venetia. But where should he go? He had already received a letter from the duke of Bavaria, couched in the most flattering terms, addressed to "The Most Illustrious Marco Bragadin, my dearest friend," * assuring him that the fame of his secret had spread throughout all Germany, and asking to be numbered among his admirers. Bavaria then was open to him. The other alternative was France. He had written to Henry IV., having reason to believe that at the French court he would find a ready welcome and honourable terms. Henry replied to his ambassador at Venice, enclosing a letter for Bragadin, and ordering De Maisse to open negotiations with the alchemist.† The letter is a curious specimen of the attitude upon which Bragadin and his fellows could always count—a mixture of curiosity and hope, a desire to see the new thing, and a lurking expectation that there was some truth in the man's pretensions; enough, at least, to justify a trial. But Bragadin never received Henry's letter; for the French ambassador replied to his master that the alchemist was a miserable charlatan, already exploded, and therefore he would not deliver the king's enclosure. So Bragadin resolved to seek refuge in Bavaria. On the 6th of August he set out for a ride in the country, as he said. He galloped to Bassano, passed the Alps without stopping, and reached Landshut, near Munich, where the duke was residing.

* "Cod. Cicogna," *ut sup*. † Daru, *op. cit.*, xxviii.

XI. "VELUT VOLATILIS FUGIT UMBRA."

Then follows a most singular series of letters * from Bragadin to his friends, announcing his honourable reception at the Bavarian court, the growing importance of his position, his intimate relations with the duke. By his own account, which the duke's letters in a measure confirm, Bragadin was once more on the full flood of success, enjoying a St. Martin's summer of renown, blossoming again in the warmth of princely favours. The duke, he says, is "a very saint, worthy to be adored for his innate goodness and his angelic temper." He has taken a wonderful fancy to Bragadin ; has promised to obtain his absolution at Rome : "My dear and sweet lord is only waiting the election of the new pope. I cannot express myself better than by saying that I seem to be dealing with an angel from Paradise. I only wish those rich old gluttons at Venice, puffed up with ignorance, could see the way my dear and only prince treats me. He often says, 'I am all-content if only Signor Bragadin be with me.'" And the duke writes to the Cornari in terms almost as warm. A very pretty duet ; Bragadin's *pura fascinatione* is clearly at work once more. Then follow invitations, in Bragadin's name, to the whole Cornaro family, and a present of four magnificent carriage horses, from the duke, to bring them to Munich. The postal service between the capital and Innsbruck is placed at Marco's disposal. He receives a monopoly

* "Revista Vienese," *ut sup.*

of all the corn in Bavaria, and offers to make a present of some to the doge ; for Venice is in need of grain, and Bragadin wishes to bear no ill will to his natural prince. But the affair did not go smoothly, and only a miserable little dribblet found its way into the granaries of Venice. Meantime Marco is not neglecting his "philosophy," * and writes continually for glass retorts, mortars, vials, jars, from the furnaces of Murano; for minerals, drugs, "Cyprian balsam of terebinth ;" all things, in short, that are " necessary for a great and skilled philosopher at work upon distillation ;" for the duke is waiting till *anima d'oro* shall generate, multiply, and finally produce gold.

But, as was inevitable with a charlatan, this apparent success rested upon a rotten foundation. This time the weak point was Bragadin's relations with Rome—a point where the ground had already trembled beneath his feet. His absolution and release from his monastic vows were not yet secured. All had been put in order through the kind offices of a Spanish priest, an intimate of the pope, and Sixtus was ready to sign the necessary dispensations whenever Bragadin should pay the sum of twelve thousand ducats into the papal treasury ; the owner of *anima d'oro* could afford that amount. But Bragadin's collapse at Venice rendered it impossible for him to come by the ducats at once, and the whole matter hung fire. Meantime, Sixtus died, and Pope Gregory, with whom the alchemist had now to deal, was a man of singular purity and austerity of manners. When

* " Filosofia " is frequently used to express both witchcraft and alchemy. Cf. " La Signora di Monza."

the duke of Bavaria's representative, Minutio, mentioned the case, his Holiness would not hear of any indulgence, and seems to have expressed an opinion that the duke should rather make an end of a scamp, an apostate friar, more than suspected of dealings with the powers of darkness. With this angry message Minutio left Rome for Munich.

While this storm was gathering in the south, the sky was still serene in Bavaria. The duet between the duke and Bragadin goes on. There is a crescendo of satisfaction in Marco's letters about himself. Suddenly these cease, and we hear that he is in prison; that he is secretly tried, confesses, and is condemned to lose his head, and to be burned as a sorcerer, his two black dogs along with him.* Minutio had arrived from Rome; the duke found himself baulked of his desire to see gold. The combination was fatal to Bragadin.

So sank his castles in the air, and vanished into thin smoke. Marco Bragadin, his dogs, his jars, his *anima d'oro*, fall back into the obscurity whence they had emerged for a while; the dark gulf closes over them—*velut volatiles fugiunt umbræ*. From the very first there was never any hope of permanent success. Bragadin is a type peculiar to his age. There were hundreds of adventurers like him roaming over Europe. The interest of their problem lies in this: What end did these men really propose to themselves? How did they forecast their career so as to secure anything like a permanent success? It is probable that they did not look for permanence; it did not

* See "Revista Vienese." He was executed April 27, 1591.

U

enter into their scheme. They traded on curiosity, greed, credulity, on the weaknesses of their contemporaries. They intended to make for each day sufficient for each day's needs. Their skill consisted in playing with circumstances, in combining or counterposing the people with whom they came in contact. The excitement of the game was its own sufficient reward. It did not matter that it was a game which could have one issue only—failure in the end.

CATERINA CORNARO, QUEEN OF CYPRUS.

IT is of Caterina Cornaro, lady of Asolo, queen of Jerusalem, Cyprus, and Armenia, that we have to speak : a daughter of Venice, born in that heyday of Venetian splendour, the close of the fifteenth century and the opening years of the sixteenth. The lust of the eye and the pride of life, the confident, unhesitating assertion of sensuous emotion, were declaring themselves as principles of being ; the flower of pleasurable existence was breaking from bud to blossom, to ripen later and fall in that Dead Sea fruit of seventeenth-century corruption. Venice had won her wealth ; she was turning now to the use of it ; baring her bosom to the joyous and seductive air, blown from the distant salt sea, bright yet soothing, languid and caressing, penetrating and pervading all with its magical perfume, that stirred the soul and drew it to a very ocean of rapturous delight. She opened her heart and throbbed to the sweetness and love of her sea-girt home ; she opened her eyes and drank the changeful symphonies of colour that, morning and evening, flamed upon her water-ways. Her artists caught upon their palettes the reflection of sunsets seen from the Zattere, and laid with free hand this glow upon their canvases;

while the golden glory of Venetian women grew there, large like their skies, soft and undulating as their ocean floor, clear as the morning light, aureoled with hair of midday splendour, robed in a colour that was learned from their sunsets. "Spartam nactus es ; hanc orna." Venice had asked for no Arcadia ; her little Sparta of the mud islands she had claimed, held, made beautiful ; and now, should she not enjoy it?

If we wish to know what the women of this ample Venetian life looked like, we must turn to the pictures of Titian. There, in his Venus of the tribune, large-limbed and golden on the white sheets, or in his Flora with full breasts and down-hanging hair, or, higher and better still, in his Madonna of the ecstatic, upraised face, with arms outstretched and breeze-lifted locks, ecstatic, it is true, but not with any super-terrestrial ecstasy—there it is that we shall find them. But should we desire to learn what these women were, not in body only, but in heart and mind ; if it be their daily life we wish to scrutinize, to see them in their homes about their business—we are left but poorly off, and have to be content with such scraps of knowledge and such inward glimpses as may be caught from the comedies of their day, or from the few Venetian novelettes of Bandello and his brother raconteurs.

One thing is clear about their manner of living ; this wide luxury, this abundant life, was not for all the women of Venice. A curious calculation * has been made, from which it would seem that, out of seven hundred noble ladies, not more than sixty or seventy

* Yriarte, "La Vie d'un Patricien de Venise" (Paris : 1874), cap. ii.

were in the habit of appearing daily in public; the others remained close shut in their houses, except upon festivals and great public functions. It was the courtesans who freely used and freely enjoyed the diurnal splendour of Venetian habit. They were always *en evidence*, present on the piazza; their gondolas to be met out on the lagoons, by San Spirito or the Lido; their liveries became well known; their doings and their sayings were the subject of the people's gossip; round them the popular interest settled. The great ladies remained, for the most part, a shadow and a name; they were seen once or twice, perhaps, in the year, upon one of those state ceremonies when the noble houses vied with each other in the wealth of jewellery and the richness of the robes worn by their *gentildonne*. But even on such occasions as a ball in the ducal palace, given to some wandering prince, the courtesans held their own, and the more renowned among them were sure of invitations, though, at times like this, the Venetian nobleman took care that, in splendour of dress at least, his mistress should not eclipse his wife. It was a free and brilliant life that these women led; they affected a gorgeousness of dress —rich coloured silks or velvets or Eastern stuffs—which distinguished them from the noble lady whose everyday wear was the long and simple black silk *cappa*. Their houses were furnished to the furthest point the sumptuary laws would allow. If a Venetian gentleman desired conversation, wit, music, even such politics as the vigilance of the Three permitted—all, in short, that we mean by a *salon*—it was to their drawing-rooms that he had to go. It was there, and not in his own house, that he would meet Titian and Sanso-vino the architect ; or, if he desired a lampoon on his foe, Pietro Aretino, with his daughters Adria and Austria. Venice was tuned to a high note of pleasure, and the atmosphere of these drawing-rooms was cal-culated to delight a trained sensibility ; for many of the women were greatly accomplished — fine musicians; brilliant talkers; sometimes, like Veronica Franco, skilled writers of the sonnet and that curious polished verse which says so little and says it so beautifully.

Very different was the lot of the noble ladies. They lived from their girlhood in an Eastern seclusion; as carefully and as jealously shut away as though they were the inmates of some Turkish seraglio. The Venetian men had imbibed their views on domestic matters from the East; in every department that which touched them intimately was coloured from Byzantium ; their deepest-rooted instincts, habits and forms were Oriental. They did not keep eunuchs as a guard upon their women, it is true ; but they had a hundred jealous eyes always on the watch, and no Venetian would think of leaving home for long without a word to some more trusted servant.* At all events, they took advantage of one fashion in favour among Venetian ladies, and by flattery they induced them to wear a veritable instrument of torture which prevented them from straying far afield : pattens of an enormous size were in vogue, and the mania for increasing the height grew, until at length

* The Arsenal museum affords a proof of the extent to which this brutal and insulting suspicion could be carried.

a lady could not walk without the help of two attendants, on whose shoulders the giantess leaned her hands. One day the French ambassador was in conversation with the doge, and touching on this topic, he remarked that such a fashion must be most incommodious. The doge admitted that no doubt ordinary shoes would be more convenient, when one of the councillors broke in with, "Yes, far, far too convenient."* The cynical suspicion expressed in this story suggests a far from happy life for nobly born Venetian dames.

The married women were not, however, the greatest sufferers in a Venetian household ; they saw the world upon the great church feasts or the public ceremonies of state, and on such occasions they received full liberty to indulge their taste for jewellery and dress. But the young girls never stirred outside their doors except to go to mass or confession in the neighbouring *parrocchia ;* and then they were jealously followed by some old and faithful nurse, and their beauty carefully hidden beneath the long white *fazzuolo.* The young men had to be content with their slight opportunities, and they made the most of them. The loves of many a Venetian story begin with some chance meeting in an aisle, some ardent glances exchanged while waiting for the *padre*, or the touch of a skirt in the narrow *calle* between the house door and the church. This jealous watchfulness was extended to all teachers as well; to music-masters, dancing-masters, governesses. The head of a Venetian household disliked the presence under his roof of any one

* St. Disdier, "La Ville et la Republique de Venise," part iii.

who was not entirely a dependent. And experience may have taught him that he was right; for, as it was, very often the old and trusted nurse would find her bowels of sympathy too deeply stirred to be withstood, and by hook or crook the lover of the church door or the *calle* would win his way to meeting, brief perhaps, but bright. But that was a happy fortune not always granted to Venetian maids; and, for the most part, the result of such jealous guarding was that the girl received no sort of education. Nor had she that other feminine resource and occupation of dress; for at home she was confined to the simplest clothing, and not a jewel was given her except, perhaps, a little gold cross or a modest silver chain; a flower from the garden, a carnation or a rosebud, she might put in her hair, just above her ear, but that was all. What else could she dream of then, the long dull day, but a lover or her wedding morning? For marriage meant liberty to her; then she would have music lessons, and a dancing-master, and servants, and a gondola, and invitations to the ducal balls. One occupation she had daily, and that was to sit for hours in the sun upon the housetop,* with all her hair drawn out through the top of a crownless straw hat, each lock soaked in unguents and carefully separated so that they fell in a veil all round her head. There she sat, bleaching her tresses in the sun till they grew to that glowing Venetian gold. Or in the afternoon girls of her own age and fate might come to keep her company, each with her old *dueña*, who

* The platforms where they sat were called *altane*. See Cesare Vecellio, "Habiti Antichi e Moderni" (Venezia; 1590), No, 119.

chattered and scolded in the inner court, while they would sit in those little squares of high-walled garden with a cypress rising on either side of the tall, barred gate. Stories they told one another, of what they fancied love was like on the other side of the walls, or floating in a gondola across the moon-lit lagoon. Songs, too, of the nursery, learned in the cradle from those old women whose voices reached them from the courtyard now—caught from

> "Bona sera ai vivi ;
> E riposo ai morti poveri ;
> Bon viaggio ai naviganti ;
> E bona notte ai tutti quanti : "

or—

> "Lei non m'amava, no ! "

some high-tenored gondolier as he rowed along the little canal below their windows. They had games of ball, with forfeits, now and then, if the weather was not too warm, in the large rooms where the balconies hung above the canal. And when the cats were away surely these prisoned mice might play a little, and steal out on to the balcony at the sound of some singing voice they knew; and then bright smiles, and the wave of an arm, and the carnation from the hair thrown down to the hands that waited for it below. And then, sometimes, love would laugh at locksmiths, and balconies seem made for rope-ladders, and night and the small canals are dark, and gondoliers may be found trusty; and a secret marriage would follow, or else a runaway one, and then came tears and scandal, unless, as Bianca Capello did, the girl should end by wedding a grand duke of

Tuscany. But these, we may suppose, were rare occurrences, and the life of a Venetian girl of quality was dull and uneventful, and her one escape, in marriage, did not offer a much brighter prospect. All she could look for were ropes of pearls, the real passion of every Venetian woman, more long and solemn ceremonies, a visit each *la sensa* to the Merceria,* where the puppet stood that changed its fashions to the Paris mode every Ascension Day; or, if her husband were a *podestà*, a captain, or *prov-veditor*, she might hold a little court at Bergamo or Brescia, and have the pleasure of being the greatest lady there.

For Caterina, however, queen of Cyprus, a more stirring though less placid fate was in store. She was born on St. Catherine's Day, in 1454, the child of Marco Cornaro and Fiorenza. his wife.† The Cornari were a very noble Venetian house, and, as so many Venetians did, they tried to heighten their ancestral value by claiming the blood of the Roman Cornelii for their veins. On her mother's side Caterina had, unquestionably, an imperial lineage; her great-grandfather was John Comnene, emperor of Trebizond. Queen of Jerusalem, Cyprus, and Armenia, child of

---

* See Yriarte, "La Vie d'un Patricien de Venise," cap. ii.

† Her descent on her mother's side was distinguished (Romanin, "Storia Docum. di Ven.," vol. iv. lib. xi. cap. iii.)—

John Comnene.
|
Valenza = Nicolo Crispo, duke of Naxos.
|
Fiorenza = Marco Cornaro.
|
Caterina.

the emperor of Trebizond, mother of the prince of Galilee—what a curious collection of vague, shadowy, half-real titles ! But as yet they lie in the distance, and Caterina is only a little Venetian girl, living the quiet home life of other Venetian maids. We may fancy her, like St. Ursula in Carpaccio's picture, asleep, lying straight out in her gaunt-posted bed with the old red hangings, the sheet tucked close beneath her chin, where the delicate hand and wrist are nestling; the small, bare room, with a seat or two, the open window where the cool, fresh, sweet sea air blows softly in with the morning light, bowing the heads of the carnation flowers in their pot by the window-sill, bearing on its wings the few and early strokes of the campanile's bell. But the angel that comes through the opened door, bringing those morning dreams that are true, brings not to her, any more than to St. Ursula, tidings of peace. The dreams that come with him are dreams of that "Fortunate Isle" floating on the far Levantine waters, of Cyprus, "the mother city of delights," of pomp and splendour, of a royal crown, of death and murder, of merciless treachery. But the angel is Destiny, and he has no tears for so much goodness, youth, and beauty born to such a fate.

We cannot now paint a portrait of Caterina with any certainty of likeness. It is impossible to obtain a close view of the queen as she really was; she speaks too seldom in history—indeed, only once, and that when the pain of her life was bitterest upon her. All that we can do is to sketch her figure upon the wide canvas of her story, catching hints for our study from contemporary chroniclers and artists. We can show her drawn to Cyprus in pride and expectation, wounded there by death and treachery, crushed by Venice of the velvet paws, sinking quietly down the hill of life at last in the sunny seclusion of Castle Asolo.

We must leave her then for the present, asleep in her Venetian chamber, and turn to the place whither she is surely drifting, to Cyprus and the court of the Lusignan. It was a dark background for Caterina's bright young life to stand relieved against. The kingdom of Cyprus passed, by sale, from Richard Cœur de Lion to Guy de Lusignan in 1192. Guy's brother and heir, Almerico, married Isabella, queen of Jerusalem and Armenia, and thus both these titles became united to that of Cyprus. The crown descended for two centuries through a succession of Ugos, Almericos, and Pierres, till 1426, when King Jan Lusignan was made a prisoner by the Mamelukes of Egypt, and bought his liberty by the promise of an annual tribute to their soldan. Jan was succeeded by his son, John the Second, a man of infirm character,[*] easily led by the women about him, and married, for the second time, to one of singular strength, ambition, and unscrupulousness, Elena Paleologus, daughter of the tyrant of the Morea. The queen Elena was a woman of that type so often produced by the palace life of Eastern courts. Like Eudoxia, Irene, or Pulcheria, she was mistress of

---

[*] " Vir muliere corruptior," says Æneas Sylvius of him, *op. omnia* (Basileæ : 1551), p. 379. Hen. Giblet, " Hist. de' re Lusignani" (Bologna : 1647), lib. x.

intrigue, and determined to govern both her husband and his kingdom. She brought with her from her home those principles of policy which shrank from no cruelty, which dwelt among the inner chambers of the seraglio, and moved by secret stairs, by venal courtiers, by treachery and poison. When Elena reached the Cyprian court, she found that King John had one child, a bastard boy, called James,* the son of his mistress, the beautiful Maria Patras. James was bright, brave, ambitious, and popular; he had inherited his mother's gift of great beauty, and the king was infinitely devoted to him. There was every probability that, though a bastard, he would be named heir to the crown. The queen, however, gradually asserted her power over her husband; and in the end, by the

* Vianoli, "Historia Veneta" (Venezia : 1680), lib. xix. b. 675 : "Restava (James) nella nudità della mera qualità naturale che riceve dalla madre ;" Æneas Sylvius, *op. omn. edit. cit.*, p. 579: "Natus est magni spiritus adolescens." This is the pedigree of James (Malipiero, "Annali Veneti," Archiv. St. Ital., vol. vii. part ii.):

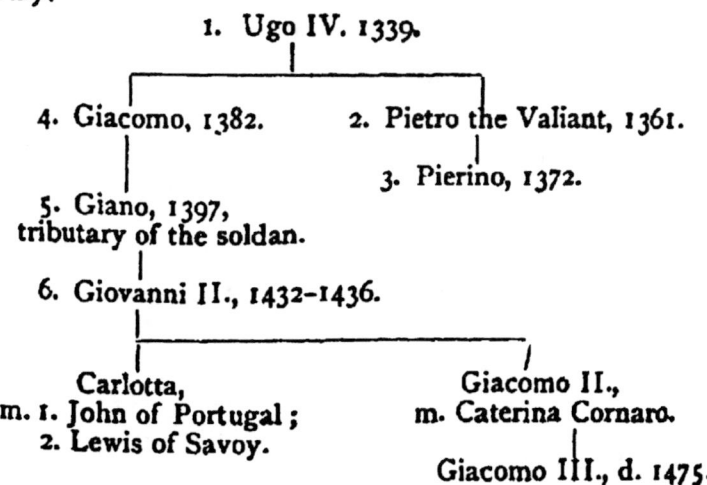

cold cruelty with which she mutilated Maria,* his mistress, she terrified John into complete submission. She saw that if she desired to rule absolutely, she must do so through her own daughter, Charlotte; but first the handsome and beloved James must be removed. Elena would have chosen his death, no doubt, as the surest way to the attainment of her object; but James's excessive popularity rendered such a course too dangerous. She determined, therefore, to destroy his hopes of the throne by compelling his father to appoint him archbishop of Nicosia. Though the boy could not then have been much more than fifteen years old, he was tonsured, consecrated in the four orders, and sent down to the palace of his See. There he led a life of considerable freedom, and mixed constantly in amours and intrigues;† but he never failed to attach all those who came near him, by his beauty and his grace. At Nicosia he also became intimately acquainted with the Venetian merchants, and especially with Andrea Cornaro, brother of Marco and uncle to Caterina. This friendship laid the foundation for the closer connection with Venice and for the marriage which were to follow.

The queen, believing that she had disposed of James, now turned her attention to the other half of her design. She intended to seek a husband for

* Queen Elena, with diabolical cruelty, deprived Maria of her nose and ears, and then sent John to visit her.

† The queen was constantly, attempting his murder, and once he nearly lost his life through the treachery of a favourite servant. But James was born under a lucky star. See Giblet, *op. cit.*, lib. x. p. 616.

Charlotte, to induce the king to resign in favour of his son-in-law, and then to reign herself, through Charlotte. Prince John, of the royal house of Portugal, was chosen. He arrived at Cyprus; the marriage was completed, and, under the direction of the queen, John assumed the reins of government. But Elena found in him a man more powerful than suited her purpose. He had resolved to rule, not in appearance only, but in fact. The queen saw her mistake, and corrected it. John was poisoned.* It now became necessary to choose a second husband for Charlotte, and this time Elena was more fortunate. Prince John's widow was betrothed to Lewis, a son of the duke of Savoy, selected because his feeble character and easy temperament made it improbable that he would oppose the queen. But before Lewis could reach Cyprus, Elena died,† and the king immediately sent for his bastard son, loaded him with caresses and favours, refused to allow him out of his sight, and showed every disposition to make him resign the mitre for the apparent title to the throne: he would certainly have named him prince of Galilee, had not death cut him short. John followed his wife within a very few months, and Charlotte, who was still waiting the arrival of her husband, was proclaimed queen.

---

* Æneas Sylvius, *op. omn. edit. cit.*, p. 379; Giblet, *op. cit.*, iib. x. p. 592.

† The queen died in 1458; King John on the 24th July the same year. See Mas Latrie, "Histoire de l'Ile de Chypre," Doc. vol. iii. No. xiv. The island was most unhealthy: death after death occurred every summer during the heats. See Capo-di-lista's journey to Cyprus, ap. Mas Latrie, *loc. cit.*

James took the oath of allegiance to his sister, and
then endeavoured to leave the court in order to return
to Nicosia. But his intentions there were suspected,
and he was arrested by the constable of the island,
detained a prisoner, and some attempt was made to
poison him.* Thanks to his innumerable friends, and
to the strength of the party which preferred a male
succession to the crown, James escaped and reached
Nicosia, with every determination to make an effort
to unseat his sister. His friend, Andrea Cornaro,
encouraged him with hopes of Venetian aid, feeling
sure that the republic, out of jealousy for Genoa, who
had espoused the cause of Charlotte, would gladly
win an ascendency in the island by helping James to
the throne. Charlotte, in the greatest alarm, urged
Lewis to hasten his coming. The prince of Savoy
passed through Venice, and reached Cyprus before
the archbishop could complete any plan of action.
James declined to risk his life, and, with the help of
the Venetians, he fled to Alexandria, to the court
of the soldan, the titular superior of the Cyprian
crown.

There James pleaded his sex, always a powerful
argument in the Eastern mind, and excused his ille-
gitimacy, which Oriental nations have seldom considered a bar to succession. He further urged upon
the soldan that a crown tributary to him was being
disposed of without his advice or consent. James
is also said to have made a formal recantation† of

* Georgio Bustron. MSS. Arund., Brit. Mus., No. 518, fol.
21ᵛᵒ., given by Mas Latrie, *op. cit.*, Doc. No. xv.

† The document is a curious one, and is given by Mas

Christianity in order to clinch the favour of the Mahomedans. The document was eventually sent to Pius the Second, and became one of the reasons why the Holy See always showed itself so hostile to James. But there is very little doubt that the whole of this episode of the recantation, as well as the document produced to attest it, was nothing but a forgery by the knights of Rhodes, who were warm partisans of Charlotte. Whether the archbishop ever signed such a monstrous deed or not, his success at the soldan's court proved complete. His beauty helped him to the favour of all who heard him plead his case, and the charm of his manner created a *furore* in his favour. In the hall of the palace and surrounded by his Mamelukes, the soldan ordered James, then twenty-two years old, to be robed and crowned king of Cyprus,† and adopted him as his own son. From his new father James received a convoy of ships and a detachment of Mamelukes; with these he sailed to claim his kingdom. He landed at Cyprus, and city after city fell or yielded without a struggle. Only two castles, those of Famagosta and Cerines, made any resistance, but they presently

Latrie, *op. cit.*, vol. iii. p. 110. Æneas Sylvius also refers to it, *op. omn. edit. cit.*, p. 580. One or two phrases will show its character: "Et negabo deitatem, et adorabo humanitatem," "luxuriabor cum hebrea super altare," etc.

† For the success of James at Alexandria, see Mas Latrie, *op. cit.*, vol. iii. Doc. p. 99, ad ann. 1460; Æneas Sylvius, *op. et edit. cit.*, p. 579; Malipiero, "Annali Veneti," p. 596; Sanudo, "Vite dei Duchi," ap. Muratori, Rer. It. Scrip., tom. xxii. p. 1185; Navagero, "Storia Veneziana," ap. Murat., *op. cit.*, tom. xxiii.

x

surrendered. Lewis fled from Cyprus and returned to his father's court. The queen Charlotte withdrew first to Rhodes, and then to Rome, there to implore the aid of Pope Pius against her brother and his infidel allies.

James was firmly placed upon the throne. But he saw arrayed against him the Genoese, whom he had expelled from the island, the duke of Savoy, in the interest of Charlotte, and the pope, who refused to acknowledge his title and had received his ambassadors with very scant courtesy. He could look for no sure support from the soldan, who was more likely to seize Cyprus for his own than to undertake wars in defence of James. It was imperative that the king should find an alliance elsewhere, and marriage seemed the easiest method for cementing one. The preponderance in Cyprus could not fail to be a tempting dowry, and the chief competitors for King James's hand were Naples, Venice, and the princes of the Morea. Venice appeared first in the field. James's old friend, Andrea Cornaro, pointed out to him that the republic was his firmest support, and that it was to her he should contract himself. Andrea therefore proposed a match between the king and his own niece, Caterina Cornaro. A romance has been made out of the circumstances of this suggestion. It is said that one day Andrea dropped upon the floor a miniature of Caterina ; the king picked it up. and the picture was so lovely that he became deeply enamoured of the original. But Andrea played with him. concealing the name and pretending that the portrait was that of his mistress, until he had worked the young man to a frenzy of passion.* Then he told James that this was in truth Caterina his niece, to be won only as queen of Cyprus. However that may be, whether James was moved by love alone or more by policy, he sent an embassy to Venice to ask, in form, the hand of Caterina as his queen. The Senate gladly accepted the offer in the name of Venice. They further promised to adopt the bride as a daughter of the republic, that her birth might in no way fall below that of her husband, and added a fitting dowry of one hundred thousand ducats.

The contract was signed, in 1468, by the doge, Cristoforo Moro, on the one hand, and Filippo Mastachelli, James's ambassador, on the other. The ceremony† of the betrothal took place in the hall of the Great Council. Forty noble ladies went to the Palazzo Cornaro to bring the bride to the ducal palace. There she was received by the doge, the council, the senators, and state officials. A consecrated ring was placed on Caterina's finger by Mastachelli, and Cristoforo Moro formally gave her away to James Lusignan. Then, with all the ceremony and incidents of royalty, her court reconducted her to her palace at San Polo. But her passage to Cyprus was delayed. A hitch occurred in the negotiations, and for the next four years Caterina remained at Venice, treated as a queen by her fellow-citizens, but

* Daru, "Storia della Repub. di Venezia" (Capolago : 1837), lib. xvii. p. 356.

† See Mas Latrie, *op. cit.*, vol. iii. Doc. p. 182. He gives a fragment of an anonymous chronicle at present in the National Library, Paris. The author is in complete accord with Malipiero, already cited.

more than doubtful whether she would ever wear the crown of Cyprus. For Ferdinand of Naples had been secretly endeavouring to detach James from his Venetian engagements, and strongly recommending a match with a daughter of his own house. He had agents at work for him in Cyprus—Lewis Fabrice, a Catalan, who had been created archbishop of Nicosia in spite of all the efforts of Venice to prevent the nomination, and Marin Rizzo, the king's chamberlain. James wavered between the Neapolitan and the Venetian alliance, and showed his coldness towards the latter by quarrelling with Andrea Cornaro, uncle of his *fiancée.* * The republic, however, determined to hold the king to his engagements; she was not in the habit of putting her hand to any work without carrying it through. The government sent an ambassador to the Cyprian court to explain that Venice would make the rupture of this match a public question; further, to urge James not to disgrace his royal word, solemnly given by his own ambassador, nor yet to put this slight upon the queen already pledged to him. Venice promised to take the island under her protection whenever the king should fulfil his contract. The attitude of Caterina's guardian and his own personal inclination determined James to abandon the Neapolitan connection. In 1471 his representatives were sent to Venice to bring his queen to Cyprus. There still remained one ceremony to be performed. Caterina was brought from her palace to the Church of St. Mark, and there, before the high altar, the doge adopted her as

* Mas Latrie, *op. cit.*, vol. iii. Doc. pp. 307, 310, 311, 312, and 316; Romanin, *op. cit.*, vol. iv. lib. xi. cap. iii.

a child of the republic.* She was now no longer a Cornaro, but Caterina Veneta Lusignan, a daughter of Venice. Venice took the parents' vows for her child; we shall see how well she kept them. Great rejoicing followed in the city, and, as a bystander remarked, "it seemed to each and all that the Signory had won a kingdom, as, by God's good grace, did actually happen." † Early in the next year, 1472, the Bucentaur came once more for Caterina, to speed her on her way to her new kingdom. In cloth of gold and regal train she appeared on the steps of her palace; the doge gave her his right hand, and side by side they seated themselves upon the daïs, while the great boat moved slowly down the grand canal and out to the Lido, where the admiral of the fleet was waiting with the ships that were to carry her to Cyprus and her home.

Caterina was eighteen years old. Titian has painted a portrait of her about this time, in a purple robe, with a crown and a veil upon her head and a flower in her hand. She is not tall, and rather slight in figure; beautiful, graceful, sprightly, with a witty mouth and happy countenance. Happy she must have been. She had passed suddenly from the cloistral quiet of her home to a splendour, a pomp, a destiny that her most far-winged dreams, in their widest flight, could hardly have revealed to her. The fate that was unfolding before her must have seemed

* Romanin, *loc. cit.*, July 14th, 1472; Malipiero, "Annali Veneti," pp. 597, 598.

† Paolo Morosini, "Historia della Citta di Venetia" (Venetia: 1637), lib. xx.

magical in its brilliancy. Queen of Jerusalem, Cyprus, and Armenia, surely it was like some Eastern tale come true. She was young, with that large capacity for enjoyment which the Venetians had; her husband she knew to be handsome and brave; he had won his kingdom, and, in his heart, had chosen her to be its queen; she might well rely upon her beauty and her charm to gain and keep his love; their two lives were being drawn together to the very home of the mother of love, to Paphos and to Fountain Amorous. The prospect was one of mingled magnificence and delight, unclouded, for her, by any prophetic vision.

Caterina reached Cyprus, and one brief year of quiet and of happiness was given to her. Then James died in the July heats of 1473, from a fever caught out hunting. He was only thirty-three years old, and the enemies of Venice did not hesitate to say that the fever was the result of Venetian poisons.* But between the foes of the republic at the Roman court, who bring this charge, and her friends, who as strenuously deny it, we cannot now decide. The young king died and left his wife with child. For other offspring there were three illegitimate children, two sons and one daughter named Zarla, a contraction for Charlotte. By his will† James bequeathed his kingdom to his queen and the child that should be born of her.

---

* Sismondi ("Rep. Ital.," cap. xxviii.) quotes Raynaldus, "Ann. Eccles.," as the authority for the poisoning.

† Giorgio Bustron, "Chron.," MSS. Arund., Brit. Mus., No. 518, fol. 69vo., the Will of James ; Mas Latrie, *op. cit.*, vol. iii. Doc. p. 445 ; Sanudo, *op. cit.*, p. 1197.

He appointed a commission of seven nobles, including Andrea Cornaro, to advise and support Caterina. On her death the crown was to descend to her child solely, with reversion to each of his bastard sons in order of birth, and then to his bastard daughter, in case the legitimate line should fail. The constitution of the queen's council did not give much promise of peace, for it contained such antagonistic elements as Andrea Cornaro, the Venetian, and Marin Rizzo, and John Fabrice, brother of the archbishop of Nicosia, both of whom we have already seen engaged by Ferdinand of Naples to break the match between James and Caterina.

Her troubles were beginning to close around the queen. No child had yet been born; and Cyprus was almost an open prey, lying ready to the swiftest or the strongest arm. Caterina, only nineteen years old, saw enemies on every hand. The Cypriot nobles were jealous of Venetian ascendency, and the archbishop had little difficulty in persuading them to think favourably of Ferdinand's pretensions as the surest counterbalance to the influence of the republic. Venice, as Caterina knew, would never hesitate to take her kingdom from her when the moment came. But just now the government was engaged in a close and single-handed struggle with the Turk; Venice had lost Negropont, and next year was to witness the heroic defence of Scutari, and Europe was presently to experience the shock of seeing the Turks before Otranto. So for the present Caterina might look for help and advice from her home, knowing that if the Venetians were themselves unable to occupy the island, they would never willingly allow another power to do so. There was yet a third danger besetting the queen : Charlotte renewed her claim to the throne as the sole legitimate Lusignan.

In August, 1473, a child was born to Caterina, and called James after his father. As grandson of the republic, his sponsors at the font were Mocenigo, the admiral, and the two *provveditori* * of the fleet. By the will of James, the birth of this boy should have settled all claims to the throne. But no sooner had the Venetian fleet sailed away than the arch-bishop of Nicosia, who had been maturing his plans with the king of Naples, rose in revolt. His scheme was to marry Alfonso, a bastard of Naples, to Zarla, James's illegitimate daughter. To carry out this design the archbishop, the counts of Tripoli and Jaffa, with Marin Rizzo, all three of whom had been named of the council by James, seized on the city of Famagosta, where Caterina was lying, recovering from childbirth. The town was roused by the uproar in the middle of the night. The conspirators forced their way into the palace ; Gabriel Gentile, the queen's physician, fled for safety to Caterina's own chamber, whither he was pursued by Marin, and, like David Rizzio, slain in the very arms of the queen. Her uncle Andrea and her cousin Marco Bembo were both stabbed under the walls of the castle, and their naked bodies thrown into the moat, where they lay many days within sight of the queen's windows, nor dared she take them up to bury them

---

* Malipiero, " Annali Veneti," p. 599 ; Ceppio Coriolan, " De Petri Mocenici gestis," lib. ii.

until they were half eaten by the dogs. The conspirators carried the young boy James away from his mother, and Alfonso was proclaimed prince of Galilee. Caterina, herself a close prisoner, they compelled to write a letter to the Venetian Senate, explaining that the murder of her uncle and her cousin was due to some private quarrel between them and the soldiers whose pay they had withheld.* But the Venetian consul sent home a true account of how matters stood, and orders were despatched to Mocenigo to sail at once for Cyprus, where he was to secure by any means the safety of Caterina and her son.† Mocenigo, however, had forestalled his instructions, and had already sent the *provveditor* Soranzo to the island, promising himself to follow. When Soranzo reached Cyprus, he found the conspirators quarrelling among themselves, while the

---

* Nov. 15, 1473. See despatch of Giosafat Barbaro to doge, Mas Latrie, *op. cit.*, vol. iii. Doc. p. 352. Barbaro gives an account of the events of that night: "Questa note preterita, cercha a hore XI., essendo nel letto, premeditando molte e diverse cose, alditi verso la piaza uno inusato son de campana . . . per la qual cossa chiamai suso el mio fameglio e disili chel sè dovesse far a la fenestra e star attento se el sentiva remor alguno, sentando mi ulular e latrar assaissimi cani." Roman., *loc. cit.*, Letter of Senate to Angelo de Adria, Jan. 22, 1474 : "Ma in la camera propria in conspecto di quella povera zoveneta taglioro a pezzi il suo proprio medico e un altro suo servitor e domestico. . . . Tolsero la cassa e le zoie, l'anello del sigilo e l'obbligarono a scriver lettere ai castellani di ceder loro le fortezze." Malipiero, "Annali Veneti," p. 600 ; Ceppio Coriolan, "De Petri Mocenici gestis," lib. iii. ; Sabellico, "Historia Veneta," Dec. iii. lib. ix. ; Navagero, *op. cit.*, p. 1138.

† Despatch of Senate to Mocenigo, Dec. 20, 1473, Secreti, xxvi. fol. 58 ; Mas Latrie, *op. cit.*, vol. iii. p. 362.

people of Famagosta and Nicosia had risen for the queen, and were clamorously demanding her liberation. On the approach of Mocenigo the chief conspirators fled. Order was restored and many executions followed. In obedience to injunctions from Venice, the forts were put into the hands of men wholly devoted to the republic. A review of all arms took place before the queen at Famagosta, as a display of power and a warning to the disaffected; and, in reward for his services, Caterina presented Mocenigo with a golden shield, emblazoned with the arms of Lusignan. Quiet was apparently secured, and the Venetian admiral sailed away.

Venice was beginning to lay her hand upon Cyprus; by this protection of the queen she established a right to a voice in the government of that island. In March of the following year the Senate appointed a *provveditor* and two councillors as permanent residents to assist Caterina in her government.*

But trouble on trouble pursued Caterina. In August, 1474, her boy died of fever. He was only one year old; and again the charge of Venetian poisoning was renewed, but the more obvious and more probable cause of his death was the deadly malaria † of the coast region. Caterina wrote to the Senate, telling them of her loss; and orders were given that her father, Marco Cornaro, should go to Cyprus,‡

---

* Secreti, xxvi. fol. 79 ; Mas Latrie, *loc. cit.*, p. 370 ; Romanin, *loc. cit.*

† Romanin, *op. cit.*, lib. xi. cap. 5.

‡ Nov. 11, 1474, Secreti, xxvi. fol. 152 ; Mas Latrie, *loc. cit.*, p. 398.

nominally to comfort his daughter and to bear the condolences of the republic, really to act as Venetian agent in conjunction with Giovanni Soranzo, their *provveditor*, in checking any revolt which might follow on the death of young James Lusignan. This dread of revolution was not groundless. When her nephew died, Charlotte renewed her claim to the throne, and many of the Cypriot noblemen declared for her as the last true Lusignan. She was a brave, determined woman, with the courage and the resource of her mother Elena. When the boy died, she was at the court of the soldan of Egypt, urging her legitimacy, as her brother James had urged his manhood and his beauty. Charlotte further promised, if the soldan helped her to the crown, that she would pay in full the annual tribute, which Caterina had allowed to fall into arrears. Venice was not at that moment able to undertake the defence of Cyprus against Charlotte and the soldan, but by diplomacy she succeeded in cutting the ground from under the ex-queen's feet. The *provveditor* was instructed to advise Caterina to send an embassy to the Alexandrian court with the tribute which was wanting,* and to excuse the delay on the score of the ravages committed by the locusts. Venice was really governing Cyprus and directing its policy, down to the minutest details of an apology. Caterina obeyed : her embassy was favourably received in Egypt, and Charlotte was dismissed. But she refused to cease her efforts. She returned to Italy, and continued to urge the dukes of Milan and Savoy, the Genoese,

* Secreti, xxvi. fol. 138 ; Mas Latrie, *loc. cit.*, p. 391.

and the pope to lend her their aid. Letters written by her to Genoa were intercepted and sent to Venice.* They disclosed a scheme for a descent on Cyprus already far advanced. The Venetian government ordered their admiral, Antonio Loredano, the hero of Scutari, to garrison the forts on the island,† and to arrest and send to Venice Maria Patras, the mother of James, along with his three bastard children. The marriage between young Alfonso of Naples and Zarla Lusignan, which formed the basis of the archbishop's plot in 1473, had never been completed; and the republic saw that if they held the young girl and her two brothers in their power, they would have one difficulty the less in this delicate business of keeping all other powers out of Cyprus till they themselves were ready to absorb it. Their orders were obeyed as promptly as though the kingdom were in fact already a province of their empire. Loredano sent the children to Venice. But Alfonso refused to renounce the marriage which had been arranged with Zarla. He pursued her to Venice, and, with the help of his father Ferdinand, he nearly succeeded in carrying her off by stealth.‡ The Venetians replied by sending the child to Padua, where she soon afterwards died of the plague,§ as was said. Alfonso was baulked; but his father would

---

* Malipiero, "Annali Veneti," p. 607.

† Council X., Misti, fol. 175; Mas Latrie, *loc. cit.*, p. 408, Oct. 30, 1476; Rom., *loc. cit.*

‡ Navagero, *op. cit.*, p. 1156.

§ Council X., Misti, xviii. fol. 182; Jan. 16, 1477; Mas Latrie, *loc. cit.*, p. 412.

not allow him to abandon the game, and in 1478 he sent him to the court of the soldan. Once more Caterina was obliged to pay the deficient tribute. This time, however, Venice instructed her to demand a formal act of investiture * in return for the discharge of her debt. The diploma came back to the court of Cyprus, and Alfonso's mission failed. He wearied of this chase after a wife and a crown; he was glad to find himself beyond the reach of his father's restless ambition; Alexandria was to his taste, and he gave himself up to the pleasures of the town.†

External danger seemed at an end for the present. But the continual pressure of hostility, the rapid and repeated blows of destiny, had shattered the royalty of Caterina's state. Her tenure of the throne hung upon the fine thread of Venetian pleasure; her tenure of life depended upon an equation between the strength of the Venetian garrison and the force or cunning of the Cypriot nobles. By the year 1478 the queen's household, her movements, her very income, now limited to eight thousand ducats, were under the direction of the *provveditor* and his councillors. The doge has to order them not to hold the reins so tight, but to allow the queen to move from one palace to another, and to see that her table is properly supplied.‡ Her liberty was gone; it was hardly possible that

---

* Malipiero, "Annali Veneti," p. 605, where the deed is given in full.

† Romanin, *loc. cit.*

‡ Colbertaldi, "Hist. di Cat. Cornara," MS. Cod. viii., It. alla Marciana.

she could, by any course of conduct, satisfy the government which intended eventually to unthrone her. One thing she certainly might not do; she must never dream of a second marriage. It might have been some consolation to Caterina had the Venetian domination secured to her peace. But there was no rest inside her island kingdom. The citizens, the people of Cerines, Famagosta, Nicosia, were faithful to her; they loved their queen. But all through the island the great nobles were her enemies, and drew with them their peasants. They were profoundly jealous of Venetian rule; they saw the weakness of the queen; some of them coveted the throne for themselves. Caterina was compelled to live in constant dread of revolution, murder, or dethronement, shut within the walls of one or other of her faithful towns. Conspiracy after conspiracy was discovered, some directed against her life, others against her liberty. At each new outbreak she could see the frown gathering upon her parent's brow. The dread of Venice was always before her eyes. Yet she was absolutely helpless; never was a queen more so; caught between rebellious subjects whom she could not rule and a cold, uncompromising guardian who desired her kingdom. For the better protection of Caterina, Venice, in 1477, had proposed to send a colony of one hundred Venetian nobles * to the island. They were to receive large fiefs and a salary of three hundred ducats each. But when the commissioners sent to prepare the draft of the scheme came to examine the Cyprian exchequer, they had to report that it would

* Malipiero, "Annali Veneti," pp. 606, 607.

not bear this additional charge. The design accordingly fell through. The government, however, continued to appoint governors, captains, treasurers, *provveditori;* * occupying every post at court and every fort in the island. Each new arrival from Venice deepened the hatred of the Cypriot nobles and increased the danger to Caterina's life. The pain of her position was so great that she may well have wished for the end ; but that was to be delayed for many years yet ; and, when it did come, it proved to her the bitterest experience of all her bitter fate. For ten years more she lived on in Cyprus, feeling her life daily curbed and crushed between her subjects and her guardians. Young, beautiful, and unhappy, called to a government beyond her powers, the fate of Caterina recalls to us the equally disastrous lot of that other lovely, hapless, and abandoned lady, Mary Stuart, queen of Scots.

At length, in 1488, Venice was ready to take her final step towards annexing Cyprus. She only required a pretext, and that was soon offered to her by two events of this year. The sultan Bajazet II. intended to subdue the Mamelukes of Egypt, and had prepared a large force for the purpose. The Venetians surmised that, on the way, he would seize Cyprus as a base of operations. They determined to remove the queen, and their action was hastened by the discovery of a plot. Marin Rizzo, the old conspirator of 1473, had met Alfonso of Naples at Alexandria. Rizzo suggested that Alfonso should sue for the hand of Caterina, and rely on his father

* Mas Latrie, *op. cit.,* vol. iii. appendix, p. 841.

Ferdinand for support. To pave the way for this match, Rizzo sailed for Cyprus in a French boat. He intended to sound the queen on the subject, and took with him Tristan Giblet, whose sister was waiting-maid to Caterina. The two landed at Fountain Amorous, and told the master of the galley to cruise off shore till he should see, up on the headland, a fire signal raised by night. The Venetian admiral Priuli, however, was aware of the whole design. He seized the Frenchman, and, after learning the hour at which the signal might be looked for, he manned the galley with his own sailors and sent it towards the Fountain Amorous. All went well; the fire was lighted and answered; Rizzo and Giblet came on board, and were arrested by Priuli's men.* Both were sent to Venice, but Giblet poisoned himself on the way. Rizzo was kept in close and secret confinement; the Ten hesitated to condemn him to death, as he pleaded that he was ambassador of the soldan.† Finally, however, a year later, he was strangled secretly in the armoury of the Council of Ten.

The discovery of this last plot determined the Venetian government to act. Venice could never permit a second marriage, which would have destroyed the shadowy title of heir to her daughter which she now claimed. On the 28th of October the Ten arrived at their final decision that Caterina should be recalled; and Priuli was instructed to carry out their orders as

---

* Malipiero, "Annali Veneti," p. 609; Navagero, *op. cit.*, p. 1197.

† Mas Latrie, *op. cit.*, vol. iii. pp. 435-444; extracts from the Chron. of Marin Sanudo, Council X., May 13, 1489; Rom., *loc. cit.*

firmly, yet as gently as might be,* only under no circumstances was he to fail. "We fully authorize you to bow her to our will, with or without her own consent." In case of refusal, he was to inform her Majesty that she had forfeited all claim on the protection of the republic, and, as a consequence, her income would be suspended and herself treated as a rebel. On obtaining her consent, Priuli was to affirm everywhere that the queen had taken this action of her own free will, and not on any compulsion from Venice. Giorgio Cornaro was also commissioned to accompany Priuli to Cyprus,† where he was to assist the general in compelling his sister to resign. And both were told how to act in case they found Caterina already fled to Rhodes, a design the unfortunate queen, in her terror, was suspected of harbouring.‡ Venice had closed her hand, and it always proved a strong one. Giorgio arrived in Cyprus, and found no pleasant or easy task before him. He had to encounter the strongest repugnance to his proposals—tears, entreaties, even, as we have seen, thoughts of flight; so closely did the queen cling to her kingdom and her shadowy semblance of a royal state. "Is it not enough," she said, "that Venice shall inherit when I am gone?"§ No, it was not enough; abdication complete and at once was demanded of her. Promises of a regal reception, of

---

* "Ultraque omnia, utemini erga majestatem suam omnibus illis dulcibus, humanis, placabilibus et gratiosis verbis que judicaveritis posse operari effectum hujus nostre intentionis."
† Misti, xxiv. fol. 29 ; Mas Latrie, *loc. cit.*, p. 420.
‡ Misti, xxiv. fol. 34 ; Mas Latrie, *loc. cit.*, p. 429.
§ Bembo, "Historia Veneta" (Basileæ : 1556), lib. i.

Y

princely treatment, of recognition as a crowned head, of a large income, of fiefs in the Veneto, were lavishly made to her, only she must obey. At last she yielded. In the piazza of Famagosta and of Nicosia solemn *Te Deums* were sung and the banner of St. Mark was blessed and unfurled, while the queen looked on from beneath a baldachino. She saw her cities taken from her one by one, the cities that had always been her own. No point in all the long ceremony of un-robing was spared her ; in every town and village the same cruel pageant was performed. She entered each one as a queen and left it discrowned. Venice was determined that all the world should see how willing had been her abdication. But the people flocked about her on her mournful progress, with tears and blessings ; tears for their liberty lost with their queen. At last, early in 1479, it was finished. Caterina and her brother sailed for Venice, and Cyprus became a part of the Venetian empire.

The government prepared an excellent constitu-tion * for the island. Venice never failed in that respect. A lieutenant, the supreme governor, with two councillors, was established at Nicosia ; a captain, or deputy governor, also with two councillors, was sent to Famagosta ; to these were added a military governor or *provveditore*.† But the Venetian title to the island had no legal ground. James Lusignan, Caterina's husband, was a usurper ; Charlotte, his legitimate sister, was the real queen, and it is in virtue

---

* Malipiero, "Annali Veneti," p. 611 ; Navagero, *op. cit.*, p. 1197.

† Mas Latrie, *op. cit.*, vol. iii., appendix, p. 844.

of her claim that the house of Savoy still bears the empty title of king of Cyprus. But, further admitting James's title as good, the succession to the crown should have been governed by his will, which bequeathed it, after the death of his last bastard, to the nearest of the blood of Lusignan. In truth, the republic had no title; she desired Cyprus and took it. It never brought her any good; it is even said to have worked much harm to her social morality, for the island was the home of a deep-seated luxury. Its influence, no doubt, did help to heighten the corruption which was then beginning to appear at Venice. The opening of the next century saw the establishment of many offices,* each, however, more powerless than its neighbour, to check the extravagance of the dress, the licence of the monasteries, the rapid growth of vice, the decay of health and spread of infectious diseases. With much trouble and expense Venice held Cyprus for a little less than a century, and then lost it to the Turks in 1571.

On the 5th of June, 1479, Caterina's galley reached the Lido. There she landed under an awning of gold and crimson stripes. She was conducted to a chamber prepared for her at San Nicolo, where she might rest and prepare for the ceremony of the next day. On the 6th the doge, accompanied by a train of noble ladies, came to wait on her and lead her to the Palazzo Ferrara,† now the Fondaco dei Turchi, where her

---

* The following offices may be noted :—The *provveditore alle pompe*, 1514 ; *contra bestemmia*, 1537 ; *sopra monasterj*, 1521 ; *della sanità*, 1485–1556.

† The building occupied by the Museo Civico.

lodging had been made ready at the public expense. But when the Bucentaur neared the Lido, a *burasco* blew down, and so disturbed the ladies that their condition seemed likely to destroy the stateliness of the occasion. The doge therefore ordered the anchor to be dropped, and waited till the wind went by. When the sea had subsided, Caterina was brought on board the barge; she was dressed in black velvet with a veil and jewels *alla Zipriota*, as we see her kneeling in Bellini's picture, "The Miracle of the Cross." The procession moved up the Grand Canal, and as it passed the Palazzo Cornaro, Giorgio received the honour of knighthood from the doge, as a reward for his services in persuading his sister to abdicate. Then followed long banquets, and three days of ceremony in the Ferrara palace.* But one last function yet remained to be performed before the republic would let the queen of Cyprus go. At St. Mark's, in the very place where nineteen years before Venice had adopted Caterina as her child, she now set the seal of the Church to her spoliation. The queen was forced to go through the long office of a second and more solemn abdication. Then the government invested her, for life only, with Castle Asolo† in the Marca Amorosa, the Trevisan march. Till Asolo should be ready to receive her, she was lodged in that palace on the Grand Canal, now the Montè di Pietà, called the Palazzo Corner della Regina after her.

---

* Marin Sanudo, "Chron.," extract by Mas Latrie, *loc. cit.*, p. 445.

† "Commemoriali," lib. xvi., ap. Mas Latrie, *loc. cit.*, p. 435; Mutinelli, "Annali Urbani," lib. v.

The castle of Asolo stood on the spurs of the Alps, between Bassano and Montebelluno, at no great distance from the Villa Masèr. Far away it looked across the plain to Padua and the Euganean Hills, those islanded mounds that rise abruptly from the rich growth of vineyards and of mulberry groves. On the other side of those hills lived another famous woman, beautiful, with golden hair—Lucrezia Borgia, duchess of Ferrara. The morning sun and clear light morning air come fresh to Asolo from the sea that lies round Venice; while behind it the Julian Alps swell upward, wave on wave, towards the boundary heights. It was here that Caterina was to taste the sweet idyllic close to all her stormy life, surrounded by her little court, her twelve maids of honour, and her eighty serving-men, her favourite negress with the parrots, her apes and peacocks and hounds, and dwarf buffoon. Here the still days went by in garden walks, or by the little brooks, or in the oak grove, where the company would talk of love as though it had no life, like some dead god that could not reach their hearts; or else would sing the sun to his setting with touch of lute strings and sweetly modulated voices. A dreamy, gentle company in a soft, rich land, where the seasons melted from glory to glory, from pure green spring, through summer, "all delights," to russet autumn and its falling leaves; where "dead-cold winter" was as brief as might be.

Caterina left Venice for Asolo, and all the people of her little principality, olive crowned and bearing olive branches in their hands, came out to meet their lady. Under a canopy of cloth of gold they led her to the piazza of Borgo d'Asolo, where an address was presented to her. "Oh, happy land of Asolo," cries the orator in peroration—"oh, happy land of Asolo, and oh, most happy flock that now hast found so just and sweet a shepherdess! Oh, ship thrice fortunate whose tiller lies in such a skilful hand. Ye then, ye laurel boughs, the victor's meed, endure the sharp tooth of our knife that carves on you the name of Caterina. Sing, birds, unwonted strains to grace the name, the glorious name, Cornelia." And so he goes on, appealing to poets, to historians, even to the very rocks, to eternize the splendour of her story; apostrophizing Apelles and Zeuxis, Zephyr and Jove, and the Delian goddess.* In spite of the unintended irony, it was all like some May masque designed by Poliziano or Lorenzo de' Medici, and executed by Piero da Cosimo, with its sham classicism, its false old gods, and its real sweet leaves and springtide air.

Caterina began to give laws to her little kingdom, and to take a queenly interest in its cares and its well-being. She opened a *monte di pietà*, or pawnbroking bank, for the relief of those in pressing need. She imported grain from Cyprus and distributed it. She appointed her treasurer of state, her *potestas regius*, and an auditor to hear and judge appeals.† She wielded her little sceptre for her people's good, and won their love by her gentleness and grace. Here, in

---

* Tentori, "Saggio d. St. Civil. e Polit. d. Venezia" (Venezia: 1790), vol. xii.

† Colbertaldi, "Vita di Caterina." From this author and from Bembo's dialogues, "Degli Asolani," I have taken the details of this part of Caterina's life.

the quiet of twenty years, she lived, surrounded by a phantom royalty; yet, unsubstantial as it might be it was as real as any she had known in Cyprus. Here she and her court listened one and all to those grave *ragionamenti* on platonic love, with their weariful, never-ending age of gold; with their gods and goddesses and mortals made immortal; with Ceres, Venus, Cupid, Mars, and Jove; with Ganymede, or Daphnis, or a Danaë.

Let us look at one day of her life that has been preserved to us. The speaker is Pietro Bembo, brilliant, handsome, twenty-eight years old. He has come across the Euganean Hills from Ferrara and Lucrezia's court, perhaps with that famous lock of her yellow hair already closed in the leaves of some book he carries. The month is September; and the occasion the marriage of one among Caterina's maids to Floriano di Floriano da Montagnana. There are many guests from the country round, and from Venice too, all of them glad to escape to the cool mountain slopes from the torrid summer heat upon the plain. They have been breakfasting about twelve o'clock in the large central hall with *loggias* on either side, open to the air, but sheltered from the sun that is growing hotter and hotter to its meridian blaze. The faint breeze reaches them through the arches of the *loggia*, curling round the wide-spanned pillars. Between each of these is framed the tall-topped cypress spires that shoot up from the gardens below, relieved in black against the deep and throbbing blue. In the woods and alleys and under the pergolas is no hush; all the pleasaunce lies quiet and silenced in the noonday heat. The meal is over, but the company is still at table, Caterina sitting at one end, while the talk flows languidly around. The musicians have played and the singers sung. At a sign from the queen, two of her maids rise up, and, moving down the hall between the rows of guests, they curtsy low to Caterina. Then the elder, like one of Gian Bellini's or Carpaccio's "Angiolini," raises her lute and with one hand holds it to her breast, while with the other she sounds some few notes of prelude, and then breaks into song :

> "A maid I lived, in mirth and jocund air ;
>   Sweet fancies fed me, with my lot content.
>   Now Love doth me afflict, doth so torment,
> Nor now nor ever will his torments spare.
>
> "I thought, ah me! to live a life of joy
>   When first, dear Love, I passed into thy train ;
>   But now for dolorous death I wait, am fain ;
> My trusting heart how could'st thou thus decoy?
>
> "While yet to love unyielded and estranged,
>   Medea looked on Colchis free and glad ;
>   But when she burned for Jason, bitter and sad
> Was all her life henceforth, to her last hour unchanged."

She, when she had finished her chaunt, played yet a little longer, returning upon the first notes of her song : then the younger took up her companion's refrain, but in an altered fashion, and, weaving around it with her lips and voice, made answer in this wise:

> "A maid I lived, in dolour and distress,
>   With comrades wroth, with my own self in rage ;
>   Now love with such sweet thoughts doth me assuage,
> What can I else but sing for mirthfulness ?

"I would have sworn, O Love, to follow thee
    Were but to make sure shipwreck on a rock ;
    Yet, while I feared this doom, heart-riving shock,
Release from all my pains is granted me.

Until that day when first Love conqueror plays,
    Andromeda knows naught but sore annoy ;
    When she to Perseus bows, delight and joy
Companion her through life, through death eternal praise."

So they go on with "nay" and "yea;" the "oh, diviner air" is caught up and answered by the "oh, diviner light." And when the girls have finished their antiphony the queen calls on her favourite maid to take her viol and sing to them, a closing note to the "yes" and the "no" of the other two Then Caterina rises from table, and she and her attendants retire to their rooms to rest and sleep through the burning hours till evening shall bring the time for supper, more music, and dancing carried to the dawn. But three young Venetian gentlemen and three Venetian ladies prefer to leave sleep behind the curtains of their beds and wander out into the deep, inviting garden shade. The gardens were the pride of Asolo; and these six people, who are presently to lose themselves in the labyrinth of Bembo's dialogue, stroll now beneath a pergola of vines that divided the garden cross-wise. The shade from the woven leaves was delicious and cool; on either side of the walk ran a square-cut hedge of juniper, breast high only, so that the eye might take in all the greenery of the close. There were other walks bounded by well-trimmed laurel walls, rising high up and at their summits, curling slightly over so as to throw a shadow

on the path beneath. Into this garden they strolled—
the young men in close-fitting hose of bright and
many coloured silks, and short black cloaks; the
ladies in velvet and brocades of gorgeous dyes
and tight-rolled masses of golden hair: a globe of
colour moving through a deep green shade. They
wandered on, rising slowly uphill, for the gardens
lay behind the house and towards the Alps, until
they came to a lawn of fine and velvety grass,
studded with flowers, where the more formal garden
lost itself. Beyond the lawn was a shrubbery of
laurel growing as it chose; through this thicket a
pathway led into a grove where the silence and the
shade alike were profound. In the middle of this
wood a clear stream bubbled from the living rock,
welling up and filling a basin hollowed for it in the
stone. Over the lips of the basin it fell, and was
caught in a runnel of marble and led, with soft
murmur and bickerings through light and shade,
down to the gardens which it watered and kept cool.
Here by this fountain the three ladies and their
cavaliers sat down, and, after some slight coyness not
quite real, spun out that cobweb of platonic love
through the long declining afternoon.* The whole
picture recalls the very spirit of Boccaccio's† intro-
ductions, of Polizian's *ballate*, of Giorgione and his
garden-parties; it is a "never-ending Decamerone."

---

* See Bembo, "Degli Asolani," lib. i. op. class. Ital., No.
135 (Milano : 1808).

† See Boccaccio, Sonnet x., p. 376 of Sig. Carducci's edition;
"Rime di Cinò d. Pistoia ed altri del secolo xiv.," Barbera
(Firenze : 1862).

For Caterina and her maids we may hope, however, that it was not all pure platonism. For her court was full of guests constantly arriving and departing; and every fifteenth day came Pandolfo Malatesta, lord of Rimini, from his castle of Cittadella, to make his suit to Caterina herself, or, as others said, to win the love of her waiting-maid Fiammeta. And her own family, the Cornari, were courting Caterina for her influence. On the strength of their sister's royalty they aspired to the title of princes; and by them she found herself forced to arrange a match between one of her nieces and a prince of the house of Naples.* But Venice watched this ambition with a jealous eye. She held that the Cornari were sufficiently rewarded by the knighthood of Giorgio and by the cardinal's hat which had been procured for his son. Venice would not permit a private family to assume exceptional rank, and administered many sharp rebukes to Caterina, warning her to live content with that state of life to which it had pleased the republic to call her, and to cease all thought of Cyprus, round which her fancy and her hopes still lingered.†

The queen really loved Asolo, her gardens, and her court, nor ever wished to leave them, summer or winter. Three times only did she make a journey from her castle. Once when the weather was so cold that men could walk from Mestre to Venice across the lagoon, the rigour of winter compelled her to return to her palace on the Grand Canal. Once too, in 1497,

---

* Malipiero, "Annali Veneti," p. 612.
† Roman., *loc. cit.*, p. 437, note 1, cap. x., April 3, 1510.

she paid a visit to her brother Giorgio, then *podestà* in Brescia.* She was splendidly and regally received. A guard of forty youths met her outside the town; on the close-fitting hose of each were blazoned the arms of Cornaro and Lusignan. Triumphs and allegorical pageants followed: Diana and her nymphs, who meet a winged dove that sings to them; but the nymphs all stay their ears, and, falling on the boy, tear his wings from his shoulders, as they do in Signorelli's picture in our National Gallery. The queen entered the city in a chariot of state drawn by four white horses horned like unicorns. Jousts by torchlight were given in the evening, and the jousters marched in procession, with helmets on their heads from whose crests burst flame. It was Caterina's last royal ceremony, and it was continued for twelve days; then the queen returned to Asolo. But Venice showed herself jealous of this play at mimic royalty, and for the honour then done to his sister Giorgio was soon after recalled from Brescia.

The troubled condition of the mainland which resulted from the wars of the League of Cambray drove the queen from her home; Asolo was occupied by the troops of Maximilian. Caterina went to Venice for greater safety, and died there on the 10th of July, 1510, fifty-six years old.† Her funeral displayed as much magnificence as Venice, on the verge of ruin, could afford. On the 11th of the month a bridge of boats was made across the Grand Canal from the Cornaro Palace to the other side. The dead queen

---

* Marin Sanudo, " Diarii," I. 741.
† Bembo, " Historia Veneta" (Basileæ : 1556), lib. x. p. 417.

was followed by the patriarch, the Signory, the vice-doge, the archbishop of Spalato, and an immense crowd of citizens with torches in their hands. There was something fitting in the manner of her burial, for the night was a stormy one, with heavy wind and rain. On her coffin lay the crown of Cyprus—outwardly, at least, Venice insisted that her daughter was a queen ; but inside her body lay shrouded in the habit of St. Francis, with cord and cowl and coarse brown cloak. Caterina was carried to the Cornaro chapel in the Church of the Sant' Apostoli, and next day the funeral service was performed. Over her grave Andrea Navagero, poet, scholar, and ambassador, made the oration that bade farewell to this unhappy queen, whose beauty, goodness, gentleness, and grace were unavailing to save her from the tyrannous cruelty of fate.

THE SPANISH CONSPIRACY:

AN EPISODE IN THE DECLINE OF VENICE.

THE Spanish Conspiracy, by the timely discovery of which Venice was believed to have narrowly escaped destruction in 1618, is one of those episodes in history which at once arrest attention by focussing the conditions of a period and throwing a flood of light upon subsequent events. In diabolical picturesqueness this conspiracy takes rank with the Gunpowder Plot or the Massacre of Saint Bartholomew. Owing partly to the doubts thrown upon its reality at the very outset, partly also to the silence of the Venetian government, to the mystification of some contemporaries, and the declared scepticism of others, the whole affair has acquired the fascination of a riddle. It has attracted abundant research, and has even found its way into dramatic literature in the best of Otway's tragedies, "Venice Preserved." At the time there was a French answer, a Spanish answer, a Neapolitan answer, a Turkish answer to this riddle, and subsequent historians, Capriata, San Real, Chambrier, Daru, have each adopted one or other of these solutions. No one of the answers, however, is quite satisfactory, nor covers the whole ground of our information so as to rebut all objections. It may be impossible now to read to the bottom of this muddy pool; and von Ranke, the most distinguished as well as the most recent of those who have attacked the problem, has confined himself to researches in the fact without expressing a decided opinion in any direction. Indeed it would be difficult to find a more tangled skein for the historian to unravel; yet the process reveals so curious a condition of society in Europe, and in Venice especially, at the opening of the seventeenth century, and throws so strong a light upon the causes which first corrupted and then destroyed the republic, that the effort to follow each clue through the labyrinth is repaid with interest.

And first for the outward and visible facts of the case as they appeared to the Venetians in the spring of 1618. Early in this year the city was full of strangers—Italians from the mainland and foreigners wandering in search of adventure, whose nature it was to be drawn at last towards the city of the sea, to "fall like spent exhalations to that centre." They were attracted thither by the splendour of Venetian state ceremonies which were gradually growing more and more sumptuous, were surely being made the pretext for a larger licence. On this occasion Venice was preparing to celebrate the election of a new doge, and the yearly pageant of wedding the sea happened to fall about the same time. The *locande*, therefore, were all full; so too were the lodging-houses which served as dependencies to the overcrowded inns. The piazza at night was thronged with foreign forms in long cloaks, slouched hats, and high leather boots, promenading and swaggering, now in shadow, now in moonlight, and filling the air with the adventurer's language, French in all its endless modifications of *patois*. The air seemed charged with vague uneasiness, and Venice had reached a highly nervous condition between her pleasures and her fears. For some time past the conduct of the Spanish governors in Naples and Milan had been the cause of serious alarm to those politicians who were not entirely dazzled by the blaze of pageantry and lost in the hunt after pleasure; but there was a wild swirl of reckless enjoyment all about them. and a warning voice, had they raised one, would have been drowned in the din of the revel.

On the morning of the 18th of May, Venice awoke to another day of amusement—to her morning bath, her midday siesta, the evening promenade upon the lagoon, the "masques and balls begun at midnight, burning ever to midday." But a thrill of terror awaited her. This morning of the 18th the early-risers found the bodies of two men, hung each by one leg to a gibbet in the piazza, in sign that they had been executed for treason. On the 23rd, two days before the Sposalizio del Mare, another body, bearing the marks of terrible torture, was also exposed in a like manner. The public emotion became intense. The people felt themselves suddenly pulled up by this evidence of death, secret, swift, and apparently causeless, in their very midst, hung full in face of their heedless enjoyment. The silence of the government heightened the alarm. The executive made no motion to postpone the ceremonies of the next few days; the three bodies hung there, unexplained, but relieved in horrible colours upon the brilliant background of civic pomp. No one knew these men who had been put to death. They belonged to the mob of vagabonds and adventurers whom Venice attracted, and upon whom she, in a measure, lived. One thing alone was clear; they were all Frenchmen. Conjecture was allowed free play; and the public soon pieced together, out of the endless rumours of the town, a consecutive story. These men were the agents of the duke of Osuna, viceroy of Naples, and of the Marquis Bedmar, Spanish ambassador in Venice. In accordance with a preconcerted design, the city was to have been seized by a Spanish fleet, which already lay outside Malamocco, the arsenal fired, the mint and treasury of St. Mark's rifled, the doge and his council blown up. When Venice had been sufficiently cowed she was to be handed over to Spain. The plot had been discovered in time, the guilty arrested and tortured; more than five hundred of their accomplices had been drowned by night in the canals. In proof of this, the inns, full to the garret a few days before, were now nearly empty. Such was the story which gained immediate acceptance. The reticence of the government neither affirmed nor denied anything, and the popular fury exploded in an attack upon the Spanish embassy. Bedmar's palace and even his life were in serious danger.

At the moment when the conspiracy was discovered the French ambassador, Bruslart, was absent from Venice on a pilgrimage to Loretto. He received information of events from his brother Broussin, who was in charge of affairs, and therefore sent a similar communication on the subject to the Minister of the Exterior in Paris. Even thus early, four days after the first executions, Broussin expresses his disbelief in the reasons popularly given for the sentence. He was sceptical as to the alleged Spanish origin of the plot, because he and all the French officials knew that there existed a French plot to which the condemned were parties, and whose centre was in their own court; a plot directed not against the republic, it is true, but against a power the republic dreaded and desired to conciliate—against the Turks. Moreover, this French design was aimed at the Levant, where Venice had always shown herself jealous of any interference. To the French embassy, therefore, it seemed clear that here lay the real reason for these sudden executions. Bruslart returned to Venice three weeks later; and since those who had suffered death were Frenchmen, a long correspondence ensued between the ambassador and the Minister in Paris. In all his despatches Bruslart denies that the Spaniards were the authors of the plot. Daru, the French historian of Venice, accepts Bruslart's negation and carries it a step further. He boldly asserts that the Spanish Conspiracy never had any existence at all.

Daru's theory is so startling, and in supporting it he deals so elaborately with the condition of the plot, that it will be of service to follow him closely for a little way. By rejecting the accredited story of the conspiracy, the French historian lays himself under the obligation to explain the action which Venice took in the matter. This he does with surprising dexterity. The duke of Osuna, Spanish viceroy of Naples, Daru affirms, was engaged in schemes to make himself king of Naples. He asked Venice to help him, and she consented. Osuna's treason was discovered at Madrid, and Venice exerted all her powers to obliterate every proof of her complicity with the viceroy. To do this effectually she hanged, drowned, or strangled five hundred men, emissaries of Osuna, whom she found in her dominions, and who were aware that she was herself a party to their designs, and who might be called as witness against her at the Spanish court. The tortures she inflicted were applied to wring from her own confederates the names of all who, by the slightest side-wind, might have obtained an inkling that the republic was a principal in the conspiracy. To the world Venice said that Spain had been compassing her ruin, and her doge celebrated a public *Te Deum* for this salvation from danger; in reality she had been plotting against Madrid, and the thanksgiving was held because she had succeeded in destroying all her accomplices, and with them every trace of her guilt towards Spain. This is a startling theory, and picturesque in the lurid light in which it places the Venetian government. If Daru's theory were correct, no more sacrilegious ceremony than the *Te Deum* in St. Mark's was ever celebrated inside a Christian church. But it is not correct; and a wider view, embracing the general condition of Europe, and more especially the attitude of France, Spain, and the viceroyalty of Naples, will prove its fallacy.

By the Peace of Lyons, France had virtually withdrawn from Italy in 1601. She had ceded Saluzzo, in Piedmont, to the duke of Savoy, in exchange for the district of La Bresse on the French side of the Alps. The French no longer possessed a claim to any portion of Italian territory; Spain was left in undisturbed possession. The withdrawal of France caused serious alarm to those Italian states which still retained their independence. No power remained in Italy to prevent Spain from suppressing the last embers of freedom; and these fears received colour when the Spanish began to harass the duke of Savoy. The peace of Madrid, however, in 1617, promised to restore quiet to Italy, and that peace was especially the work of the Spanish court. Indeed the centre of disturbance lay by no means in Spain itself. There the attitude was pacific. The court of Madrid was virtually asleep, sunk in a deathlike inactivity. The king, Philip III., was consumed by a gloomy religious fervour, unrelieved by any vital interest beyond the preservation of a rigid and stifling etiquette. He was completely dominated by the dukes of Lerma and Uzeda, who dreaded a war which might rouse his Majesty from this lethargy or should call into notice men of action who would prove rivals. In contrast to the paralysis of Madrid, the provinces were feverishly restless, owing to the active ambition of their governors. It was Inojosa, Fuentes, Toledo, Osuna, Bedmar, who threatened the remnants of Italian freedom. They, and not their court, were the source of that alarm which Italy felt. These men were powerful and fully aware of the weakness of their home government. They seldom received instructions from Madrid, and still seldomer obeyed them. Virtually independent princes, it was in war. in conspiracy, and in movement that they came to the fullest consciousness of their power. To the Spanish representatives in Italy the peace of 1617 was distasteful, as any peace must have been, and they agreed to ignore it. Toledo and Osuna both continued to annoy Venice, in spite of repeated orders to disarm.

The viceroy of Naples plays so important a part in the story of the Spanish Conspiracy, that we must look a little closer at the course of his life. Don Pedro y Giron, grandee of Spain, knight of the Golden Fleece, and gentleman of the bed-chamber, was the head of a powerful Spanish house, and had increased his influence by an alliance with the family of the duke of Lerma, favourite and all-powerful minister of King Philip. By nature Don Pedro was ambitious and impetuous, and the restless air of his century raised his pulse still higher. At the age of twenty-five he conceived himself neglected by his court. He therefore formed a company of troops at his own charge, and took them to the Netherlands, where he served under the archduke of Austria. On the close of the campaign he returned to Madrid with a fine reputation for valour, and was soon after appointed viceroy of Sicily. In his kingdom he made himself unboundedly popular. His manners were distinguished by courtly Spanish grace, relieved by flashes of humour which appealed to the popular taste. He soon became a favourite with nobles and people alike. But he committed one fatal mistake; he allowed himself too great a freedom in matters of religion. Already he was suspected by the Church for his fearless defence of the heretics against the rigours of his own court. And now many stories of his levity were set afloat, and came to the ears of his enemies the Jesuits, who stored them up against the day of his disgrace. When Venice fell out with Ferdinand of Austria, Osuna was sent as viceroy to Naples, under orders to support the archduke. At Naples he continued his popular policy, taking special care to conciliate the people. He even went so far as to execute certain barons for cruelty to their dependents. The populace of Naples adored him. They called him the "good viceroy;" but the nobility, whom he curbed, united with his old enemies the Jesuits to work his ruin, and the combination in the end proved too strong for Osuna. On the Peace of Madrid being signed, the viceroy refused to disarm, and continued to attack Venice in the Adriatic. With a frankness characteristic of himself, Osuna again and again told the Venetian resident that he had no intention of observing the treaty. "I am resolved," he said, "to send the fleet into Venetian waters, in spite of the world, in spite of the king, in spite of God." The fleet sailed under Osuna's own colours, and his enemies were not slow to comment on the viceroy's flag flying from the ships of Spain. His army steadily grew in numbers, and became the asylum for all the *bravi* and broken men who were wandering in swarms over Europe. The Jesuits and the nobility had little difficulty in surmising that Osuna's object was the crown of Naples. They gave him another year to commit himself, and then they struck. In October of 1618—that is, five months after the Spanish plot was discovered at Venice—a formal information against Osuna was lodged at the court of Madrid. Early in the following year the government determined to recall him ; and then, for the first time, Osuna secretly sounded the Venetian resident as to whether the republic would support him in case he determined to resist the authority of his own court. The Venetian answer was prompt and decisive. The Ten declined to treat upon the subject at all. Osuna saw that his case was hopeless, and quietly resigned his office to his successor, Cardinal Borgia. He returned to Madrid, where, contrary to all expectation, he met with a most favourable reception ; and it is probable that the government did not consider his treason proved. The Venetian ambassador wrote from Madrid that the duke of Osuna lived in greater state than ever he did in Italy ; adding, however, "we must not praise the day till night fall." A stormy night soon closed upon Osuna. The king died in 1621, and the ex-viceroy lost the protection of his relation the duke of Uzeda, whose reign ended with his master's life. Osuna's enemy, the Church, revived the old charge of heresy, and he was put upon his trial. For more than three years the process lasted, spun out to an interminable length by the Jesuits, who had at length involved their prey. For these three years Osuna languished in prison ; finally he died at the castle of Almeda, poisoned, it is said, by the hand of his wife, to save the family honour from the shame of a public execution.

The whole of Daru's argument in explanation of the Spanish Conspiracy rests upon the relations between the viceroy of Naples and the Venetian republic. It is more than probable that Osuna did meditate seizing the crown of Naples. The scheme may appear to us now little better than a mere bubble certain to burst. But it is just one of the notes of this period that a thousand such mad and vague designs were in the air. That Osuna asked Venice to aid him, and that the republic lent a willing ear, is incorrect. The Viceroy made no overtures to Venice until a year after the plot was discovered, and then they were at once rejected.

Thus far, then, the French historian has carried us, and we have obtained no explanation of the Spanish Conspiracy. Nor can we, without taking into consideration the force which was moving the whole continent at this time. The human spirit had for long been busy, fusing and amalgamating much diverse matter inside the crucible of Italy. Now the crucible was broken by foreign invasion, and its contents flowed out to work in the innermost core of European society. The North was vivified at last, and returned upon its vivifier. After long years it had caught the element of life and became intellectualized in its constant and brutal violations of Italy. It left its mistress dead, but itself arose, quickened to a nobler life by her undying and invincible spirit. It was an age of liberation, of freedom beyond the borders of Italy, who died in the effort to project the ideas she created. She, "the lamp of other nations, the sepulchre of her own splendour," had taught the world how to tread firmly in the path where the spirit guides. But this liberation, this firm tread, brought with them, as of necessity they must, certain defects ; and so we find side by side freedom and licence, the steady step and the headlong rush. The motto of the age was—"attempt ;" *Perge! ne timeas!* Luther obeyed the spirit in his own bold, rough fashion ; rejoicing like a lad in his new found strength ; almost hoping that he might find as many devils in Augsburg as there were tiles on the roof; gladly accepting the devil as a bodily fact for the sake of a blow at him, for the pleasure of a well-aimed ink-pot. But in Italy they were long past this boyhood they once knew so well; they had now struggled so long that they were weary of movement and desirous of rest. For ages past the Italians had been active, creating the Roman Empire, the Roman Church, reawaking the arts and rediscovering humanity. They might look at Luther as a man looks at a child, but they could not feel with him even in memory. Italy was old. She had not that directness which comes from partial understanding, nor the youth nor the brutality to free herself as entirely in outward form from Rome, as she was already freed in spirit. Campanella, Bruno, and Sarpi are intellectually as bold as Luther and of far further vision, far more prophetic. But just there lay the cause of their defect as agents. In their wide and almost universal view the points for which Luther was struggling seemed of such trifling moment. The raw muscle for an external blow they had not, though the intellectual courage to deal one was theirs in abundance. See the hardihood, the audacity, the adventurous spirit of Sarpi. At each moment you expect him to falter, to stay his hand, hearing behind him the thunder of Rome, or dreading the gleam of her assassin's dagger. But no! step by step he advances; each proposition stated and established becomes to him, as it were, a spring-board whence to take a wider and a bolder flight; till from apologist he becomes accuser: Venice, his client, quits the dock for the judgment-seat; and the pope, no longer the terrible judge, is in his turn arraigned, tried, and condemned. Yet all the while Sarpi remains inside the Church, not outside it with Luther. Luther passed outside the Church through an intellectual defect, through a boyishness of understanding, because he did not go the whole length of his argument, because he was about to found a new Church. Sarpi remained inside the Church because he was intellectually complete, a full-grown man, following his argument to its close, because, in short, he was a man of no Church.

But these men are the fine phenomena of the spirit, the brilliant side of the mirror. We may be sure there was also a darker side. Nothing is more open to infection than the human mind; the quality of its flame depends on the air which feeds and surrounds it. When such world-moving forces as freedom are at work no portion of the social organism can escape the shock, or refuse to share in the impulse. But the nature of the manifestation depends upon the medium; and so, while we look with pride on a Luther or a Sarpi as brilliant examples of spiritual liberation, we are warned to read a lesson of humility in the motiveless anarchy of a Guy Fawkes or a

Jacques Pierre. In men of coarser fibre, the boldness and self-reliance which constituted the strength of Luther became licence and unreasoned restlessness. What could be done by pushing audaciously onward, by adopting the motto "Attempt," was constantly receiving illustration in countless instances of successful adventure. Concini, the Italian, was marshal of France and virtual sovereign; handsome George Villiers was ruling England to the ruin of the Crown. For all the men who were obeying the spirit of their age, whose minds were being ruffled to unrest, some such success seemed possible. They turned their eyes from the failures—from D'Ancre's dead body in the courtyard of the Louvre, from Ravaillac torn in pieces by horses, from the three corpses in St. Mark's Square;—they turned their eyes from these, or rather their desire made them single-eyed, with vision only for the impossible goal. The how, the when, the probabilities, they forgot to think of; their delirium overlaid all such back-drawing thoughts. There was a South Sea bubble always floating within their ken; an El Dorado about to be won by them, as others had just failed to win it. That the bubble was never caught before it burst, that the El Dorado was never gained, but ended only in a Raleigh's death, merely added a keener zest to the pursuit which fruition would have satiated. Adventure for adventure's sake, *querer por sol querer*, that was the real joy of life's game.

The Reformation had shaken Europe to its foundations, and the tremulous condition of the powers afforded the very medium in which this restless spirit of adventure might most freely indulge itself. Plot after plot, hazy in outline, undefined in object, impossible of execution, appears in the political world; "perplexing kings with fear of change," no one of whom could find the sore place, nor lay their hand on it to heal it. Conspiracy was epidemic, infecting the social atmosphere, breathed by princes and adventurers alike. Men born to great estate recklessly embarked upon schemes of which they only dimly saw the value or the issue. The duke of Nevers meditated establishing a principality in Greece and resuscitating the empire of the East. Pope Gregory was in close connection with the adventurer Stukeley, concocting designs for a revolution in Ireland. The duke of Osuna saw himself king of Naples and Sicily. Even if the passion for intrigue had not been so rife in Europe, this gambling spirit of its princes and nobles would inevitably have created a lower class of doubtful characters—men who became denationalized and ready, on sufficient bribe, to turn their hand to any disgraceful work. But as it was, circumstances had already created such a class. The civil wars in France and the Spanish wars in the Netherlands turned loose upon the continent a number of men reared in camps, living by brawls and intrigues, cosmopolitan in the most vicious sense. They passed freely from one capital to another, and offered themselves for hire wherever anything was stirring. Their credentials were the rough outlines of a hundred plots, and with these in their pockets they presented themselves to men like Nevers, Osuna, or Toledo. Should any one of these schemes happen to take the fancy of these princes, the details received the necessary alteration and expansion ; and then the whole work was put in hand, with the adventurer as manager. In fact, these men were the promoters of bubble companies. The chief difference between our day and theirs is that the bubbles they blew were not railroads or silver mines, but political conspiracies. Their designs are marked by reckless and meaningless audacity. The number of assassinations planned or effected at this time was very large. William the Silent is shot ; Henry IV. stabbed ; James and the lords nearly blown up ; the doge of Venice escapes a like fate by a hair's breadth. Yet no reasonable explanation based upon political necessity can be found for these multitudinous conspiracies. It was madness to imagine that England or Venice could be overthrown by a Gunpowder Plot or a Spanish Conspiracy, and it is still more impossible to see what advantage Guy Fawkes or Pierre could have reaped from their ruin. There was the pleasure of the long and secret preparation, the excitement of the scramble for the plunder and the hurried flight ; but nothing more. Yet it is among men such as these, who owned no allegiance but to the spirit of revolutionizing adventure, that we must look for the authors and agents of these diabolical schemes. The whole air was disturbed. For the North this disturbance meant life, vitality, and growth. England was about to develop her Parliamentary liberty. France was approaching the brilliant epoch of Lewis XIV. But for Italy this invasion of the North, this rejection upon herself of her own spirit, this apparition of Machiavelli as an avenging ghost, was preparing a *tenebræ* from which there could be no resurrection.

Italy was breaking down into the abyss of the seventeenth and eighteenth centuries, and Venice shared in the general declension. She had reached her apogee and was steadily declining. After the Peace of Cateau-Cambresis in 1558, she had enjoyed nearly forty years of comparative quiet. She appeared in her fullest splendour. Never before had the republic made so magnificent a display in the eyes of Europe; nor was she slow to invite the princes of Europe to visit her. Palaces rose along the Grand Canal; state ceremonies increased in number and in pomp; life in the sea city appeared like one prolonged *fête.* But there were two ominous symptoms manifesting themselves, almost unobserved, at the very heart of Venice. The banking system caught the general fever, became inflated, and burst with ruinous results; and the population of Venice continued steadily to decrease. Not only did the population fall off in numbers, it also began to deteriorate in quality. The race for distinction in wealth and splendour shattered the poorer noble families, and the collapse of the banking system completed their ruin. The young men of these broken *case nobili* refused to embark on business; and nothing remained for them but a life of mischievous adventure, centring round the churches and the piazza. There was decay in the noble class and a corresponding decay among the artisans. Commerce and shipbuilding steadily declined. The

number of pauper and foundling children increased
so rapidly that the government was compelled to
make provision for their support. A large part of
the population was living on the charity or the vices
of the rich. But this general collapse of a wide-
spread prosperity had a reflex action; and, while it
ruined the smaller nobility and the smaller traders,
it confined the flow of money to the larger houses
who had weathered the storm. And so side by side
there existed enormous private fortunes, luxury, and
display, and a desperate poverty which hated the
luxury while serving it. In fact, there was a schism
inside the state; and this schism showed itself in the
art no less than in the social life of Venice. The
great schools of painting and of architecture, magnificent, rich, ornate, were a fitting expression of the
wealth, the pomp, and pride of Venice. But from
the people came a poetry that was spontaneous,
native, licentious, irreligious, because it felt the reflex
of the Reformation. Profanity invaded the altar.
The Père Duchesne of Venice appeared. The Senate
was obliged to prosecute those who chaunted fictitious
psalms and obscene litanies, to take action against
mock priests who administered the sacraments or received confessions. Everywhere there was an insurgence of dialect; a reformation directed not against
the dogma of Rome, but against the pedantry of Rome.
Comedy rose once more from the heart of the people
to answer the Ciceronian phrase or the Platonic
refinement. "This was the apparition of the people
in letters, of Luther in poetry, of free judgment on
the stage. Harlequin is opposed to the Inquisition:

Pulcinella to pontifical wrath ; Pantaloon to the last session of the Council of Trent. Beltran counterbalances S. Carlo Borromeo ; Florindo neutralizes S. Filippo dei Neri."* While Europe is at the reformation, Italy had reached the revolution.

Here, then, is Venice divided. And the division is marked in its strongest tones of splendour and of corruption by two events: the reception of Henry III., king of France and Poland, and the Spanish Conspiracy. Henry passed through Venice in 1574, on his way to take the crown of France. The republic determined to receive him as became his rank and her desire to secure the friendship of France. The sumptuary laws were suspended during the ten days of Henry's stay. The great ladies were invited to vie with one another in magnificence of dress and jewellery. The guilds were ordered to prepare a splendid pageant. The Palazzo Foscari, the destined lodging of the king, was hung with cloth of gold, with crimson velvet, with sky-blue silk *semé* of fleurs-de-lys.† Forty pages, the youth, the beauty, the nobility of Venice, were appointed for service on the king. They met him as he came in his barge from the shore near Mestre, each in his gondola, and his gondolier in silken shirt and hose embroidered with the family arms. They swept in a semicircle round the royal barge and conducted the king to Murano. Then, on the following day, in grand procession, they brought him to the palace of the

* See Ferrari, *op. cit.*

† See Marsilio della Croce for a detailed account of Henry's visit, " Historia della publica e famosa entrata in Vinegia del Serenissimo Henrico III.," etc.

Foscari. For ten days the king was fêted as no prince had ever been before. There were the gorgeous liveries of France and of Venice; fantastic barges, sea monsters on whose backs the workmen of Murano fashioned crystal vases at the furnace mouth; water pageants; triumphal arches designed by Palladio and painted by Tintoret; regattas; serenades; fireworks on the canal by night; banquets where the plates, the knives, the forks, the food were all of sugar; a ball in the Sala del Maggior Consiglio, and that parterre of lovely ladies whose perfume of beauty intoxicated the royal senses past all waking. The king never forgot it nor recovered. His life after was a long mad dream. Henry is said to have left the remains of his vigour in Venice. We cannot wonder, for he brought very little with him, and Venice was a siren tangling the hearts of men in that network of woven light and colour, the silver-golden waters of her lagoons. Or shall we say that she was a harlot, selling herself for her own pleasure; buying a doubtful political importance by bartering her body, not by the force and weight of her arms?

Underneath all this pomp which Henry saw, there lay a starving and a dangerous population, casting up as a froth a mob of varied nationality; men who haunted the piazza and gained a livelihood by all disgraceful means—by spying, by informations, and by murder. The *bravi* were a source of constant alarm, and in 1600 the government passed a stringent decree of banishment against them all; but in vain. These ruffians were thoroughly acquainted with all the hiding-places of the intricate city; a favourite refuge

2 A

was the palace of some ambassador, where they were sure to find a ready asylum. The police magistrates have constantly to complain that their *sbirri* are mocked and insulted from the grille in the basement of some embassy by the man they were sent to arrest. These basements were, in fact, hives of scoundrels of all sorts, petted, caressed, embraced by men like Bedmar or like Bruslart, who required their services to obtain information or to remove a foe. The difficulty of dealing with these people, the rapid spread of political corruption, and the continual murders, induced the government to encourage a class of men who were in themselves as dangerous as the *bravi.* Denouncement became a trade. The *bocca del leone* was opened and a reign of terror began, very similar to that produced by the *delatores* of imperial Rome. No one was safe—the charge of treason offered such a sure and secret method of securing vengeance on an enemy. In every great house some servants were to be found who were informers by profession. The fearful lengths to which this system of espionage might be pushed received an illustration in the fate of the unfortunate Foscarini, accused of plotting in the house of Lady Arundel, with whom he was only in love. Foscarini was put to death ; and the lady herself only escaped humiliation by compelling Wotton, the English ambassador, to plead her cause before the Senate ; so powerful were informers and so dangerous the confidence reposed in them by the government. Spies, *bravi*, courtesans, footmen, barbers, quack doctors—in short, all the evil spirits of the place stood together in a kind of freemasonry of iniquity with which the police were quite unable to cope. These were the elements of a corrupt society, banded together to prey on all from whom they could wring any money or other advantage. Their numbers were constantly recruited by fresh arrivals from Naples, from Spain, above all from France. The Venetian ambassador writes from Paris, "Every day my house is crowded with people who declare themselves desirous to serve the republic; the applications are numberless; so full is this kingdom of idle men." No one of these adventurers who arrived at Venice was likely to remain outside the floating population of his brothers whom he found already established there. His initiation would take no long time, and he would soon learn that under the life of the Venetians themselves there was a life of foreigners, *roués, déclassés*—men all of them engaged in intrigue of some sort. Before long he might find himself committed to a plot as wild as that for blowing up the doge and sacking the city.

There were three Frenchmen, Jacques Pierre, Regnault, and Langlade, living in this seething society. They had come to Venice in 1617, in the course of their profession as adventurers. Pierre was a Norman by birth, and had served with distinction against the Turks. Owing to the knowledge of the East which he had thus acquired, the duke of Nevers frequently consulted him in the preparation of his schemes for a descent on the Levant. The matter, however, had grown cold, and Pierre quitted France to seek a fresh field in Italy. Venice was the point he determined to make for eventually, but he wished to go there in the pay of the government. With that object in view he presented himself to Simon Contarini, the Venetian ambassador at Rome, and produced the usual credentials of his class—the assertion that he was in possession of secrets important to the state of Venice. Contarini, whose suspicions were aroused, pressed Pierre for an exact statement of what he meant. The adventurer replied that the viceroy of Naples entertained vast designs against the Turk in the Levant and on the coast of Albania, but showed great vagueness as to details. Contarini wished to forward profitable information to his government and therefore continued to urge Pierre, asking, "Are you sure that the points are the Archipelago and Albania?" The Frenchman pressed Contarini's hand and answered, "Somewhere thereabouts." This was enough for the ambassador, who now knew the type of man he was dealing with. He dismissed Pierre and made a note that he was a man to mistrust. Pierre then took service with the duke of Osuna, and soon discovered his hatred of Venice and surmised his desire to make himself king of Naples. Pierre continued some time at Naples, acquiring importance in the service of the duke, discussing plans for attacking the republic, and adding to his stock-in-trade by mastering the viceroy's political secrets. The adventurer was growing conscious of one serious drawback. He could not write fluently and spoke no Italian. To remedy this defect he attached to himself another Frenchman, Regnault; described as "an old scamp, a man of no spirit, a drunkard, a gamester, and a smoker, . . . branded with a lily on the shoulder for misdeeds in France." But Regnault was ready with his pen, and willingly entered into partnership with his brother adventurer; his duty was to act as secretary to this company which Pierre was forming. To complete the trio, Langlade was also admitted to partnership; and all three applied to the Venetian resident at Naples for pay in the service of the republic, bidding, as usual, for his countenance by offering to disclose political secrets affecting his government. This time they were successful. Spinelli, the resident, was less sharp sighted than Contarini, and Langlade and Regnault were more plausible than Pierre. They left Naples for Venice with letters of introduction; but they did not find the reception they expected. Langlade, who had secured a written contract from Spinelli, was sent to the arsenal to carry on his trade of Greek-fire maker; but the other two were left out in the cold. The reason for this conduct on the part of the government was the repeated warnings against Pierre, which Contarini forwarded from Rome. Pierre, however, was not a man to be baulked. He understood the character of Spinelli and believed he could frighten the resident. Accordingly, he wrote to Spinelli, "As yet I have not received a penny from the government. I believe I am being trifled with. While acknowledging every obligation for the trouble you have taken, I will come to Naples myself to thank you." Spinelli believed this to be a threat against his life; and, at his earnest request, the Venetians gave Pierre an appointment in the fleet.

Meanwhile Pierre and Regnault had presented

themselves to their ambassador, Leon Bruslart. Their object was, if possible, to reopen negotiations with the duke of Nevers concerning his designs in the Levant. Furthermore, through the help of Bruillard, Bedmar's secretary, a thorough scamp like themselves, they had obtained a footing in the Palazzo di Spagna, and had even gained an interview with the ambassador, in whose presence they freely discussed Osuna's designs against Venice. These were no secret, but no doubt Pierre, by an adroit management of the information he had picked up at Naples, induced Bedmar to believe that he was deeper in the viceroy's confidence than was really the case. However that may be, Pierre and his party had opened relations with two great ambassadors at Venice. It remained for Regnault to attempt the like with Wotton, who represented England. Regnault met Wotton one day, by accident, in a bookseller's shop, and asked for a private interview, on the plea that he possessed important political information, which he wished to take to England himself, but required letters and money. Wotton, however, was as wary as Contarini, and Regnault as ignorant and maladroit as Pierre, and the whole matter fell through. Nothing could more thoroughly bear the stamp of charlatanism than the conduct of Pierre and his friends. They were spinning such a tangled web that to unravel it became impossible. The high personages with whom they were playing had only partial light upon their movements. Bruslart knew nothing, or only by rumour, of the Bedmar connection ; Bedmar had heard nothing of the Nevers scheme; Wotton had no inkling of either;

and the Venetian government was, as yet, in perfect darkness. It was impossible that any one of these, when called upon, should have been able to give an adequate account of the plot.

The Frenchmen had now obtained what they required to float them. They had established apparent connections with three ambassadors in Venice. They might be seen going in and out of their palaces; familiar with side doors, and known to the servants. They could use these powerful names, and hint at more powerful ones in the background. It was time now to water the stock, to enlarge the number of shareholders. The great recruiting ground, the piazza, was always open to them, teeming with idlers ready for any mischief. Pierre had no difficulty in finding adherents who would not press too rudely for the how or the when of his scheme. Enough that there was a plot. Its vagueness merely rendered it the more fascinating; the imagination had the freer scope to magnify the possible prizes. One day, as Pierre was sauntering in St. Mark's, he passed a young Frenchman, whom he at once determined to enlist. He proved to be a native of Languedoc, Gabriel Moncassin by name, and a soldier of fortune by profession. Pierre carried him off to dine with him, and afterwards established him in his own room. Then, under a promise of secrecy, the plot was hinted at, and, on hearing the names of Osuna and Bedmar, Moncassin consented to join. A day or two later, Pierre took his recruits, now a band of four or five, to the top of the campanile. From that height he unfolded to them the plan of the conspiracy, so far as it had any. He pointed to the treasury of St. Mark's, right below them ; to the mint, looking towards San Giorgio and the sea ; to the otiose crowd of nobles sauntering on the *broglio;* to the unarmed throng of citizens at the piazza's end. "A handful of stout men with sticks might make themselves masters of it all, and drive this herd of pantaloons into the water." "Is it not a wonder," he cried, "that Venice has remained so long a virgin?" Then he turned and pointed to the two ports of Lido and Malamocco, promising that the Neapolitan fleet should sail in there to second their enterprise when the right moment arrived. But Osuna's ships, whether promised to Pierre or only sailing in the gulf to damage Venetian shipping, never came. They were wrecked off Manfredonia ; and the chief had to tell his followers that the execution must be delayed till autumn, as he and Langlade had been ordered to join the fleet. So the company separated—Pierre and Langlade to their posts ; the two brothers, Desbouleaux, to Naples ; Regnault for France, to see the duke of Nevers. The Ten had received an anonymous warning to be upon their guard ; hence the orders to Pierre and Langlade. Pierre endeavoured to avoid compliance by submitting to the government an elaborate statement of alleged designs entertained by Osuna against some place and some power not named. He hoped that the desire to read to the bottom of this communication would induce the Ten to keep him in Venice. But the ruse did not serve his turn.

In the middle of April another young Frenchman had come to Venice. His name was Balthassar

Juven ; a man well connected, the nephew of Marshal Lesdigueres, and altogether of a better character than the men with whom he chose to associate. He lodged at the Locanda Trombetta, and there he fell in with Moncassin. The two compatriots soon became friends, and Moncassin, who was uneasy under the weight of his secret, unbosomed himself to his new acquaintance. Balthassar made up his mind at once. He took Moncassin with him to the doge's palace, on the pretext of some business, and left him in the anteroom, while he related all that he knew to the doge and his council. Moncassin was then called in and frightened and cajoled into completing Balthassar's story where it was wanting. Then, having gone so far, he offered his whole services to the Signory. The name of Osuna had alarmed the council, and they desired to have proof of his complicity. Moncassin assured them that such proofs would be found, in the shape of letters under Osuna's signature, upon the person of Bedmar's secretary. At first the council proposed to arrest Bruillard at the Palazzo di Spagna, but this course was abandoned as too violent. Moncassin then offered to tempt Bruillard to a certain house where he might easily be seized. The secretary, however, proved wary. He had already committed a murder, and refused to venture beyond the embassy, whose right of asylum the government were unwilling to violate. The Venetians never obtained any conclusive proof that Osuna was the author, or even an accomplice of the plot. Foiled here, the government, with the help of Moncassin, introduced a spy at one of the conspirators' meetings, and the faces of all were noted. The brothers Desbouleaux and Regnault were arrested, examined by torture, executed, and hung on the piazza. Four others suffered death in the ducal prisons. Pierre and another conspirator, Rossetti, were drowned at sea by order of the admiral. Langlade was shot at Zara, along with a soldier and a boy, whom he had attached to himself. These twelve men were all who suffered death; but the excitement of the moment made the popular voice multiply these twelve into five hundred, and the sudden flight of so many foreigners from the city, gave some colour to their calculation. The fury of the populace fastened upon the Spanish ambassador, and Bedmar was soon afterwards recalled.

The discovery of the conspiracy coming with such startling rapidity, and in the midst of apparent security, gave a violent shock to the Venetian imagination, and the danger was magnified beyond all reasonable bounds. The government kept silence because they were unwilling to exaggerate an event which they knew to be, after all, more mad than perilous. But their silence had an effect the reverse of that intended. Indeed, the conspiracy in itself was of no vital moment. It is only as a symptom that it acquires importance, and as a symptom it is terribly significant. That it was localized at Venice draws attention to the curious and abnormal social condition of the sea city—sure precursor of her decline and ruin. Her vital force was gone, her growth stayed. Death and decay were at her heart. That beautiful body, beautiful still with a siren's fascination, was irrevocably doomed. "Esto perpetua," the last prayer, the last words of her great patriot Sarpi, could not save Venice from the fate that was coming past reprieve. The prophet of the "sun-girt city," looking upon her from her campanile's top, might well have wept and closed his prophecy with these words: " Piangi, che ben hai donde."

OLIVER CROMWELL AND THE VENETIAN REPUBLIC.

DURING the course of these essays we have frequently had occasion to point out the excellence of the Venetian diplomatic papers—the "Relazioni," or reports made by ambassadors on their return from their missions, and the almost daily despatches from the courts to which they were accredited. The despatches contain the minister's first impressions, the details of court life, and the events of the political world; while the "Relazioni" are elaborate synopses of the general aspect and conditions of those kingdoms whence the ministers had returned. The reports are largely based upon the despatches; but, being written at leisure, they are frequently cast in a more literary form.

The Venetian school of diplomacy has always enjoyed a deserved reputation. Our readers will not have forgotten Lord Chesterfield's advice to his son to cultivate, in whatever capital he found himself, the Venetian ambassador as the man from whom he would learn more than from any other. There were two classes of diplomatic agents employed by the republic, ambassadors and residents. Ambassadors were always patricians; they were elected in the Senate; and the post, though usually onerous, was valued as a mark of esteem. The Senate elected none but its ablest members to an embassy, and the mission was frequently a stepping-stone to the dukedom. The residents were chosen from among the secretaries to the Senate and the Ten. These secretaries all belonged to the class known as *cittadini originarii*—a sort of middle-class aristocracy; not admitted, it is true, to the Great Council, but possessing various privileges—the right to bear arms, for example—and standing between the patricians and the people. The proper title of a resident was "Circumspect;" the title of an ambassador was "Most illustrious and most excellent." Both ambassadors and residents were men who had enjoyed ample training in political life; skilled observers; bred in the school of *pensieri stretti e viso sciolto;* and the standard of fulness and accuracy demanded by the Senate was so rigid and exacting that these Venetian despatches and reports—now that they are open to inspection—acquire a singular value for us. Mistakes in detail inevitably occur, for it was impossible that a Venetian should thoroughly master all the minutiæ of daily life in the country to which he was accredited; but in these documents we have the perfectly honest and candid opinion of a skilled foreign observer, writing with the freedom and frankness engendered by the knowledge that his comments were made for his master's eye and for none other. Of course the value of the despatches and reports varies with the natural ability of the writer; but we believe no one will quarrel with the fulness and acuteness of the noble specimen we shall give in the following pages.

The documents which we purpose to use have been collected and transcribed by Signor Berchet, and cover the period of English history from the death of Charles I. to the fall of Richard Cromwell. We have selected them for two reasons : first, because of the striking portrait they present to us of the great Protector ; and, secondly, because they are in themselves an excellent example of the Venetian diplomatic style.

Venice had always maintained friendly relations with the house of Stuart. On the fall of that house the Venetians were in doubt how to act. They disliked a republican form of government, and they had no confidence that the Parliamentary *régime* would last, and were therefore unwilling to commit themselves to any acknowledgment of its supremacy. But the pressure of the war of Candia, the loss of that island, and the perpetual danger from the Turks compelled them to seek assistance wherever it could be found. No alliance seemed more desirable to them than that with England, whose fleet was rapidly becoming the most powerful in Europe, and whose interests in the East were growing steadily under the care of the Levant Company. We shall see that Venice was compelled to acknowledge first the Parliament, then Oliver, and finally Richard Cromwell, and all without obtaining the object she had in view.

We come now to the documents ; and we shall leave them to speak for themselves ; adding merely such connecting matter as may serve to make them clear, and to lead us up to the main purpose of this essay, the portrait of Cromwell drawn by Giovanni Sagredo.

As we have pointed out in a previous essay, Charles II., when in exile, sent Tom Killigrew to represent him in Venice. The Venetians expected that the Stuarts would soon return to England, and accordingly the resident was received with due honours on the 17th of February, 1650. This action on the part of Venice gave the greatest offence in England, and it subsequently cost the Venetian representative much time and trouble before he could remove the ill effects of the slight put upon Parliament. It was not long, however, before the Venetians discovered that the Stuart cause was still on the wane. The Turkish war was pressing hard upon the republic, and it resolved to abandon the royal house of England, to make peace, if possible, with Parliament, and to secure the co-operation of the English fleet against the common foe. The first step towards these objects was to dismiss Killigrew. We have already recounted the amusing details of the resident's expulsion for keeping "a bit of a butcher's shop." Killigrew left Venice in June, 1652. Previous to this, however, the Senate had sent orders to Morosini, the ambassador in Paris, to despatch his secretary, Lorenzo Pauluzzi, to London; to open relations with Parliament; to urge the Levant Company to assist Venice; to raise troops and ships for the Turkish war; and generally to report upon the condition and the prospects of that government. But Pauluzzi was sent without credentials and without any recognized official position. This was an error which cost Venice dear ; for Parliament was determined to accept nothing short of a full acknowledgment of its sovereign position. Pauluzzi left Paris for London. The duty of receiving him fell upon Sir Oliver Fleming, master of the ceremonies, a man whom Carlyle has described as "a most gaseous but indisputable historical figure, of uncertain genesis, uncertain habitat, gliding through the old books as master of the ceremonies—master of one knows not what." Pauluzzi seems to have found Sir Oliver solid enough, and certainly quite master of the situation. On the 2nd of May, Pauluzzi reports to Morosini as follows : —"I went to Fleming, master of the ceremonies, and began by explaining to him that I was your Excellencies' secretary, sent to England in Venetian interests, to raise ships and men. For that purpose I had desired to be put in communication with some of the gentlemen of Parliament; but, since the forms of the present government did not permit of this, I had come to him to assure him that if the republic thought that its friendship was desired and would be returned, it would not withhold it. At these words of friendship desired and returned Sir Oliver broke in, 'I beg you not to use such language. This republic has no need to court the good will of Venice. Let us leave these rigmaroles and formalities, and speak frankly. If you have credentials proving you the accredited minister of the Serene Republic, well and good—you will get what you want. Pray tell me distinctly ; for if you have I will adopt one tone, if you have not I will adopt another.' I found myself obliged to confess that I had no credentials, as I had only come to raise ships; but I believed that if credentials were necessary the republic would send them to me at once. Sir Oliver then grew very angry, and said, 'I am surprised that you should come here in this fashion even for the object you mention. If I, let us suppose, were to go to Venice in this way, pray tell me, what would the Serene Republic say?' I replied that he would, no doubt, receive every satisfaction, and that I expected the same. Sir Oliver answered, 'I am willing to believe it, and, no doubt, you know better than I do. But I am amazed, and so will Parliament be amazed, all the more as we have frequently been advised that the Serene Republic intended to send a commission to recognize this republic, and the delay can only proceed from aversion to the present government.' I wished to disabuse him, but he interrupted: 'Well, you have come here to raise ships and men: I believe it: but perhaps also to play the spy, as a Frenchman did lately; I must tell you that we compelled him to leave the kingdom. Up to the present time the republic acknowledges a minister of Charles Stuart; what good can such irresolution do you? If you want our friendship we are ready. And now your prudence will tell you how you ought to act.'" With this sharp lesson Pauluzzi was dismissed.

Venice proceeded to repair her mistake. On the 1st of June, 1652, Pauluzzi's credentials, addressed "To the Parliament of England," passed the Senate. But the republic had to wait seven months before Parlia-

2 B

ment considered its honour vindicated and consented to acknowledge the representative of Venice. On the 8th of January, 1653, Speaker Lenthal replied, receiving Pauluzzi as agent for the republic. Meantime Morosini had been removed from Paris, and Giovanni Sagredo filled his place. Sagredo was now Pauluzzi's immediate master, through whom he communicated with the Senate and received their orders. On the 17th of May Pauluzzi is instructed to sound the Constituent Convention as to its willingness to send an embassy to Venice should the republic send one to London. To this an affirmative answer, signed by "E. Montagu, President of the Council of State," came from Whitehall, under date November 25. But before this reciprocal intention could be carried out, Oliver Cromwell had been created Protector, and Pauluzzi remained in London in the quality of resident.

Throughout his despatches Pauluzzi is hostile to Cromwell. He announces in these words Cromwell's assumption of the Protectorate: "London, January 3, 1654. Friday last the general was created Protector of the three kingdoms. The Parliamentarians do not cease to bite their nails for having allowed him, step by step, to mount to such a height of authority as renders him odious to the people." On the 21st of February we have an account of Cromwell's first public appearance after his elevation to the Protectorship: "On his appearance not the slightest sound of applause or of satisfaction was heard, nor any blessings on the name and person of the Protector. Very different from that which used to happen when the late king appeared in public.

In general the Protector enjoys but little affection; nay, there are not wanting signs of that hatred against him, which grows daily because, under cloak of humility and care for the nation's and the people's weal, he has arrogated all authority and sovereignty. Only the title of king is wanting, while his actual power certainly exceeds that of the late king. At present, however, though they feel themselves downtrodden, dissatisfied, and deluded, they dare attempt no action ; nor do they speak except through their teeth. But every one hopes to see fulfilled some day the prophesy that this government cannot last long." And again, on March 1st. he writes, "Every day the ill humour against the Protector and the disobedience of the troops increases. Cromwell, however, persists in his habitual attitude of humility and retirement. He protests that he is only what they have made him ; that he will never be other than they wish him to be. Traits of an insincere humility, under cloak of which he aims, perhaps, at glory greater than his present ; and on this ground his headlong fall is continually foretold and desired. But he will save himself with all the greater astuteness that he knows it to be the general expectation and desire."

Pauluzzi had already had an audience of Cromwell on the 29th of January, which he thus describes : "The day before yesterday was appointed for my audience. I was received with the same ceremonial as that observed towards other ministers. I was met by Sir Oliver Fleming, and conducted to his Highness, whom I found in a chamber surrounded by twenty gentlemen, arranged on either side, and Cromwell in the middle. On my appearance in the chamber he uncovered, and remained so till I began to speak. He uncovered again at every act of reverence I made when naming the most Serene Republic. I expressed myself as follows : congratulating the Protector on his elevation, assuring him of the good will of Venice, and begging his aid against the Turks. He remained attentive to all I said, without interrupting me ; and Sir Oliver translated the whole into English. Cromwell replied in the following terms, translated into Italian by Sir Oliver, expressing his good will towards Venice ; declaring that he had every desire to assist the republic, which he considered the buckler of religion against its most powerful foe. I bowed at these expressions, and promised to report them to my government ; and with that I took my leave, accompanied by Sir Oliver to my carriage, as is the etiquette adopted towards all who are recognized as representatives of their princes and masters."

In August of the same year, Pauluzzi again had an audience of the Protector, in order to present letters of congratulation from the Senate. He was treated with greater ceremony on this occasion, having the compliment of a guard of honour of one hundred halberdiers of the Protector's household troops. Pauluzzi again raised the question of assistance against the Turk. Cromwell replied that he always admired the courage of the republic ; he would inform Pauluzzi, later on, of his decision in the matter. In January of the following year, the Senate write to Sagredo that they can no longer delay the despatch of an embassy to England. They were anxious to clinch what appeared to be a favourable disposition on the part of Cromwell. The ambassador is to receive six hundred gold ducats a month as salary; four months paid in advance, and no obligation to render accounts; a present of one thousand five hundred gold ducats for outfit; three hundred Venetian ducats for horses, boxes, rugs; three hundred for vails, of which account is to be rendered. He is to take a secretary at twenty-five ducats a month, and one hundred ducats paid down; two couriers at thirty ducats each, as usual; an interpreter and a chaplain at ten scudi a month, as usual. On the 5th of June Sagredo himself was elected for the English embassy, and received his credentials. Sagredo endeavoured to excuse himself on the ground that he was already nearly ruined by the expenses of his embassy at Paris; but the Senate declined to relieve him of his duties. Sagredo accordingly began preparations for his new mission. His carriage alone cost him one thousand five hundred crowns, and his liveries as much again. On the 1st of September he left Paris with a large suite, including, over and above his embassy staff, five Venetian noblemen and their servants. Cromwell was pleased at this mark of attention on the part of the republic, and showed his sense of the compliment by sending a man-of-war to meet Sagredo at Dieppe, which the ambassador had chosen as the point of embarkation in preference to Calais, owing to the frequent robberies committed by the garrisons of Gravelinghen and Dunkirk. Sagredo was much impressed by the size and strength of this man-of-war, and wrote to the Senate, " If your Serenity had twelve such ships, no power in the world could resist the onset. It has seven hundred men and one hundred guns." The ship crossed the Channel to Dungeness in seven hours, and landed the ambassador in England. His public reception took place by water. The grand master of the ceremonies, accompanied by thirty gentlemen and the Protector's trumpeters, came to meet him, "in sixteen feluccas," at Greenwich, whence, after a sumptuous repast, they conducted him to the Tower. At the Tower the Protector's carriage was waiting him; and, followed by five other carriages and a guard of fifty horse, he was conducted to the lodgings reserved for ambassadors and other distinguished foreigners.

Sagredo sent the Senate an account of his first audience in these terms: "On the fourth day after my public entry I was informed that, owing to the colic which had attacked his Highness, my audience was to be postponed for three days. Cromwell sent the master of the ceremonies to assure me of the regret which he felt at this delay, and to inform me that, notwithstanding the sickness which confined him to bed, he would rise on purpose to receive me, if I thought it necessary. I did not fail to thank his Highness for such obliging expressions, and added that his well-being was too valuable to be exposed to any imaginable risk; that I would wait his recovery, nothing complaining of this delay if it were employed in restoring his health.

"Three days later, he sent his carriages and two councillors of state to my lodging to fetch me. I was conducted to Whitehall, that is, the palace of the late king. On my entering the great royal hall, hung with the richest tapestry and crowded with people, Cromwell took two short steps towards me. He begged me to be covered, and I then expressed myself as follows : that the republic, wishing still further to mark their regard for the Protector, had sent me as special envoy to repeat to him what Pauluzzi had already communicated. Cromwell replied, thanking the republic, and declaring that their ambassador should receive the same treatment as that accorded to the representatives of other crowned heads. On my withdrawing, he again took two short steps towards me, hat in hand. I found him somewhat pulled down, with signs of a health not absolutely and entirely established, for I noticed that while he remained uncovered, the hand which held his hat trembled. For the rest, he is a man of fifty-six years ; a thin beard; a full habit; short, robust and martial in appearance. His countenance is dark and profound ; he carries a large sword by his side. Soldier as well as orator, he is gifted with talents to persuade and to act."

Sagredo's next despatches, dated the 5th, 6th, and 12th of November, dwell upon the difficulties he encountered in securing the object of his mission, Cromwell's aid against the Turk : "The Protector, in order to maintain the credit of his arms, and to justify his heavy taxation, resolved to attack either Turkey or the West Indies. Various considerations inclined him to the latter. I shall do all I can to induce him to attack the Turk, but there are two grave obstacles. The first is the Spanish war ; the second, the Turkey merchants, who form the most powerful party in the city, and who fear the sequestration of their wealth in the Levant. His Highness sent me last week a pamphlet setting forth the reasons which oblige England to go to war with Spain. The conjuncture is little favourable to my designs. I resolved, however, to neglect no efforts which might conduce to the public benefit. I demanded an audience of his Highness, which was granted me in his private cabinet. He met me in the middle of the room, and on my departure he accompanied me to the door. My interview had for object to win him round by playing on his religious feelings, which he displays with all palpable demonstrations of zeal, even going so far as to preach every Sunday to the soldiers, exhorting them to live godly lives. And this preaching he accompanies not merely with efficacious persuasions, but also with the example of his tears, which he holds ready at a moment's notice. By these means he excites and controls the spirit of the troops at his pleasure. In the second place, I did not fail to ply him with the stimulus of glory and fame, as follows: 'I am instructed to remind your Highness that Venice has now for eleven years been the buckler of all Christendom against the Turk. These barbarians are preparing to complete the conquest of Candia, the outwork of Italy. The zeal your Highness has for the Christian faith, that piety and religion which are the noble ornaments of your generous spirit, will surely set on fire the sacred flame of your great courage, and put a keen edge on your valorous sword, which cannot be drawn in a more glorious cause than the cause of the gospel.' To this Cromwell replied that the generous and constant defence offered by Venice against the common foe laid every Christian prince under obligations to your Serenity; that he had frequently felt the pricks and goads of zeal for the service of God; that it would have been better had I come to this court earlier—I should then have found the conjuncture favourable to my wishes; that he would take the opinion of his council. He personally was much disposed to all that might profit your Serenity, for whom he entertained a particular esteem."

These negotiations, however, produced no fruit, and Sagredo, perceiving that he could make no way with the purpose of his mission, demanded his recall. The Senate granted his request, and he left England on the 18th of February, 1656, in the middle of a violent snowstorm, having spent five months in London. He left his secretary, Francesco Giavarina, behind him as resident for the republic.

On his return to Venice, Sagredo, according to custom, read, in the Senate, an account of his embassy. This *relazione* is so interesting in itself, as a fine specimen of what these Venetian reports were like, and contains so succinct and instructive a view of the great rebellion and the Protectorate as observed by a foreign ambassador, that we shall venture to give it almost *in extenso.*

"MOST SERENE PRINCE,
    "The position, size and population of England, Scotland, and Ireland are so well known to

you, from books and from the reports of ambassadors to that court, that it would be superfluous and tedious to recite them here.

"I, Giovanni Sagredo, knight, find it more opportune that I, as your first ambassador to London after the downfall of the royal house, should give you a distinct account of how the civil war began, of the causes of that change of government, of the character of the man who at present directs and commands, of the forces and the alliances of England, and of the designs she now entertains.

"For an uninterrupted period of fifteen years that kingdom has been tossed on the troublous sea of civil war, whereon at last the royal authority made lamentable and disastrous shipwreck.

"The causes of this shipwreck are various; and perhaps the essential causes are not those which live in the mouth of the vulgar and by the notoriety of common report.

"The hatred against Charles I. of England was augmented by a certain instability in religious matters, an instability which he clearly proved by professing himself first Calvinist, then Lutheran, and finally by his passionate endeavours to render the ceremonies of the Protestant Church as similar as possible to those of Catholicism. His subjects, who had imbibed from their ministers an implacable aversion to the Catholic faith, hated him for this policy, which proved him entirely Catholic at heart. It is true, however, that his Majesty on the scaffold, guided by a diabolical desire to prove the injustice of his condemnation, publicly professed the dogmas of Protestantism, and, to the damnation of his own soul, endeavoured to give the lie to the rumour that he leaned towards the Catholic faith. We must add, as no unimportant agent in his ruin, that he lacked the spirit to govern by himself, and availed himself of ministers whose wits were slow and heavy, such as Lord Holland, or of austere prelates like the bishop of Canterbury, who desired to govern London as though it had been a college or a religious house.

"His Majesty was gifted with a placid nature, infinite goodness, and incomparable sincerity, and his breast, as though it had been made of crystal, allowed all his most secret thoughts to shine through; so that his Scotch servants, by whom he was surrounded, treacherously published his most intimate intentions, and made service to him impossible by giving his foes the opportunity to traverse his designs.

"That he did not, at the outset, present a bold front to Parliament contributed much to his misfortunes. He suffered meetings and assemblies where, under cloak of urgent reforms, the royal prerogative was attacked, and the first seeds of revolution were sown.

"The Parliament, perceiving the occasion favourable to its designs, grew in courage and audacity as the king's council showed itself lacking in credit and esteem. And, as frequently happens in civil convulsions, the first movements of Parliament were received with approval by those who love to fish in troubled waters, and think to better their own fortunes by the misfortunes of their country.

"Matters having come to an open rupture, and to the arbitrament of arms, the earl of Essex was the first who took the field against the king. In the opening encounter Essex was so thoroughly crushed and defeated, that eight thousand Parliamentarians yielded themselves prisoners to the king; among them many of his bitterest foes. But the king, always prone to clemency, and neglecting the sound advice to make a summary and deserved example of these men, let them all go free upon their oath not to bear arms against him again.

"Fairfax, successor of Essex who had been poisoned by the Parliamentarians on suspicion of his personal ambition, defeated the royal troops twice; and, after various reverses, the king resolved to place himself in the hands of the Scotch, in the hope that, as he was their countryman, they would espouse his just cause. But the Scotch, who had already ruined his Majesty by selling his secrets, now actually sold the king himself to the Parliament for two hundred thousand pounds sterling. His Majesty was closely guarded by the Scotch in a certain castle; and being asked by them whether he preferred to stay where he was or to be consigned to the English, he replied that he would rather be in the hands of those who had bought than of those who had sold him.

"When they had the king in their power the Parliamentarians deliberated long. The more moderate were of opinion that, when abuses had been reformed and pledges taken, the king should be restored to authority. Others, and among them Cromwell, who was then second in command and who enjoyed the highest esteem, represented that affairs were already reduced to extremities, admitting no adjustment and no compromise ; that the hatred between the king and Parliament was too deeply rooted, and mutual injuries too far advanced, to allow of retreat ; that the king restored would take revenge ; that those who feared to smite a crowned head would find a hundred of their own heads smitten in its place ; that the safety of Parliament must be weighed against the safety of the king; and, in short, that, holding the king a prisoner, they should proceed to condemn him as a criminal. This opinion, which gave security to guilty consciences, met with approval ; and Charles I., king of England, was condemned to be publicly executed.

"The charges against him turned on his share in the late disturbances ; on his subservience to vicious and greedy favourites ; and on the sufferings of the people during the civil war.

"The scaffold was raised level with a window of the palace, and hung with black velvet. And because they were afraid that his Majesty might resist the execution of the sentence, and refuse to lay his neck on the block, two iron rings were fastened to the foot of the scaffold, through which a cord was passed to be placed round his Majesty's neck, and so to compel him by force to extend his neck to the axe should he refuse to bow to the fatal blow.

"But the king, warned in time, without coming to these extremes, begged that no violence might be used, as he would of his own accord yield to the law of necessity and the rigour of force. He died with constancy on the 30th of January, 1648,* amid

* More Veneto.

universal silence and amazement ; for, owing to the strong detachments of troops posted in various parts, no one dared to show his sorrow except in his heart of hearts. So he died ; an example without example which struck pity not only among men, but also among the very beasts. For an old lion, who still lives in the Tower of London, showed his emotion by fierce roars, not only on the day of the execution, but even now, every year on the anniversary of the same, to the wonder and observation of all people.

"London was the chief and the most obstinate centre of the war. The people advanced from their private purses untold treasures for the maintenance of their army. The goldsmiths alone are still creditors for eight hundred thousand crowns.

"Fairfax, who was at that time in supreme command, was unwilling to sign the death-warrant. He gave a forced consent, however, when urged by Cromwell, who brought him the order from Parliament. Fairfax also refused to advance against the Scots, as that would have been a violation of treaty. Parliament compelled him to resign his baton to Cromwell, his lieutenant. Cromwell, though then only second in titular command, was in every way supreme in authority. For Fairfax was a practical soldier only, whose sword was his sole resource ; while Cromwell knew how to use his sword and his tongue equally well, and to such purpose that, after unhorsing his own general, he also unseated Parliament, though that had been the chief cause of his aggrandizement. They say that Cromwell, foreseeing that the supreme power must one day fall into his hands owing to the weakness of others and his own ability, insisted that the execution of the king should follow an act of Parliament—that is, a decree of the people—in order that the breach between the people and the king's descendants might become impassable. And to render any return of the royal family all the more difficult, the royal property, to the amount of eight hundred thousand crowns of income, was sold, along with the furnishings of the king's wardrobe, which was put up to auction.

"And as upon the wreck of some fallen palace we may see another and more magnificent edifice arise, so upon the ruins of the royal house Cromwell piled up the portentous splendour of his fortunes, until he reached that culminating point where he now stands.

"And, because all subsequent events of moment are either the result of his councils or the fruit of his actions, my report will now deal with nothing but the deeds of this man, who has become, through his fortune and his ability, the most famous figure of our day.

"On the fall of the royal authority all government and the entire control of public affairs passed into the hands of Parliament. Although Cromwell had only one vote, yet, as representative of the army, his opinion was venerated and supported by the majority. We must remember that Parliament was deliberative, the army executive.

"Cromwell's success in Ireland, and his personal courage there, rendered him all the more powerful. The reduction of Scotland, accomplished with only nine thousand men, added to his renown. Before going into battle, he encouraged his troops by telling them that God had assured him of victory by a voice which spoke to him in the midnight; and such was the confidence which his soldiers had in him, that their attack was irresistible. The Scotch broke, and there was not a man of the English army who did not bring in a prisoner apiece.

"Civil war being thus ended, a foreign war with Holland followed, on the question of the herring fisheries.

"The navies of former days were far inferior in tonnage and in guns to those of to-day, and so one may say without exaggeration that the ocean never saw more formidable armaments nor more bloody battles between two nations braver or more ferocious. As many as three hundred ships, English and Dutch, took the sea, and with such a letting of blood that many times the very waves have blushed for the shame of such cruel slaughter.

"The Dutch have received a heavy blow. They have spent more in two years' war with England than in one hundred with Spain. Their disadvantages fall under three heads.

"First, their merchant navy is out of all proportion to their fleet. Secondly, they have no bronze cannon, in which the English are well found. The English range and weight being superior, they disable the enemy before coming to close quarters.

"The third and most notable disadvantage is that the English intelligences are so good, that at the very outbreak of the war they were able to seize Dutch shipping in various waters; and in this way one may say that the Dutch have indemnified England for the expenses of the war.

"Parliament taxed the nation heavily for the maintenance of the fleet. This rendered it odious to the people. Cromwell fomented the disgust. Questions between the Parliament and the army began to arise. The army refused to submit to reforms which would weaken its power. Cromwell, foreseeing an attack on himself, with masculine resolution, placed guards at the strategical points of the city, and entering Parliament, accompanied by a few officers, said, 'You have too long sucked the purest blood from English veins; the nation is weary of suffering the ruinous consequences of your misgovernment; you have overplayed the prince, a *rôle* that does not belong to you; now, stripped of the royal mantle and kingly authority, get you about your business; the comedy is over.'

"The members, in amazement, kept silence; but the Speaker demanded by what authority Cromwell dared to sack Parliament. Then Cromwell, showing his sword, replied that his authority lay there. He drove the Speaker from his seat, removed the mace, and the other members, in terror and confusion, went their ways.

"This change of government took place without any rising. Those who pitied the king rejoiced to see the authors of his disasters humiliated. The people applauded the vigour of Cromwell, whose authority and esteem served to justify his acts.

"The Dutch war continued; but after the fierce battle in which Tromp was killed, peace was concluded upon terms most advantageous to England. By this peace Cromwell became yet more respected and feared. He summoned two other Parliaments, but these proving restive under his orders were presently dissolved. Cromwell was unwilling any longer to submit his towering and dominating prosperity to public criticism. He accordingly established the military government which now exists. He caused himself to be proclaimed Protector of the three kingdoms, with the council, which he retained in order to preserve the fiction of a republic, and to lessen the odium which his despotic government creates. He has declined the crown ; for, after overthrowing the royal dignity, it would have been a too naked display of hypocrisy to place the crown on his own head. Cromwell cares nothing for a name. He is content with his authority and power, beyond all comparison greater, not only than that of any king who ever reigned in England, but than that of any monarch who wields a sceptre in the world just now.

"The fundamental laws of the nation are upset, and Cromwell is the sole legislator. His laws are dictated by his own judgments and his own desires. All offices issue from his hands. The members of the council must be nominated by him ; nor can they rise to power except through him ; and, that no one may become master of the army, he has left the office of lieutenant-general vacant.

"As for his wealth, no king ever raised so much from his subjects. England pays at present one hundred and twenty thousand pounds sterling a month in burdens ; besides this, the duty of five per cent. on all merchandise sold or bought in a city of such flourishing commerce as London amounts to three million two hundred thousand crowns a year; add to this the dues on export and import for the whole kingdom, and the confiscations of private fortunes, such as the duke of Buckingham's, which amount to an enormous sum—for the revenue of the English nobility exceeds that of any other nobility. The Catholics, on a payment of two-thirds of their income, are permitted to continue in the exercise of their creed. In spite of all this wealth the Protector is not rich. His expenditure exceeds his income. There are twelve millions a year for the armament; for Cromwell is obliged to support those who supported him. At the beginning of the civil war the pay of the Parliamentary troops and sailors was increased, in order to entice the king's forces away from him. But the durability of a government founded on force depends upon the troops; it is therefore necessary to pay the soldiers punctually to avoid revolt. The army is well fed and clad, but rigorously disciplined. Neglect of duty is punished by the rod; for an ordinary oath, instant cashiering; for excesses, imprisonment, and sometimes hanging. Promotion by merit, not by seniority, causes complaints against the government. These are reported to the Protector by his numerous spies. He purifies the army by sending mutinous troops to the Indies, or to the extreme parts of the kingdom; by these purgatives he cures the disease, and prevents it from increasing and infecting the principal members.

"It is a remarkable point among the maxims of his

supersubtle policy, that, knowing he could not rely on the aristocracy, he began to raise to the highest commands in the army people of low degree, on purpose that they, seeing their whole fortunes to depend on him, might be bound to support his pre-eminence. This policy, which has welded the existence of the Protector and of the army in indissoluble bands, leaves but faint hopes that the king of Scotland will ever be able to untie and dissolve a union based upon such reciprocal interests. It is certain that the troops live with as much regularity as a religious body. It was observed during the late war that when the king's soldiers gained a victory they abandoned themselves to wine and debauchery; those commanded by Cromwell were compelled, after their greatest successes, to pray and fast.

"And here I must touch upon Cromwell's religion. He makes no regular external professions, and so it is impossible to know what rites he follows. In the late civil war he professed himself Anabaptist. This is a sect which abhors princedom and pretends to hold off God alone. Cromwell, immediately on his elevation to the command, not only separated from the Anabaptists, or Independents, but disavowed and persecuted them. Guided by interests of state he changes his religion. He holds that it comports with his policy that in London they profess two hundred and forty-six religions, all united in alienation from the pontiff, but among themselves very dissimilar and antagonistic. The disunion of so many various sects renders them all weak, and none can waken his apprehension.

"If at this point I were to represent to your Excellencies the dissonance and variation of these sects, I should waste much time and merely stir your pity and your smiles. Near my house there lives a noble lord with six grown sons, all of different religions ; they are always in disputes perpetual and infinite, and sometimes come to blows, so that their father's whole time is employed and embarrassed in separating and pacifying them.

"Cromwell, in short, is master of the most beautiful island in the world, of great circumference and width, abounding in men, and so happy in its fertility that in the most rigid winter season the animals always find green pastures ; where, though the land produce no wine, one drinks better than in viniferous countries; for the wine acquires strength and flavour on its journey, and by its passage over sea.

"What the land produces not is nevertheless abundant ; it is drawn thither by the copious and flourishing commerce of London—a city which yields not to Paris in population, in the wealth of its merchants, in extent, and, above all, in its convenience to the sea, which wafts in such abundance of shipping that, on my arrival, I counted more than two thousand sail upon the famous river Thames.

" And yet it is true that, after the change of government, the glory and the grandeur of London have altered much. For the most illustrious nobility which gathered there and made it brilliant is now crushed and mortified and scattered over the country. And the delicacy of the court, the gayest and most sumptuous in the world, is changed now to a perpetual march and countermarch of troops, an incessant noise of drums and trumpets, and a long train of officers and soldiers at their posts.

"The government knows that it possesses a kingdom separated from the rest of the world—a kingdom that fears not invasion, and needs no foreign support, for it has abundant forces to protect itself and to cause alarm in others with its fleet of choice ships that hold the sea in obedience and give the law wherever they pass.

"And foreign powers are held of so much the less account that they have vied with one another in open demonstrations of respect and esteem for the man who now rules England.

"In short, I can assure your Serenity that England fears no other power; nay, she claims to waken fear in them.

"And therefore they receive without returning embassies, as do the Turks; nor do they seek alliances, but expect to be sought.

"As regards your Serenity, I am bound to report with frankness events as they occurred; and I say that the despatch of Pauluzzi without credentials was taken ill. For this reason they refused him audience for seven months, nor would they ever have granted it had not credentials been given him in quality of resident.

"Then the tardy despatch of an ambassador extraordinary was taken in bad part; for Venice was the last of all the powers to send one.

"It was openly said that the Senate entertained an aversion to this form of government, and stigmatized it as illegitimate. It cost me some pains, before my arrival, to remove this suspicion. I succeeded in convincing his Highness that the despatch of an embassy to him, when none had been sent to Parliament, was a sign of peculiar respect for his person and rank. This argument made a breach in his mind. He sent a man-of-war to France for me, and I was received with all the distinctions and prerogatives in use towards other ambassadors. When the French and Spanish ambassadors left London my chapel was crowded with Catholics. The ministers objected, but Cromwell refused to interfere with my liberty.

"I reached England at a moment unfortunate for the object of my mission, when the West Indian campaign was already resolved upon. It is true, moreover, that the Levant Company—that is to say, the wealthiest Turkey merchants—watched my negotiations jealously. They insisted that, as the company had four millions of capital in Turkish ports, the slightest suspicion would suffice to induce the Turk to confiscate it, as had lately happened in Spain.

"Having now succinctly reported the changes, the forces, alliances, designs, and form of the English government, I must return to certain particulars about Cromwell, who has become so conspicuous and so famous throughout the world.

"Certain it is that history will have to dwell at length on all that I have compressed into this compendium, and that Cromwell must be considered as a favourite of Fortune's partiality. It is impossible to deny that by his genius and activity he has contributed to his own glory. But although he is rich in courage, wit, and natural prudence, all those parts would have served him nothing had he lacked the opportunity to become great. He made use of his talents and he seized his opportunity.

"Born at Huntingdon of a father whose blood was noble, but whose fortune was less than moderate, Cromwell was first a cornet, then a captain in the cavalry. Cambridge elected him as its member and sent him to Parliament.

"He is a man of the sword as well as of the tongue, and hence it is that he has climbed by such great strides. He rose to be colonel, sergeant-general, lieutenant-general, and finally general of the whole army. Favoured by fortune in many a battle, he proved himself a man of iron courage and fearless in the sharpest and most dangerous encounters.

"When he was general, two thousand sailors mutinied and betook themselves to his house, demanding their pay. He heard the noise, and went downstairs with four officers who were dining with him. He thrust himself into the crowd, sword in hand, killed one and mortally wounded another, with such speed and dexterity that the rest, terrified at this example and overawed by their veneration for his person, fled to their ships.

"Outwardly religious in the extreme, he preaches with eloquence to the soldiers, exhorting them to live according to the law of God; and, to render his persuasions more efficacious, he often makes use of tears, weeping more for the sins of others than for his own. He is a man of a solid and massive judgment; and he knows the character of the English as a horseman knows horses of his *manége,* and so with the smallest sign of his whip he guides them whither he will.

"He is not severe except with those of the opposite party; courteous and civil with his own, and liberal in rewards to those who have served him well.

"For the rest, in general he is more feared than loved—mortally hated by the Royalists, who are no small body, but who are powerless, being spoiled of wealth and arms.

"His pleasure is to ride often in his coach to Hampton Court, a country house of the late king. He never shows himself in London because of the accident which happened to him there when he was going to the City to take the Protectorate. A large stone was thrown from a window and fell on the top of his carriage, breaking it in and passing close to his head. In spite of every effort the author was never discovered.

"He lives in perpetual suspicion. The smallest gathering of men rouses his apprehension; and therefore plays, horse-races, and all recreations which might collect a crowd, are forbidden. At the public audience which is open to all, I have seen, at various doors, officers of the guard with drawn swords in their hands.

"They say he never sleeps twice in the same room, and often changes his bed for fear of some mine. Some have even been discovered. It is true, however, that the government often invents conspiracies to afford a pretext against the Royalists, and therefore to increase the army and the guards.

"Cromwell is deeply mortified that he has no children of spirit and intelligence. His two sons lack the vigour of their father, and therefore he takes no pains to make his greatness hereditary; being sure the edifice must fall when it has such weak supports as these two sons of tardy and heavy intellect.

"The first man in the army is Sergeant-General Lambert. They say that in his heart he does not love Cromwell, though outwardly he professes the closest union with him. In any case, no one is more able than Lambert to cause a change and form a party.

"Whether the present government will last long is a difficult question. It is likely, however, that after the death of Cromwell we may see some change of scene, in accordance with the universal law that violence can never endure."

Giavarina, late secretary to the embassy, remained in London as Venetian resident at the Protector's court. His instructions were to urge, upon every possible occasion, the advisability of assisting the Venetians against the Turks. This he did, but without success. On the death of Cromwell, Giavarina conveyed the condolences of the Senate to his son Richard. Giavarina was treated with all ceremonious respect. Five court carriages, drawn by six horses each, were sent to take him to Whitehall. Richard Cromwell held out every prospect of being willing to satisfy the Venetians' request. But Giavarina warned his government not to place much reliance on these promises, which he considered were made more with a view to induce the republic to acknowledge Cromwell by the despatch of a special envoy, than with any idea of their actual fulfilment. Giavarina's residence in London was not more pleasant than it was profitable. He found himself in difficulties on account of the asylum and shelter which he gave at the residency to twenty Catholic priests, whom the Spanish ambassador had left behind him when he was recalled. Giavarina was still further embarrassed by the superior place assigned to the legate of Brandenburg at court ceremonies. He considered it his duty to absent himself on this ground from the festivities attending the confirmation of Richard Cromwell as Protector. The Senate, however, disapproved his conduct, and even proposed to recall him from his post. Nor were these the only troubles which Giavarina had to endure. The Senate paid him very poorly and very irregularly; the expenses of the residency were heavy; he found himself overwhelmed with debt; and, to put a crown to his misfortunes, on the night of the 18th of October, 1657, the residency was broken into by twelve thieves, who bound and beat the resident, and, as he says himself, " robbed me of everything, even my hat ; the public ciphers and despatches alone escaping by a miracle."

But better days were in store for Giavarina. The Protectorate fell, the Stuarts were restored, and the Venetian resident had the honour to be the first foreign representative to welcome Charles at Canterbury the day after his landing in England.

VENICE OF TO-DAY.

So much has been written, and is being written daily, about Venice from the picturesque point of view, that one is tempted to cry " Enough," to declare that the subject is exhausted for the present. Such, however, is not the case. For some reasons, which we will presently try to indicate, the fascination which the sea-girt city exercises over her devotees is inexhaustible. The lover returns to the contemplation of his mistress with ardour ever new; he resumes the endless task of cataloguing her charms, only to find that having said all, he has not said half enough. The truth is that we must number Venice among the "cities of the soul;" she ranks with Oxford, Rome, Siena, Prague; she has the fatal gift to touch the imagination, to awaken a permanent desire. Of course I do not mean that every one feels thus about Venice. I cannot forget, when the floods of 1882 had destroyed the exits from the city, that row of discontented Englishmen who lined the hall of one hotel, cursing the place and glowering at the porter as though he were responsible for the downpour on the Alps. For these the language of the Venice-lover must seem as the crackling of thorns under the pot, like sheer moon-madness ; but they are always at liberty to keep away, to read nothing that bears the name of Venice, not so much as to have heard whether there be a Venice or no.

Perhaps the æsthetic quality which most emphatically belongs to the Venetian landscape, the quality wherein resides the secret of her charm, is infinite variety. As a proof of this assertion, I would adduce the fact that no one is quite satisfied with what others write or say about the city, is not satisfied with what he says himself; something is said, but not all—part of the truth, but not the whole truth. The aspects of Venice are as various, as manifold as the hues held in solution upon her waters beneath a scirocco sky. There is a perpetual miracle of change; one day is not like another, one hour varies from the next; there is no stable outline, such as one finds among the mountains, no permanent vista, as in a view across a plain. The two great constituents of the Venetian landscape, the sea and the sky, are precisely the two features in nature which undergo most incessant change. The cloud-wreaths of this evening's sunset will never be repeated again ; the bold and buttressed piles of those cloud-mountains will never be built again just so for us ; the grain of orange and crimson that stains the water before our prow, we cannot be sure that we shall look upon its like again. The revolution of the seasons will, no doubt, repeat certain effects : spring will chill the waters to a cold, hard green ; summer will spread its breadth of golden light on palace front and water-way ; autumn will come with its pearly grey scirocco days, and sunsets flaming with a myriad hues; the stars of a cloudless winter night, the whole vast dome of heaven, will be reflected in the mirror of the still lagoon. But in spite of this general order of the seasons, one day is less like another day in Venice than anywhere else; the lagoon wears a different aspect each morning when you rise, the sky offers a varied composition of cloud each evening as the sun sets. Words cannot describe Venice, nor brush portray her ever-fleeting, ever-varying charm. At most they can give one mood that Venice creates, one aspect of the light and colour upon her palace walls and water streets. Venice is to be felt, not reproduced; to live there is to live a poem, to be daily surfeited with a wealth of beauty enough to madden an artist with despair at its ungraspability; and hence it may be that Venice has had so few adequate portrayers among the thousands who have essayed the task, and not a single poet, if we except Shelley, who better than any one else has, incidentally in "Julian and Maddolo," caught and expressed the general spirit of the lagoon landscape; and Mr. Pinkerton, who has seized another of the more prominent qualities of that landscape, the all-pervading, sad, caressing grey, characteristic of the lagoons in scirocco weather, and has translated this quality into its corresponding mood of mind with a touch at once so true and delicate, that I know not where to look for a more faithful portrayal of this emotion.

It is remarkable that the most frequent efforts to express the feeling of Venice in words, should have been cast in prose and not in verse, and should be the work of foreigners, not of Venetians. George Sand, Ruskin, Théophile Gautier, all strangers over whom has been thrown the spell of the siren, who, leaving her, have borne away with them an incurable wound, for which the only solace has been to dwell again in memory with the features of the beloved, and to reproduce her lineaments on the mirror of the mind. The Venetians love their Venice, but they do not write about her; they live with her, and that is enough. With painters, on the other hand, the case is different; though here again we feel that the artists have given us a part of Venice, not the whole, a quality of light or of colour, one aspect of her infinitely various beauty. Although the great Venetian masters are chiefly concerned with the external life of their city, her pomp and circumstance, incidentally we find them influenced to the very depths of their art by the æsthetic qualities of their native place. The dome-like spaces which Bellini leaves above his throned Madonnas' heads, recall the infinite sweep of the vast Venetian sky; nowhere in painting do we feel, as we feel in Tintoret, that shimmer of light, that blending of tones which belong to the waters of the lagoon; nowhere are the flaming glories of the sunset sky more vividly reproduced than in the triumphant splendours of Titian's canvases. Turner perceived the diffusion and blending of light and colour which we note as a principal feature in the Venetian landscape, and strove to reproduce it in the radiant morning light of " Returning from the Ball," and in the marvellous blending of colour in sky, sail, and sea, in " The Sun of Venice." Turner came near to grasping the spirit of Venetian landscape; but even he found that there were more tones in heaven and sea than dwelt upon his palette.

In writing about the charm of Venice, it is difficult for those who feel it to avoid becoming dithyrambic. Venice admits no Laodiceans; hot or cold you must be. The spell begins the moment the traveller leaves the dust and roar of the railway station, and finds himself suddenly, and without warning, on the borders of the Grand Canal. No one who has once felt the thrill of delight that revelation brings is likely to forget it. And day by day the spell is deepened as the stranger grows familiar with the city's winding ways, and with the waters upon which she floats. Hitherto we have asked what is the chief character- istic in this landscape which acts so swiftly and so potently, and we have found that, in its widest terms, the dominant external, æsthetic quality of the lagoons is vastness and variety; the vast dome of heaven above, the vast expanse of water below, the infinite variety of light and colour in both.

But this wide external setting of sea and sky is not the only ingredient in the Circe-cup. There is the city itself and her people. And, coming a little closer, we may dwell for a while on the singularity of Venice's geographical position, and the uniqueness of her history and life. An old Venetian writer has styled one of his books, "Venezia, Città Nobilissima Singolare;" and singular, indeed, is the position of this city, lying spread out like a lotus, her palaces and campanili thrown up from the long level of the water, a boss upon the silver shield of the lagoon. Perhaps no piece of water in the world is more remarkable than this hundred and eighty-four square miles of Venetian lagoon, shut off from the sea by the narrow breakwater of sandy islands, called the Lidi. Whether the lagoons were formed by a subsidence of the land and an inroad of the sea, leaving the Lidi as high points unsubmerged; or whether the Lidi were originally bars built by the rivers Brenta, Sile, and Piave, across their mouths, eventually causing those streams to flood their deltas, is an open. question. But whatever may be the history of their formation, the lagoons are an essential feature in the landscape and the life of Venice. They gave protection to her first founders, when flying from the ruin wrought by the Huns upon the mainland; and to-day the health and safety of the city still depend upon the regular ebb and flow of their waters. The rivers which helped to make the lagoon have long been banished from their ancient courses, and now discharge their streams direct into the sea. All the varied movement of this water-system depends upon the Adriatic for its life and being. The lagoon is not a lake, still less is it a swamp, nor is it like the open sea. The internal economy of the lagoons is a piece of most singular natural engineering, for the circumference of these hundred and eighty-four square miles, which at high tide seems to inclose one unbroken stretch of water, really contains four distinct water-systems, with separate watersheds, main arteries, and confluent streams by which the sea, twice a day, as from a great heart, comes pulsing in through the four breaks in the Lido barrier, performing its task of cleansing and purifying the lagoon, and bearing away with it, on its outgoing, all the refuse of the city. At low tide these channels and arteries are quite distinctly marked, as they wind between the oozy banks of mud, which in spring are green with long trails of sea-grass, and in autumn are brown and bare, taking the reflection of colour from the sky. But at high tide the whole surface is flooded, and there lies Venice with her adjacent islets—San Servolo, San Clemente, Poveglia—set like gems upon a silver targe. On the mainland shore of the lagoon there is a strange debatable territory called the Laguna Morta, where the sea and land are in doubt, blending with one another, and producing a region that is neither sea nor land. This dead lagoon is the home of wild fowl, and of pungent, salt sea-plants, tamarisk and samphire, and above all, in autumn, wide fields of pale sea-lavender. Beyond the Laguna Morta the ground consolidates, and the Venetian plain, studded with villas, poplars, vineyards, and mulberry-groves trends up to the foot of the barrier Alps. The lagoon, the Alps, and Venice, floating upon the one and guarded and circled by the other, are the noblest features in the landscape. From the water you can see the whole vast sweep of mountain chain, beginning far in the east with the snowy hills of Carnia, curving round the broad Fruili plain, and springing to exquisite proportions and jewelled shape in Monte Cavallo, Antelao, and Tofana, finally dying away in filmy pale-blue crests beyond Verona and the Lago di Garda, and under the battlemented snows of Adamello. Here again we enjoy a sense of vastness and of space. These long and immovable lines of serrated peaks, touched, even in summer, now and again with snow, and in winter white and cold and clear to their very roots—peaks with beloved names that invite the climbing spirit, are all yours to gaze at and to dream about, lazily rocked in your gondola on the bosom of the still lagoon.

Such is the general external aspect of Venice. The history of the city is no less singular. When those first refugees from the mainland sought an asylum on the shoal mud-banks, drove their first piles, and built their wattled walls, they little thought that they were founding a community whose history would flow in unbroken current for more than a thousand years, that their descendants would be the richest lords in Europe, that their navies would ride supreme in all known waters, and pour the wealth and opulence of the East through Venice upon the Western world. In the isolation of their lagoons the Venetians acquired freedom and learned self-government. The obscurity of their position permitted them to grow undisturbed. The first seed, blown by the gust of invasion from the mainland to the mud islands, had time to mature in quiet, to strike deep roots into the soil, and to spring into a lofty and beautiful tree. The chief feature in the early history of Venice is that she belonged neither to the East nor to the West; neither to the empire of Constantinople, nor to the kingdoms which sprang up on the ruins of Rome. She lay between the two, a nest of hardy islanders, determined and ready to assert her independence. If the Lombards claimed her, she appealed to Constantinople; if the emperor wished to interfere, she flung herself on the Western side. She drew from East and West alike that nourishment which went to make her what she really was—a nation by herself, a peculiar people, Venetians of Venice. The history of this singular growth falls broadly into four great periods: these we may distinguish as the period of consolidation, the period of empire, the period of entanglement, and the period of decline.

When the early settlers, flying before the Hunnish terror, first took to the lagoons, they fell upon the various islands of the Archipelago and upon the long ridges of sand that guard the lagoon from the sea; and each little group of immigrants began a separate life for itself, retaining as far as possible the customs, religion, and constitution of their ruined home on the mainland. The Lidi, as being furthest removed from the danger of invasion, were the favourite asylum; the largest townships sprang up there—Heraclea, Jesolo, and Malamocco. These townships gradually drew together into a federation of twelve communes, each governed by its own tribune, and meeting in general assembly for the settlement of business which affected the general interest of the lagoons. Jealousy and internecine feuds soon appeared, as one or other of these townships came to the front, and endeavoured to impose its will upon its neighbours. Now it was Heraclea which claimed to lead, and destroyed its neighbour and rival Jesolo, and was in its turn attacked and razed to the ground by Malamocco. It is possible that had this period of internal rivalry continued for long, the lagoon communities might have frittered away their strength in private quarrels, and the state of Venice might never have emerged at all. But external pressure came in time to save the confederation and to compel the lagoon town-ships to consolidate. The perils of ·the mainland sowed the first seeds of Venice; the peril of the sea was to form and complete her. Pipin's attack taught the Venetians for the first time how impregnable was their sea-girt home; and they never forgot the lesson. For long months the Frankish chivalry was held at bay, defied by the impenetrable network of small canals and oozy mud-banks, through which no passage could be found. Finally the assault was shaken off, and Pipin retired to Milan. At this moment of their great victory a fusion between the Venetians and their home took place; henceforth each belongs essentially to the other. It is to this triumph over Pipin that the Venetians looked back as to their birth-hour: the story of the victory is haloed in romance, and cherished as the sacredest record in all Venetian history. The Hunnish invasion proved the dangers of the mainland; Pipin's attack demonstrated the peril of the sea. The Venetians now effected a compromise, and chose as the future home of their state that group of islands, midway between the sea and the land, then known as Rialto, but henceforth to bear the proud name of Venice.

The consolidation at Rialto closes the first period of Venetian history; the period of deepest interest for us. Modern Venice, with all her pride of palaces, wealth of art, variety and picturesqueness of life, dates from the repulse of the Franks. The people of Venice in this struggle attained to manhood; they learned their power ; their union gave them force. They began to create their constitution, that singular monument of rigidity and durability, which persisted, with hardly a break in its structure, for the next ten centuries. The aristocracy of Venice emerges ; her empire extends, following the lines of her commerce in the East ; St. Mark is substituted for St. Theodore as patron ; the Crusades are used as a means to conquer Dalmatia and to plant the lion in the Greek Archipelago. Venice clashes with her rival Genoa, and struggles for this Eastern Empire ; from the shock she emerges victorious. Into her state coffers and her private banks poured all that wealth which was presently to issue in the pomp of art, the pageantry of existence, her palace fronts along the Grand Canal, her learned academies, her printing press, her schools of painting, her regal receptions, the splendour of her state functions, the sumptuousness of private life ; all, in short, that made her what she was—the dazzling pleasure-garden of Europe, the envied of other states, although she had already overpassed her apogee. For her greatness and her pride were leading her towards her doom. Not content with her commercial empire in the East, Venice could not resist the temptation to put out her hand and to seize the wrecks of the Visconti's dukedom ; to build herself an empire on the land. She was caught and entangled in the mesh of Italian intrigue ; she became a factor in continental politics, and was brought face to face with the great powers of Europe. Her progress upon the mainland aroused jealousy ; the other states of Italy became uneasy for their own safety. Rome seized the opportunity to form the League of Cambray, whose object was to annihilate the republic. The league failed of its object; but the wars it entailed left Venice crippled, and other disasters poured upon her head. Her commerce in the East received an irreparable blow by the discovery of the Cape of Good Hope, which took the carrying trade out of her hands. She ceased to be the mart of Europe.* She was left to battle alone against the Turk; slowly expending blood and money, vainly appealing to indifferent Europe. Under this weight of misfortunes her strength was broken; she declined, and sank. The rigidity of her constitution held her still together; there were flashes of her old brilliancy and power in Morosini's conquest of the Peloponnese. But her day was past, and Venice gradually wasted away till she was but a wreck and hollow show of her former glory; the last of her doges yields the state to Napoleon without a blow, and, laying the ducal biretta on the table, calls to his servant, "Take it away, I shall not use it more."

But, though the republic fell, Venice still remains; Venice, the place and the people. There are two ways of seeing Venice intimately, of obtaining a closer view of both as they are to-day: one is by sea, with help of a gondola; the other is by land, wandering through that curious maze of narrow streets in which it is a delight to lose one's self. No conveyance can be more delightful, more easy, more romantic than the gondola: it is the most beautiful boat in the world,

* It is not impossible that the Suez Canal may restore to Venice her lost position.

and the most luxurious carriage ; and, like all things connected with Venice, is essentially a child of the place ; its form is adapted to the needs of the strange city that created it ; the lines of its structure are governed by the purpose it has to serve, the passage of the narrow Venetian water-ways. The visitor who is interested in his carriage cannot do better than pay a visit to the *squero*, or building-yard, where his gondola was made. His gondolier will be proud to take him. The *squeri* are picturesque though pitchy places. The long lines of boats drawn up to be cleaned or mended lie like a row of stranded whales. At one corner the pitch-pot stands always ready boiling, sending its thick black smoke into the air ; and the boys rush round the caldron, grimy as imps, each with a smearing brush brandished in his hands. Or, perhaps, the bottom of some boat has to be dried thoroughly and in haste, before receiving its coating of melted tallow. This is done by kindling a brisk blaze of reeds under the boat ; the flames leap high into the air ; volumes of pale smoke roll up over the housetops, and are swept away seaward by the breeze; the boys dance about in front of the flames, like demons officiating at some sacrifice ; there is much shouting and noise; the whole scene is strange and picturesque.

The art of gondola-building is one which requires great nicety and exactness. Three qualities are especially demanded of the boat : that it should draw little water, that it should turn easily, and that it should be rowable by one oarsman. To secure these conditions the hull is built of light thin boards ; only a very small portion of its flat bottom, thirty-six feet in length, rests upon the water, and the boat swings as on a pivot; and, finally, the boat is not equally divided by a line drawn from stern-post to bow—there is more bottom on one side than on the other, in order to counterbalance the weight of the rower behind. The ornaments of the gondola, the familiar steel prow or *ferro*, the sea-horses or dolphins, the rude carving of some scene from Tasso, all that makes the vessel the picturesque object we know, are furnished elsewhere than at the *squero*. Should any one be curious about the natural history of these ornaments, and their gradual development through the centuries, he cannot do better than consult the pictures in the Academy by Gentile Bellini and Carpaccio, and the later works of Guardi and Canaletto. In the former he will see the Venetian noblemen in their gondolas, with the bright covering of Eastern rugs for a *tenda;* the *ferro* not shaped as now, with its hatchet-head and six teeth, but merely a round club of metal; the tall rower, graceful then as ever, in his party-coloured hose and slashed doublet. In the pictures of Guardi and Canaletto the gondola has undergone a great change; it is the modern gondola that we see: the boat has lost its brilliant colouring, but, as a compensation, it has certainly gained in grace.

The gondola is so intimately connected with life in the sea-city, that, of the pictures and impressions which one carries away, stored in the portfolio of the mind, a very large number must be associated with one's boat. And what can be more delightful than to start some morning early to spend a day upon the lagoon? Venice is never more lovely than on a clear summer morning; the air is sweet, the light falls on palace fronts in broad white flakes, the breeze blows fresh from the Lido, whither we are bound. As we row past the green point of the public gardens the fishing-boats are coming in from their night's toil, laden with fish for the Rialto market; some are not yet come to anchor, and cross and recross one another as they tack, threading the figures of their sea *sarabande;* others lie, bow by painted bow, their nets hauled mast-high to be mended and dried in the sun, and their great coloured sails close together, and folded like the wings of a butterfly just alighted on a flower. The sails of Venice are a constant object of beauty in the landscape; their deep oranges and reds, their fantastic designs—here a heart pierced by a sword, there a rose in bloom, or a star with a flash of lightning breaking from it—contrast so vividly with the cool grey of the waters upon which they float. On the Lido itself, when one has reached the Adriatic side, one may wander for miles in either direction along the shore, where the lizards bask in the hot sand, where the pale sea-holly, with its delicate purple bloom, grows to perfection, mingled with the faint yellow of the evening primrose. The Adriatic, the great water avenue to Venice, opens away to south-east, while on the furthest horizon you can just discern the faint blue line of hills above Trieste, and the top of Monte Maggiore that overhangs Fiume and the Quarnero Gulf. A little way along the shore, and out of reach of those crowds that flock to the bathing establishment, is an unfinished wooden châlet;

standing in grounds partially enclosed, and planted with euonymus, a shrub that grows luxuriantly in Venice. The house was begun for Victor Emanuel, but never completed; and from its upper windows you command a glorious view of Venice, backed by her chain of guardian Alps. The city lies like a flower upon the water; the rosy front of the ducal palace, the slender campanili of San Giorgio and San Francesco, set on either side of St. Mark's more massive tower; on the one hand the bright green woods of the public garden, and far away on the other the cones of the Euganean Hills, that rise like islands above the misty levels of the plain: over all, the vault of the vast Venetian sky, cut by the serrated line of silent and eternal snow. It is pleasant, as the day grows hotter, to leave the glare of the more open shore of Sant' Elizabetta, and to seek the woods of the Favorita, where the acacia groves and catalpas yield some shade, where the whole ground is carpeted with the white and gemlike star of Bethlehem; or, better still, to wander down the English-looking lane and water-meadows that lead to the fort of San Nicolo, where the gondola can be sent to meet us. Inside the fort the grass is greener and the boskage more profound than anywhere else within easy reach of Venice. In late spring the perfume from the pure acacia blooms is borne far out across the water, and in the grass sweet violets grow in abundance. Behind the acacia grove is a Protestant burial-ground, now disused, where lie the bones of many an Englishman who came to Venice for pleasure, and remained to die: here is the tomb of Sir Francis Vincent, last

English ambassador to the republic; and here, too, that distinguished Anglo-Venetian, Mr. Rawdon Brown, prepared himself a grave, and daily came to tend the shrubs and flowers at whose feet he hoped to sleep. The Austrians granted Mr. Brown this exceptional privilege; but the present masters of Venice refused to carry it into effect, and nothing now remains except the thick and rankly growing hedge which surrounds the empty grave. There is no more beautiful promenade in Venice than that around the ramparts of the San Nicolo; past the little red *osteria*, the Buon Pesce, where the blackbirds sing in the ivy-mantled walls of the old convent garden, out by the Custom House, and on to the ramparts themselves. In summer the broad earthworks are spread with a carpet of more than Persian brilliancy; crimson poppies, purple salvias, and vivid green grass. Round the corner of the fort the current sweeps in or out of the Lido mouth, the ancient water entrance to the city, and marks the water surface in swirls and varying tones of silver grey. Far to the east, in the offing, the sunlight falls upon the congregated sails of the fishing-boats plying their business by the Piave's mouth, where fish are most abundant. Everywhere there is a sense of space in sky and sea, and the pungent odour of sea-brine upon the air.

In the evening we may return by the island convent of San Lazzaro, where the Armenian monks spend their placid lives in study and the culture of their garden lands here and on the Lido. The island is a veritable gem of colour set upon the lagoon; for the monks have painted their convent a deep crimson, and all day long San Lazzaro glows upon the water like an oleander bloom blown from one of its own garden bowers. Ungrudging access is granted to this garden and cloister rich in flowers. The terraced walk looks towards Venice, and is planted with alternate cypress and oleander trees. Between these exquisite settings are framed vignettes of the city; San Giorgio and San Marco, San Giovanni and San Francesco; and the green point of the public gardens. This terrace is a place on which to bask and dream the evening through; watching the crabs sunning themselves and fighting on the sloping wall-foundations, or noting the ripples stirred by some fish upon the shoal lagoons; watching, too, the sunset flame itself to death behind the Euganean Hills, while the heavens slowly change from gold to orange, to crimson, to purple, to pale transparent azure, till night comes silently over the Eastern waters, veiling the brilliant hues of day; the first stars begin to tremble in the blue; it is time to seek the gondola and to row home towards the long line of piazza lights that make a broad inviting path for us across the lagoon.

The lagoon offers many expeditions more distant than the one to which we have just referred. Torcello, with its ancient Basilica and mosaics, its Greek church of Santa Fosca, its old traditions of early lagoon history, and its present desolation, will always prove a favourite. The way to Torcello takes us through six miles of lagoon scenery. After leaving Venice behind us, our prow is set towards the easternmost corner of the lagoon, that desolate unexplored tract of marshland, formerly known as the " Dogado," where the doge had his preserves of fishing and shooting, and whence came the wild-duck, which by custom he was obliged to present to every noble on St. Barbara's Day. Torcello lies between Venice and the Dogado; and to reach it we have to pass Murano, with its glass furnaces sending their long black streamers of smoke into the air. Presently we reach Mazzorbo, once the greater city, the *major urbs,* now composed of a few scattered houses, a wine-shop, and a church, whose campanile is riddled with Austrian shot. The Alps go with us all the way to Mazzorbo, marching along, pace for pace; but at the entrance to the village we forsake the open lagoon, and pass into a narrow canal that winds between high garden walls, over whose coping hangs a mantle of ivy, with here and there a burning spot of pomegranate flower. Spring and autumn are equally delightful at Torcello. In spring the orchards and the hedges of thorn are in full bloom; the delicate sprays of pink or white are thrown up in relief against the blue sky. In autumn all the water-meadows are a shimmer of purple-red, from the feathery plumes of the sea-lavender that gives to the waste spaces the colour and feeling of a Scotch moor. The island of Torcello is a desolate place, with a world's-end atmosphere about it. Once it was populous, but now marshes and malaria render it almost uninhabitable. There is a little museum of antiquities that have been found on the spot. But the *custode* of the museum, one of the few natives of Torcello, is more interesting than any of the antiquities which he guards. He is a robust and healthy young fellow, but with a manner so mellow, so dreamy, so far away, such a sense of ancient half-remembered things in his blue eyes, that it seems as though the very spirit of Torcello had passed into his soul. He will take you round the museum, laying a light hand here on a torso, there on a Roman tomb. "A *cippus*," he will say, in gentle, lingering tones, "a Roman *cippus ;*" and then, as you pass on, he adds lower, as though quite to himself, and caressing some secret all his own, "a Roman *cippus*." The campanile of Torcello is, as usual in Venice, a solid, square brick tower, rising to a great height, and the view from it, when you have climbed the rickety wooden ladders that led to the bell-chamber, is most striking. To the east the broken land—half sea, half land—begins; and the whole country is cut by wide ditches which intersect one another. These are the "Valli," where fish are bred for the Venice market; and a very valuable property the "Valli" are. To the south is the Adriatic, and the long line of Lidi breakwaters, curving away to Chioggia ; Venice and the Euganean Hills to the west ; and north, the ever-present Alps, visible from Torcello as hardly from anywhere else, for there is absolutely nothing to interrupt the view ; the plain runs right up to their roots, and the eye may wander on and on till it finds the eternal snows of Tofana, Antelao, or Pelmo. The sea and sky, Venice and the mountains, these are the four chords on which the music of the Venetian landscape is played.

A sail home from Torcello in the evening is a delightful experience ; and some of the gondoliers are skilful at handling their boats, without keel or rudder, steering them with an·oar behind, like the Vikings of old. If it be summer or autumn, a storm, sudden and furious, is not at all improbable, and will make no bad close to such a day. The great masses of cloud gather in the east, and sail slowly and stately towards us, surely gaining upon us. The van of the storm-clouds is curved into an arc by the pressure of the wind behind, though here upon the water there is only breeze enough to fill the sail. Steadily the billowy battalions advance until, as we are off Murano, the colour of the water begins to change to a pale pea-green, no longer transparent, but thick as jade. There is a feeling of oppression in the air, a brooding stillness, then suddenly the wind drops; not a breath, not a hush for five minutes, while the storm-clouds overtake us. Then, far away behind Murano, one catches a low humming, like the noise of a threshing-machine; it is the wind in the city — you must down sail and make for the nearest post. The hurricane leaps out from the city, striking the water, tearing it into foam, and flinging the spray high into the air. There is fury and confusion in the sky. The thundery masses are rent and riven; through the gaps of dun-coloured vapour you catch the steely blue of storm-clouds, boiling as in a caldron; and beyond them even again, pure blue sky and sunlight. A rain-bow rises high in the air, relieved against the turbulent heavens, and spans the lagoon. Then the whole tornado sweeps away south-westward. The sunset reasserts itself, and dashes the sky with streamers of crimson and orange; then darkness, with lightning and storm slowly dying away into the west, leaving the heavens serene and the night breeze fresh and cool. These summer storms are sudden and almost tropical in their fury, but they are quickly spent; and, like tropical cyclones, their path is a narrow one, confined to one line on the lagoon, but where they strike they have been known to unroof houses.

Besides these better known expeditions to the Lido, Torcello, and San Lazzaro, there are many others quite as worthy the attention of any one who has time and to spare in Venice. A little to the right of the canal that leads to Torcello, lies the island of San Francesco in Deserto. In a desert of water and mudbanks, Saint Francis's island certainly stands. It is easily distinguished and always remembered by its solitary stone pine, which spreads its umbrella of sunproof boughs over one angle of the convent garth. For San Francesco is still a convent of the Franciscan order, and the brothers show the stone coffin in which their founder used to acclimatize himself to death. But the large square of rich deep grass which the island walls inclose is by far the most enticing feature of San Francesco. A noble avenue of cypresses, the finest to be found near Venice, runs down one side; and in spring the air is heavy with the perfume of the narcissus, which grows here luxuriantly. Some way off to the south lies Treporti, on the outermost bank of sand that keeps the Adriatic from invading the lagoon. At Treporti the scenery is very different from that of the other places we have visited: long sweeps of sandy dune, covered with coarse bent grass and heather, and broken into pools of brackish water that reflect the sky like a mirror. The ground is all uncultivated ; the air is filled with pungent aromatic odours born of the sea and the wild sea-loving plants. On the shores, which seem to stretch illimitably on either hand, the sand is fine and soft and yellow ; there is no choicer place for a bathe ; the sea is wide open before you, warm, limpid, pure, and inviting ; and as you swim far out, the domes and campanili of Venice rise up in low relief upon the water-level, and the sound of her bells comes mellowed and blended across the blue expanse.

Or if the western lagoon is to be explored, no expedition is more favourable for this purpose than the one to Fusina. Through Fusina once lay the main road between Venice and Padua ; but the Austrian railway bridge has, until lately, diverted the current of traffic from Fusina to Mestre, and any one making the journey to Fusina was almost sure to have the lagoon to himself, or, at most, to share it with some sparse and scattered fishermen. Within the last year, however, a tramway has been opened between Fusina and Padua, and a small steamboat plies from Venice to meet the trains ; but this will not seriously break the loneliness of the voyage, nor rob of its inalienable charm that great sweep of lagoon that opens away from the mouth of the Giudecca, and stretches on and on to the lagoon's end at Chioggia and Brondolo. It is well to choose a grey day for this expedition—one of those pearly silver-grey days, so subdued, so delicate in suggested colour, that come every now and then in autumn. As the gondola leaves the Giudecca canal and makes for the island of Saint George-among-the-Seaweeds, the surface of the lagoon has an oily appearance, and is almost pallid in its grey whiteness. In the offing you can see the few trees which stand in a group near the port of Malamocco, and the spars of some big shipping; nearer still the fort of Sant' Angelo and the island of Saint George itself. Everything is mellowed by an all-pervading semi-transparent haze, which, on the horizon, confounds the limits of the sea and sky. Upon the surface of this silver-grey mirror rise the black silhouettes of the fishermen; each solitary figure upright and poised upon the stem of his narrow boat. The gondola passes under the red brick wall of San Giorgio, where the Madonna stands guardian at the corner, and the saint in stone charges and slays the dragon. The island was once a convent belonging to the Benedictine order, and the home of the Venetian Saint Lorenzo Guistiniani; but now the church has lost its campanile, and the church itself, refectory, and cloisters are converted to the base uses of a powder magazine. At Fusina the Brenta used to flow into the lagoon, and a considerable portion of its waters still discharge here—sufficient to allow the gondola to proceed up this branch till it joins the present main stream. This is worth doing; for in spring the Brenta is rich in water-lilies, yellow ranunculus, and flags. From the banks of the Brenta one looks westward across a curious flat country— so low-lying that one hardly perceives any difference between its level and that of the lagoon—until the eye reaches the Euganean Hills, thirty miles away, whose cones and pyramids form such a beautiful episode in every Venetian sunset.

The expeditions to be made upon the lagoon are

so numerous and so various that it is impossible to catalogue them here, nor is it our intention to offer such a catalogue. Our object was to show how great is the variety in the Venetian landscape, in Venice as seen from outside. But it must not be supposed that the lagoons are always steeped in sunlight. They have their moods: now black beneath a sudden storm; now cold and hard as steel under the piercing east wind—the *bora* that reaches Venice from the hills above Trieste; and sometimes in winter wrapped in an impenetrable blanket of damp mist, so thick and heavy that one may easily lose one's course between the Lido and Venice; and the steamers, slowly feeling their way in or out, loom for an instant and then disappear, swallowed up in that dense wall of vapour, and the sound of their fog-horns dies away down the wind. All the shipping looks ghostly, tall, and gaunt as one passes it, and the whole scene is like the sea-traffic in a world of dead men.

Nor is the variety less remarkable or less enchanting if we forsake the gondola and take to the land. Nothing can be more full of charm than a walk through Venice; the infinite variety and windings of the *calli*, the sudden debouchment upon some open *campiello*, the perpetual changes of scene. There is usually some surprise in store for any one who takes a walk through the city; either some piece of architecture, some balcony or doorway that has escaped notice, or some vivid picture of popular life.

The beauty of the city itself is, of course, more subject to destruction than the beauty of the lagoon. It seems impossible that "progress" should ever be able really to ruin the vast dome of the sky and the wide expanse of sea-floor; but inside the town, restoration, new streets, iron bridges have entailed a decided loss in picturesqueness. Yet even on this point Venice is more fortunate than many other Italian towns. It is not long before salt winds and sun begin their labour upon the newest stone, and insensibly man's handiwork suffers a sea-change that gradually brings the most glaring restorations into harmony with their surroundings. There are two moments particularly favourable for an artist to take his walks in Venice. One is after a rain shower, when the old *intonaco* upon the walls has every tone brought out, and is vivid with colour ranging from grey through pale sea-green to red—the old Venetian red with which so many houses used to be stained. The other choice moment for a walk is in the early morning before the business of the day has begun. The sunlight falls in such broad cool flakes upon the Istrian stone, the islands San Clemente and San Servolo look exquisitely pure and white upon the water, San Giorgio Maggiore springs up like a goddess new risen from her bath. As one wanders about the deserted *calli*, the birds sing in the inclosures; and on the *zattere* the air is laden with the perfume of honeysuckle and other creepers that trail over the wall of Princess Dolgorouki's garden. Indeed, the gardens in Venice, like everything else in the city, have a character all their own. In the first place, they are greatly prized, for space is scarce in this city built upon islands won from the very sea. The soil of Venice, composed of lagoon mud, is rich and heavy, but so impregnated with salt that only certain plants will grow freely in it; and it hardly repays the labour to force reluctant flowers towards an imperfect and precarious bloom. But the variety of plants that thrive and are happy in Venetian soil is quite sufficient to furnish forth a lordly show. Many flowering and aromatic shrubs take kindly to the soil; then roses, and above all the banksia; most bulbs; and, freest and happiest of all, carnations—the *garofoli* that play so large a part in Italian love-stories. There are two gardens on the Giudecca, very different in their character, but each illustrating in its way what a Venetian garden may be. In the one every resource of wealth and art has been lavished to produce a succession of brilliant beds. In the middle of this desert of colour is a green oasis, a sort of English orchard, where the fruit trees are gathered together, and fling their laced and flickering shadows on turf as fine, as velvety, and of as deep a green as any to be found in England. On either side the walks meander away among beds of splendid colour that varies with the varying seasons. There is an Oriental lavishness about the scene; the eye is surfeited, and the scent of flowers almost oppresses the air. The other garden is not less beautiful; but it has been left in the condition given to it by its old Venetian proprietors. A narrow strip is divided from the rest of the garden by a thick hedge; and here are congregated all the flowers that grow freely in Venice. The flame-coloured trumpets of the bignonia hang from the cypress, up which it has climbed; the walks are overarched by bowers of roses; banksias festoon the wall; one corner is filled by a *Daphne odorifera* that draws to its perfume innumerable butterflies. At intervals openings in the hedge give access to that part of the garden which is set apart for profit rather than for pleasure; aisle upon aisle of vine-covered pergolas cross each other; and down these cool promenades, where the sun is never too strong, one can saunter on and on, till the boundary wall is reached, and before one open out the long reaches of the lagoon that stretch away to Malamocco and the fort of Alberoni.

It is in the streets of Venice that one comes to know the people and the manner of life they lead. And it will be strange if one does not like them, in spite of all their faults. There is a gaiety, a laughter and light-heartedness about these children of the lagoons that is very winning; a disengagement and apparent frankness of manner that captivate, for all their indifference to truth, and that fatal desire to find out what you want them to say and to say it.

I doubt if there was ever much decided costume in Venice except among the nobles and the gondoliers, and what there was has disappeared. The women, however, still wear that most graceful of all garments —a shawl large enough to cover the head and to fall below the waist—handkerchiefs, they call them,—and they have unerring taste in the choice of colours. These shawls are seldom gaudy, their tone is usually subdued—fawn, pale mauve, sometimes a tawny red; the strong colours are reserved for the bodices and neckcloths. The linen of Venice is famed for its whiteness, and of this the women make abundant display on *festas* and holy days. Nothing can surpass the grace of these shawl-clad figures, seen down the long perspective of a narrow street, or gathered in groups round the carved well-head in some open *campiello.*

Although there is not much colour and variety of costume to be met with in Venice, the streets themselves are full of picturesque suggestions. Most of the shops are quite open in front, and the whole contents may be seen—part, indeed, overflows and straggles on to the narrow pathway. Here is a corn-dealer's shop, with open sacks of polenta flour of every shade of yellow ; there an old-clothes shop, with dresses of every hue and shade ; and next door to it is a worker in bronze, whose rows of burnished pots and plates serve as a red-gold background. Then, again, up at the Rialto, where the vegetables are sold, what a wealth of colour in the piles of tomatoes, vegetable marrow, and great pumpkins cut down the middle, and displaying all their orange insides. One of the charms of a stroll through Venice, of losing one's self, as is easily done, in that labyrinth of streets, is that one never knows what surprise may be in store. Now it is some scene of market or popular life ; again it is a great stone angel standing guardian at some *calle*-head ; here a coat-of-arms that sets you blazoning, there a Gothic door with terra-cotta mouldings : the place seems inexhaustible ; and for ambient to all this variety and richness of art and life, there is the singularly limpid air and light of the lagoon.

Few crowds are more cheerful or better ordered than a Venetian crowd. The people love to congregate ; every one is out on the business of pleasure, and determined to enjoy themselves to the full. There are flashes of a ready wit in repartee that play across the throng. I remember once—the government was then in a critical state, and the ministry was likely to go out—there was a man who had drunk more wine than would allow him to walk steadily: "Take care," said some one, "you'll fall." "Well," came the instant reply, "Depretis is going to fall, and so mayn't I?" Touches of sentiment, too, are sometimes displayed, the sentiment that finds expression in the quaint *villotte* or Venetian popular songs. The struggle between the sea-wind and the land-wind is regarded as a battle for ever being waged ; the clouds are the victims of this endless strife—"They are going to the mountains, but the mountains will not receive them." The immortal wanderings of the moon strike the Venetian fancy as they struck the fancy of Shelley and of Leopardi : "Povaretta! viaggia sempre e non riposa mai ;" and sometimes a profounder note is struck, as in the remark, "Quando viene il desiderio non c'è mai troppo." But these are rarer touches, depths that are seldom stirred ; as a rule the Venetian *popolo* is the lightest and most easy-going in the world, free as a child from care or doubt about right or wrong. Indeed, this carelessness, so disturbing to a northern temper, apt to take all things seriously, is characteristic not of the Venetian *popolo* only, but of the race in general. The writer once had the misfortune to be summoned as a witness before the pretor. His fellow-witness, the only one, was an old woman dressed in a thick flannel petticoat. After weary waiting in the ante-room, where every one was smoking and throwing their matches about, we were summoned into the crowded court, made to stand up, and were lectured on the nature of an oath and the terrible consequences of perjury. While this was going on, one of the policemen suddenly said to the old woman, "You're burning," but he never moved; and sure enough a thin thread of smoke was rising from the old lady's petticoat. "Santissima Vergine Maria!" she cried in horror, but no one moved. The judge on the bench put his finger-tips together, observed the witness for a second, and confirmed the policeman's remark, "Yes, you are burning;" and prosecutor, counsel, and general public confirmed the judge, and said, "Yes, she's burning." The old lady's fellow-witness could not let her burn in this way quite quietly, so he caught her petticoats tight in his hands, while the judge, still with his finger-tips together, nodded approval from the bench and said, "Squeeze her, squeeze her, squeeze her well." The smouldering flame was soon put out. The judge smiled, the policemen smiled, the public smiled, and the case went on.

The Venetians have always been, and still are, a *festa*-loving people. In the days of its wealth and pride the republic spent lavishly upon its State entertainments. The natural capacities of the city for a great spectacle, the winding waterway of the Grand Canal, opening upon the basin of St. Mark, with San Giorgio on one side, and the ducal palace, the Piazzetta, and the Basilica upon the other, the curve of the Riva closed by the public gardens, all seem to invite and require the compliment of some scenic display. The pictures of the old Venetian masters—Bellini, Carpaccio, Veronese—prove how deeply the Venetians revelled in the pageants of state. But when the republic fell the great ceremonies came to an end. Only among the people the roots of the original passion were kept alive. The people have lost most of their old sports in which they delighted : the battle on the bridge between the rival factions of black and red, the Nicolotti and Castellani ; the human towers and pyramids, piled up in many a fanciful shape, called the *Forze d'Ercole;* but one sport—the national sport of the Venetians—the regatta, still lives on ; and lately, since Venice became a part of United Italy, the Town Council has done much to revive the splendour of the show. The regatta is frequently combined with a serenade on the Grand Canal in the evening, and the two together form a spectacle which can be surpassed by no other city in Europe. The race is rowed in light gondolas, much smaller than the gondola in ordinary use. The course is from the stairs of the public garden up to the station and back again to the Palazzo Foscari, the traditional winning-post. The prizes are money and flags for the first three, and a pig and a flag with a pig upon it for the last. Long before the race begins the Grand Canal is crowded with boats of every sort and size: gondolas, *sandolos, barche, barchette, topos, cavaline, vipere, bissoni*—there is no end to the names and kinds of Venetian craft. The façades of the palaces are all a-flutter with flags, and from the windows hang tapestries, carpets, curtains, anything that will add to the dance of colour. The balconies are filled with people ; every window has its bevy of heads; the very roofs are black with sightseers. Down below on the water the scene is no less animated and brilliant. The course is kept by large boats with twelve oars, called *bissoni.* Each of these is decorated symbolically. One represents the Arctic regions ; its rowers are clad like walruses, a Polar bear lies on its bows, and a block of ice serves as a seat for its captain and steersman. Another represents the tropic regions, with palms and gorgeous flowers for decoration. A third is a trophy of the Murano glassworkers' art. These great boats, crossing and recrossing one another on the waters of the canal, weave, as it were, a web of colour. The eye is ever charmed by some new combination of the water-loom. Presently comes the boom of a distant cannon. The race has begun. A hush falls upon the crowd, only to be broken when the first boat appears round the curve, and it becomes certain whether Nicolotto or Castellano leads. The race sweeps by, and disappears again behind the Rialto, which swallows it up like a yawning mouth. There is a perpetual buzz of voices—criticism, comment, bets flying about—until the boats come in sight on their journey home ; a moment of breathless excitement, then a roar of the victor's name as he shoots his bow past the winning post and snatches up his flag as he passes. The race is finished. All the while, overhead is the wide, blue, quiet sky, and, underneath, the water silently, persistently, heedlessly going its way to the sea.

In the evening the serenade starts from some point above the Rialto. The singers and orchestra are placed on a barge which is decorated and lighted by numbers of little lamps arranged sometimes like a pyramid, sometimes like a fountain of fire. The object of every good gondolier is to take his *padroni* as near to the music as possible, whether they like it or not. The result is that the singers' barge soon becomes wedged in between a solid mass of gondolas, like a ship in an ice-floe; and it is only with the greatest difficulty that any progress can be made. The whole of the solid mass floats slowly down with the tide, getting more and more closely jammed as the canal narrows to pass the Rialto bridge. Under that wide arch the scene is most fantastic. The electric light casts its cold white ray down the Grand Canal, falling now on this palace front and now on that, causing them to start into sudden and ghastly prominence, like ghosts unmasked. The smoke of the Bengal lights streams out from under the arch in dense coloured masses, and wavers away on the night air. The figures of the poised and statuesque gondoliers, each one standing upright on the stern of his boat, oar in hand and hair blown by the breeze, form a series of varied and beautiful silhouettes against the darker background of the houses or the sky. The serenade is a long affair; and when one has had enough of the whole strange and fantastic scene, escape is easy down one of the innumerable side canals that lead to the quiet quarters of the town.

Besides these great spectacles of regatta and serenade, there are many other *feste* in Venice, chiefly of a religious character. Each parish church, for example, honours the feast of its patron saint by a procession to all the shrines within the parish boundaries. It is a picturesque sight to see one of these bright trains of priests and people streaming across the bridges and along the *fondamenta* of some small canal. First come the porters of the church clad in long blouses of white, red, and blue, bearing the candles, the pictures, the banners, and images of the church; then a band of music, playing the gayest of operatic airs, and behind the music the priests surrounding the *parocco*, who carries the Host under a canopy of a cloth of gold; more music, a long file of the devout bearing candles, and boys with crackers and guns bring up the rear of the procession. The day ends with public dancing in the largest *campo* of the parish. Venice still records her gratitude for salvation from plague in two annual ceremonies, the *Madonna della Salute* in November and the *Redentore* in July. On both occasions the priests of every parish in Venice go in procession from St. Mark's to the respective churches of the Salute and Redentore. As the *festa* of the Redentore falls in high summer the occasion is seized to make its vigil a night-long water-frolic. As soon as the sun has set, the broad Giudecca canal begins to swarm with boats, gaily dressed with boughs and lanterns, forming an arbour under which a supper-table is spread for a party of friends. There are fireworks and prizes for the best-dressed boats; and towards two o'clock all the crowd move off to the Lido to salute the rising sun, and rush into the sea to meet it.

One of the most curious and characteristic of Venetian popular ceremonies is the way in which they keep Good Friday, and with an account of this function we will close this attempted picture of Venice of to-day, the place, and the people, as seen in its general external aspects.

If a stranger arrived in Venice on Good Friday, he would certainly take that day for a feast and not for a fast. The streets are full of people in their Sunday best. The inevitable sign and signature of a *festa* is present everywhere in the herds of children who rush, roll, and romp among the passengers, whirling their rattles to frighten Judas, or turning somersaults and calling them *Carpaccio* for the benefit of æsthetic foreigners. But, upon this day, the chief delight of the Venetian children is to fit up a *Santo Sepolcro*, and to appeal, on the strength of it, to the crowd for coppers. In most of the churches there are representations of the Holy Sepulchre, and the children of Venice follow the lead of their Church, but they are content with less apparatus. Indeed, almost anything will do for a *Santo Sepolcro*. I saw one little creature, about six or seven, who had constructed her sepulchre from an old bottle, a sprig of bay, and two candle-ends, and who appealed most successfully to the passers-by, winning as much for her pretty face and gentle mien, as for her idea of the Holy Grave.

It is at night, however, and in the more populous quarters of the city, little frequented by strangers, that the most characteristic sight of a Venetian Good Friday is to be seen. The people of the quarter, the shopkeepers, wine-sellers, fishermen, agree to sing the Twenty-four Hours, a long chaunt in twenty-four verses, following the life of our Lord through His Passion. The ceremony is a purely popular one; the Church has no part in it. The natives of the quarter subscribe among themselves, in kind or in money, to bear the expenses of the function; one gives oil for the lamps, another the wick, another wine for the singers, who are usually a company of gondoliers or porters from the district. At one end of the *calle*, a shrine is raised in the shape of a temple; the pillars and pediment and all its lines defined by little glass lamps, whose flames flicker and waver in the evening breeze. The yellow light of these altar-lamps contrasts strangely with the stronger and whiter light of the ordinary gas-jet that projects from the middle of the shrine; and this blended light is thrown upon the faces of the men and women who stand in a dense group waiting till the singing shall begin. On either side of the *calle* the upper windows of the houses are open, and filled with heads, leaning out, looking down and chatting to friends below. At the far end of the street, crowning the angle of a garden wall, stands a Madonna, carved in stone, with the Infant in her arms, a lamp and rose-wreaths about her feet, and behind her the thick clusters of a westeria that has climbed up and falls in delicate violet showers about her head. Over all is the long narrow strip of dusky sky that the house-roofs cut, lit by one large star.

Presently the singing begins. In harsh, but powerful voice, the leader of the band strikes up the first of the twenty-four hours, and the rest of his company join in as they catch the note. The tune is a grave and sombre chaunt, and the whole reminds one of psalm-singing in a Scotch kirk, with the precentor leading the way. Each verse takes about three minutes to sing, and there is a pause of five minutes between one verse and the next. The crowd is quiet during the singing; but in the interval the women begin to chatter, the men take a pull at their long virginias, and the thin blue smoke floats lazily up into the night; the boys rush and tumble, until the precentor's voice, commencing the next verse, bids silence fall upon the throng once more.

The ceremony lasts about three hours, and ends, of course, in the inevitable supper at the nearest wineshop. As we return to go down the *calle* they are singing the fourteenth hour. The light from the altar falls upon the hair of the women, the bronzed necks and faces of the men, and the fairer faces of the children they hold in their arms to see the sight. One moment, and we turn the corner by the garden wall. There all is quiet; not a footfall in the streets, and above us the silence and the fragrance of the rich Venetian night.

THE END.

PRINTED BY WILLIAM CLOWES AND SONS, LIMITED, LONDON AND BECCLES.

Printed in the United States
67110LVS00004B/64